ZUMANOMICS

Which way to shared prosperity in South Africa?

Challenges for a new government

edited by Raymond Parsons

PREVIOUS BOOKS BY RAYMOND PARSONS
The Mbeki Inheritance: SA's Economy 1999–2004 (2000)
Parsons' Perspective: Focus on the Economy (2002)
Manuel, Markets and Money: Essays in Appraisal (2004)

This edition first published by Jacana Media (Pty) Ltd in 2009

10 Orange Street
Sunnyside
Auckland Park 2092
South Africa
(+27 11) 628-3200
www.jacana.co.za

© The editor and individual authors, 2009

All rights reserved.

ISBN 978-1-77009-647-9

Cover design by banana republic
Text design and layout by Claudine Willatt-Bate
Set in Bembo
Printed by CTP Book Printers
Job No. 000936

See a complete list of Jacana titles at www.jacana.co.za

Contents

	List of contributors	iv
	Acknowledgements	vi
1	**Overture: theme and variations** Raymond Parsons	1
2	**South Africa's economic performance since 1994: can we do better?** Charlotte du Toit and Johann van Tonder	15
3	**Economic policy: some lessons from Southeast Asia** Lefentse Nokaneng and Chris Harmse	41
4	**Inflation targeting: a pillar of post-Polokwane prosperity** Stan du Plessis	57
5	**Fiscal policy beyond 2008: prospects, risks and opportunities** Iraj Abedian and Tania Ajam	79
6	**Trade, industrial and competition policy** Riaan de Lange and Reyno Seymore	103
7	**Industrial policy and national competitiveness: the spatial dimension** Glen Robbins	117
8	**Labour policy and job creation: too many holy cows?** Carel van Aardt	129
9	**Health policy and growth** Oludele A. Akinboade, Thabisa Tokwe and Mandisa Mokwena	149
10	**Politics and human-oriented development** Adam Habib	163
11	**The role of the state** Raymond Parsons	185
12	**Recapitulation and coda: 70 key findings and recommendations**	209

Contributors

Raymond Parsons
Extraordinary Professor, Department of Economic and Management Studies, University of Pretoria. Overall business convenor, Nedlac. Former director-general, Sacob. Immediate past president, Essa.

Iraj Abedian
Chief economist, Pan-African Investment and Research Services. Ex-director and group chief economist, Standard Bank. Former Professor of Economics, University of Cape Town.

Tania Ajam
Director, Knowledge Centre, at the Applied Fiscal Research Centre (AFReC), University of Cape Town. Managing Director, PBS.

Oludele A. Akinboade
Professor, School of Economic Sciences, Unisa.

Riaan de Lange
Lecturer in International Economics, University of Pretoria. Associate, ATII.

Stan du Plessis
Professor in Economics, University of Stellenbosch.

Charlotte du Toit
Professor in Economics, University of Pretoria. Director, Afrinem.

Adam Habib
Deputy Vice-Chancellor, Research Innovation and Advancement, University of Johannesburg.

Chris Harmse
Chief Economist, Dynamic Wealth. Extraordinary Professor of Economics, University of Pretoria.

Mandisa Mokwena
Business Intelligence Unit, South African Revenue Service (SARS)

Lefentse Nokaneng
Executive Director, Polybond (Pty) Ltd.

Glen Robbins
School of Development Studies, University of KwaZulu-Natal.

Reyno Seymore
Lecturer in International Economics, University of Pretoria. Associate, Afrinem.

Thabisa Tokwe
School of Economic Sciences, Unisa.

Carel van Aardt
Research Professor, Income and Expenditure Research Division, Bureau of Market Research, Unisa.

Johann van Tonder
Economist, Dynamic Wealth.

Acknowledgements

A book of essays which seeks to help shape the post-2009 socio-economic agenda in South Africa owes a debt to many people. There are several who deserve to be thanked. At the outset my deep gratitude goes to the other fifteen esteemed contributors, who have critically helped to identify some of the key issues that will confront a new government in South Africa this year. My thanks also go to the Jacana team who have so ably assisted in bringing the book to finality within tight timeframes, especially Bridget Impey and Russell Martin.

Professor Evan Gilbert of the University of Stellenbosch has been indispensable in sharing the editorial load, and I am most appreciative of his excellent assistance. My grateful thanks also go to my secretary, Frieda Garvie, who has provided secretarial assistance as well as applying discipline where necessary. To all those whose time I took to take advice on various aspects of the book's contents, I also convey my appreciation for their willingness to assist, without holding them responsible for the final version.

The usual caveat applies, in that the views I have expressed here are personal and do not necessarily represent those of any organisation or institution with which I am associated. Likewise, essayists are responsible only for their own views, and not for those of other contributors.

Raymond Parsons
Department of Economic and Management Sciences
University of Pretoria
February 2009

1
Overture: theme and variations

Raymond Parsons

> The developmental state will play a central and strategic role in the economy. We will ensure a more effective government; improve the coordination and planning efforts of the developmental state by means of a planning entity to ensure faster change ...
> – *ANC 2009 Election Manifesto*

> It is not possible to remain stationary.
> We can only choose between two possibilities:
> Moving backwards or moving forwards.
> – *Erich Fromm*

When the former long-serving chairman of the US Federal Reserve Board, Alan Greenspan, chose *The Age of Turbulence* as the title of his autobiography in 2007, almost nobody else was better placed to observe, and describe, the balloons that were about to go up, some with a loud bang, others with an unnerving plop. In 2009, as governments and stakeholders everywhere grapple with the global economic crisis – and its impact on opportunities and livelihoods for millions around the world – they must see the 'creative destruction' which economist Joseph Schumpeter (recently echoed by Greenspan) once so positively correlated with market economies, as a mixed blessing. Just at present. Over the past twelve months or so the economic dislocation has been painful and widely spread, albeit unevenly. World economic growth in 2009 is expected to be at its lowest since the Second World War. Economic contagion has spread.

And whatever other solutions global and national decision-makers may have crafted, or may still be considering, to stabilise the situation, it remains critically important for debate to revert to the economic fundamentals in addressing the risks and opportunities that lie ahead. In a period of serious economic contraction, the misery of poverty also becomes even more apparent and insistent, as the gains from global finance and trade recede – rather as the rocks appear when the tide goes out. More than ever before we need to examine, both globally and domestically, which policies and institutions can genuinely ameliorate, and hopefully eventually eliminate, unemployment and poverty.

Over two hundred years ago, when Adam Smith was trying to systematise his ideas about economic development, he chose as the title of his analysis *The Wealth of Nations*. Today if he were addressing the same theme, he would be more likely to include in the title a reference to poverty as well as wealth. For it is only within living memory that the systematic eradication of poverty has come to be seen as a real social and political possibility, even though very difficult to attain. The most challenging problem confronting economists therefore remains what it was in Adam Smith's era: to bring to light the forces that from time to time determine the economic growth and development of countries – and how best to mobilise such forces to promote prosperity.

> Prosperity is the ability of an individual, group, or nation to provide shelter, nutrition, and other material goods that enable people to live a good life, according to their own definition. Prosperity helps create space in people's hearts and minds so that they may develop a healthy emotional and spiritual life according to their preferences ... prosperity is also the broadening environment that improves productivity. (Fairbanks, 2000: 270)

This is the challenge facing this country and hence the title of this book. Why 'Zumanomics'? The title of this book is predicated on the assumption that the present ANC–Cosatu–SACP Alliance will be returned to office in the 2009 elections, with ANC president Jacob Zuma becoming the President of South Africa. This at present appears likely, whether or not the political landscape in Parliament may change somewhat in the wake of a vigorous, lively and longish election campaign, involving some so-called 'new formations' or even potential post-election formations, against a backdrop of robust debate on socio-economic issues among politicians and other stakeholders.

By mid-2009, consequently, the major present-day policy directions may to all intents and purposes have been settled for the time being. Not only would Jacob Zuma then be South Africa's President, but it is possible that some at least of the economic policies by which the country has recently been governed would be about to change or, at any rate, to be significantly modified, for at least five years. Once the 2009 elections are over, however, rhetoric must give way to sober reality – and should most certainly be given every encouragement to do so rapidly. The election will have done nothing to change – less still to eliminate – the socio-economic realities and challenges facing South Africa. Out of its policy manifesto, the new government will, with any benefits of early hindsight, need to prioritise and formulate an action plan to govern South Africa, and to manage the economy, over the next five years. General elections, after all, should mostly be referendums on the future, rather than on the past.

This collection of essays is committed to making a modest contribution toward identifying some of the key issues that will be relevant at this point in time. Its purpose is to initiate, not exhaust, discussion and at the same time to offer some policy proposals which may influence decision-making. The authors have been encouraged to consider President Zuma's choices in the light of both the ANC's campaign promises and the unavoidable reality that narrowed options will have been dictated by world-wide economic events. Essayists have been invited to say where they think he may go wrong or be seriously in danger of doing so. They have carte blanche to outline and justify their own policy preferences for growth policies.

In a lighter vein, the story is told of Soviet leader Leonid Brezhnev on the reviewing stand at Lenin's tomb in Moscow, surrounded by staff, watching the May Day parade. The Soviet Union's full military might was on display. Vast battalions of elite soldiers; phalanxes of state-of-the art artillery and tanks; an array of impressive nuclear missiles: all in all, an awesome show of military strength. Bringing up the rear came a straggle of half-a-dozen civilians, unkempt, shabbily dressed, completely out of place. An aide rushes up to Brezhnev and begs forgiveness. 'Comrade Secretary, my apologies, I do not know who these people are or how they got into the parade.' 'Do not worry, comrade', replies Brezhnev, 'I arranged it – they are our economists and you have no idea how much damage they can do' (Greenspan, 2007: 88).

More seriously, economists have singled out, at different times, a wide variety of causes of the wealth of nations. South Africa is no exception. Among them are three that have been given particular emphasis – the growth of markets, the accumulation of capital, and the progress of technology. All three, like everything else that economists write about, interact with one another, so that the influence of any one of them makes itself felt as much through its repercussions on the other two as by its direct impact. A high level of capital investment, for example, allows new techniques to be exploited more quickly and in its labour-intensive form creates more jobs. Both economic and social investment widens markets by enlarging the economy's productive powers and capacity to deliver goods and services. Interactions so complex and far-reaching make it difficult to isolate the consequences of any single factor in economic growth and development. They permit economists, indulging in individualism that is at once the attraction and the reproach of our science, to pick their own thread to guide us through the maze, and to set up their own signposts to shared prosperity.

No effort is made here to establish the measures of agreement or disagreement among the authors. Readers will nonetheless be able to discern several common threads running through the essays; and what does certainly unite them is a common purpose in offering contributions to the economic debate and to future public policy choices. South Africa's long-term outlook will be driven by political, economic and social transformation and its successful implementation. Important policy decisions have to be taken by a new government in the years ahead and mistakes minimised as far as possible.

Countries differ considerably in the quality of their policy structures and in the cost to the economy of the burden caused by the accumulation through time of policy mistakes or misjudgements. Perhaps the most important task of a collection of essays from professional economists and analysts in a country like South Africa is to help reduce this cost when it is large, and at the very least to keep it from growing when it is small. Here, as in many other aspects of life, it is easier to break down something worthwhile than it is to try to restore it. Where change is inevitable, how can we help to ensure it will be for the better?

One of the dangers in the current situation in South Africa is the tendency, on seeing something wrong, to assume that almost any change must be for the better. Such observers cannot easily be persuaded, sometimes despite mounds of chilling evidence, that the alternative policy has had an earlier and equally unsatisfactory incarnation. Hence, the importance of historical analogy and empirical evidence. Where there are no facts, sentiments prevail. The room for policy error has narrowed considerably in the light of the changed global and domestic economic circumstances with which a President Zuma and a new Cabinet will be confronted in 2009. We must therefore try harder to get more things right the first time round in future.

These essays must thus be seen in the context of critical global economic and political developments to which they owe much of their relevance and topicality, and no less so to on-going trends or factors that may take time, perhaps years, to work themselves out of the reckoning. These include a number of key perspectives.

Firstly, South Africa's longest business cycle upswing (since September 1999) has drawn to a close. How to manage this economic downswing presents important new challenges to policy decision-makers and to the private sector, so as to lay the right foundations for the next upswing. We also need to look beyond the current challenges to the longer-term requirements for growth and development in South Africa as well as address any future resource constraints. The economic slowdown at least gives the country breathing space to 'get the infrastructure right' for the time when growth regains momentum. It is also necessary to address the challenge presented by the chronic low level of domestic savings.

Secondly, superimposed on the cyclical downswing in South Africa have been the consequences of the traumatic global financial meltdown inflicting real economic pain on many countries to varying degrees, including South Africa. We are now in the middle of one of the major global slumps in recent economic history, with its widespread impact on incomes, confidence and expectations. A few months ago our challenge was mainly to navigate a domestic economic downswing; now the international economic outlook is at least equally important. Understandably, when a country has begun to taste the fruits of higher growth, the threat of an ebb is hard to take.

Thirdly, South Africa is still committed to achieving a 6% growth rate and halving unemployment and poverty by 2014 through the Accelerated and Shared Growth Initiative for South Africa (Asgisa) programme, which identified a number of 'binding constraints' that seriously hinder South Africa's economic performance. We must see whether we can be more successful in unlocking South Africa's true economic potential. The identification of binding constraints is 'disciplined art' more than science, as Nobel Prize laureate Michael Spence put it recently.

Finally, changes in the business cycle in South Africa are coinciding with major political shifts – which could have important implications for South Africa's economic direction after the 2009 elections. This has provoked wide debate. As one leading publication posed it: 'Will Jacob Zuma be president or populist?' (*M&G*, 14.11.2008). Would he fail miserably were he to aspire to both? 'Manuel warns of danger of leftward policy shift,' says another headline (*Business Day*, 19.11.2008). 'If you said "it's my way or the highway" you would not be wrong,' said a person who knows Manuel well, speculating that he would stay only until the 2009 election (*M&G*, 21.11.2008). In the conventional political terminology of the 'left' and the 'right', the battle is on for the centre in economic policy in South Africa – and is likely to continue after the elections.

And what is the perspective regarding Finance Minister Trevor Manuel's possible departure? Manuel may well remain for a while, but with the issue of succession planning inevitably growing much closer in time. And this focuses our collective mind on the particular importance for emerging markets of just who occupy key economic portfolios, including the governorship of the Central Bank. Emerging economies undergoing economic restructuring and transformation – particularly where the process is unfinished – are vulnerable to a shift in senior personnel. This is partly because economic policies are not seen to be as entrenched as appearances may suggest.

All the financial markets and international credit agencies want is to be reassured that the nation's finances will remain in safe hands, whoever the minister of finance is in future. The record shows that, given the nature of our political dynamics, a minister of finance needs the full and constant support of the President for sensible fiscal policies embodying the necessary degree of prudence. This will continue to have to be the case. In recent years Manuel and the National Treasury have successfully presided over three key stages of fiscal reform: stabilisation, consolidation and sustainable expansion of fiscal policy. Positive economic assessments of South Africa have emphasised the extent to which prudent management of state finances has contributed to a more resilient economy – and this is serving South Africa well in present economic circumstances.

The latest economic downswing will test the extent to which fiscal achievements to date leave room for an effective anti-cyclical policy to act as a 'shock absorber'. Adjusting to external shocks is never easy. What is important here is a realistic grasp of the challenge and a willingness to make hard choices, depending on how long the external shock is expected to last. It is a sign of how rapidly events moved globally in 2008 that the otherwise balanced and realistic 2025 scenario study published by the Presidency in September 2008 could still plausibly suggest that 'the scenarios presented here only occasionally hint at such [worse-case] 'Black Swan' events (PCAS, 2008). Other official statements and Manuel's 13th Budget Speech in February 2009 have indicated how much further South Africa will go in devising its own fiscal 'package' to deal with the domestic impact of the global economic crisis. The rest we know. Once the current phase is over, and any 'package' has served its purpose, South Africa will need to return to its normal fiscal flight path.

In the longer run a great deal depends on how entrenched the fiscal 'culture' and financial systems are which have been developed so far. How much of the fiscal reform and discipline will endure to provide the necessary continuity? Have Manuel and the National Treasury already succeeded in laying down fiscal policies like a railway track, along which sound fiscal policies *must* in future run? As long as the fiscal approach reflects a credible policy course, it will facilitate growth and stability – and promote a climate of confidence within which South Africa can pursue an appropriate development strategy. Markets, government and individuals – as well as community – lie at the heart of a successful development strategy. This is the centre around which the balance must be sought and leadership provided. We must walk a fine line between flexibility and consistency. Shades of populism and lopsided sectoral pressures could undermine the foundations of sound economic development, as has happened elsewhere. What Manuel has represented is what he believes to have been soundly conceived and is appropriate for South Africa to hold its own internationally.

At a time when the market economy and globalisation are under great strain – and some are happy to proclaim their imminent demise – we need to retain perspective. To paraphrase Mark Twain, reports of their death are grossly exaggerated. The so-called 'capitalist system' (there are no pristine examples – invariably a mixed bag of freedoms and imposed constraints) has shown a remarkable capacity over time to adapt to new challenges and to reinvent itself in diverse socio-economic circumstances. But it will not be 'business as usual'. Globally, the system needs a future with a difference.

The 'rules of the game' will be changed as a result of the latest global crisis in order to facilitate greater stability and equity.

Systemic financial risks will have to be far better managed in future. Financial innovation in recent years had outstripped regulatory frameworks. As the world economy undergoes a once-in-a-century shock, reforms are needed to make it work better in future. The problem often is that when the intellectual and public opinion pendulums swing, they sometimes go too far. We need a proper balance that evolves over time. This must include improved global economic cooperation and coordination. In the meantime, policy-makers have demonstrated far more flexible and appropriate responses to the global 'meltdown' than did their predecessors in the 1930s. Whatever the future pace of globalisation, it will remain something to be successfully managed by every country desiring economic progress, despite current setbacks.

And when the current world economic crisis has eventually passed, as it will do – and is superseded by renewed economic growth – South Africa must needs have taken steps to ensure that it has remained, and will continue to be, globally competitive in a world in which the culture of productivity remains firmly entrenched. South Africa has not gained ground in recent World Economic Forum global competitiveness surveys, although it is still dominant economically in the southern African region. The policies and behaviour that support competitiveness are becoming better known in South Africa – Asgisa is one testimonial to that – but the challenge is getting true acceptance and implementation of them. Unlocking growth potential requires an economy that is reasonably flexible and sensibly managed. In such an economy – and the South African economy is reasonably flexible, and can be sensibly managed – well-wishers would urge that public policy choices should reflect the balance needed to maximise productivity gains in the longer term. The nature of South Africa's trade and investment links with the outside world assumes great importance here, especially given balance of payments considerations and the need to tap into global savings.

The more ambitious a nation's socio-economic programme, the bigger the productivity gains it needs to generate to underpin it. Election promises in 2009 portend four substantial inroads into the fruits of any gains in productivity that may be secured in future years: once to increase the wage-bill (the provision of decent work); once in lowering prices (stable growth); once in more free time (a shorter working week); and once in improved social services (education, health and social security). It follows that unless the future policy framework also creates a favourable environment for efficiency gains, the constraints identified by Asgisa and other authoritative studies will constantly hamper us in seeking to boost South Africa's economic performance.

Globalisation offers choices and governments still have great sway over both the extent and the form of economic integration. South Africa must strategically engage globalisation to the best advantage of the country. Events suggest that for many countries, including South Africa, international economics may even become a dominant foreign policy issue as well. In the long run the big challenge is to make the opportunities of globality all the more apparent, its dangers less threatening. We still want to make South Africa a leading emerging market and destination of first choice for investors. It has often been argued that this approach leads to policies designed exclusively for foreign investors, not local South Africans. In truth, the interests of the two are not mutually exclusive and the involvement of (foreign) investment is an essential component of growth, development and a reduction in poverty. It is not a sufficient condition but a necessary one. South Africa simply needs to play its cards skilfully.

It is against this broad backdrop that these eleven essays have been prepared. Readers will have to decide whether to read the essays as a whole, or to choose those of greatest interest and accessibility to them. Our readers, of whatever persuasion, will be able to pick out the authors they find most interesting or perhaps most disagreeable. A 'recapitulation and coda' at the end summarises 70 key findings and recommendations arising from the various essays. While every effort has been made to minimise it, it is inevitable that the essays will overlap but this is not necessarily a bad thing. The interdependence of key economic and political variables must not be forgotten, nor that what we are ultimately engaged in here is the overall political economy of South Africa. This requires a broader conceptual framework than would normally be the case in a book of this nature. So what is in store here?

Charlotte du Toit and *Johan van Tonder* open the series of essays by reviewing aspects of South Africa's economic performance to date. They conclude that the country's enhanced growth performance of 5% over the period 2004–2007 has revealed the serious policy and implementation constraints limiting South Africa's future growth, labour absorption and poverty alleviation – and what could be some of the solutions.

Lefentse Nokaneng and *Chris Harmse* assess what South Africa can learn about economic policy from some key East Asian countries. Among the factors identified as relevant to South Africa are the role of small and medium-sized manufacturing, the importance of foreign direct investment, land reform policies, and effective social policies in shaping growth and development strategies.

Stan du Plessis focuses on monetary policy, inflation targeting and interest rates. He highlights the role of inflation targeting and concludes that, unless the inflation-targeting regime is retained in South Africa, the country will be served with a bill of higher inflation and no gain in growth – a bill for which the poor will pay the most.

Iraj Abedian and *Tania Ajam* analyse fiscal policy beyond 2008 – its prospects, risks and opportunities. Despite financial reform and achievements to date, they caution against creating a populist, welfarist fiscal framework in future that is detrimental to the sustainable upliftment of the poor and inimical to economic performance.

Riaan de Lange and *Reyno Seymore* traverse the terrains of trade, industrial and competition policy. They stress the interdependence of these policies and, drawing on the lessons of past experience, make some recommendations regarding tariff restructuring as well as other aspects of tariff and trade policy.

Glen Robbins comes to grips with industrial policy and its relationship to national competitiveness. Although South Africa needs a bold industrial policy, he is critical of the degree of centralisation in current policy and believes that an industrial policy focused on mobilising more local entities and actors would be more successful.

Carel van Aardt deals with the labour market and job creation. He looks at what he calls the 'holy cows' of present labour market policies and advocates the need for 'pillar-based' policies to address the constraints on higher levels of employment in South Africa. The creation of 'decent work' opportunities should be the primary focus of appropriate policies.

Oludele Akinboade, *Thabisa Tokwe* and *Mandisa Mokwena* tackle the important question of health policy and economic development. In their overview of the health sector in South Africa, they explore the link between health issues and economic development. They conclude that, while improving health requires changing the allocation of healthcare resources, the alleviation of poverty itself is also crucial in making the health status of South Africans more equitable.

Adam Habib reflects on what needs to be done politically to facilitate a human-oriented development agenda in South Africa. He also examines the political dynamics of the recent ANC–Cosatu–SACP Alliance succession dispute. His thesis is that it is the accountability of the political elite resulting from effective competition for political power that is necessary for human-oriented development.

Raymond Parsons addresses complex and long-standing questions around the appropriate role of the state in South African circumstances, given a changing global environment. He evaluates the role of the state to date and analyses the track record of public sector delivery in South Africa. He makes some proposals about how the performance of both the state and the private sector can be improved and better coordinated in future.

In essence, therefore, these essays have sought to present some of the major factors that have driven the South African economy over the past few years to where it is now – and where it may go beyond 2009 under a new president and a new cabinet. They assess several of the weighty challenges facing a Zuma presidency and outline some of the options available to decision-makers. Several of the essays offer a different route to familiar goals. International experience nonetheless suggests that it does not take policy miracles to generate good results. If key policies are broadly perceived to be in the right direction, then economic performance is likely to be quite successful. This has nonetheless to be achieved against a global economic context which is now extremely challenging.

At the same time, after the election in 2009, the prospect of a new ANC–Cosatu–SACP team in government will bring fresh political energy to the governance process. To the extent that the discipline of the ANC–Cosatu–SACP Polokwane Conference 'collective' allows it, a new government will hopefully be open to new ideas on aspects of policy. A careful scrutiny of the ANC 2009 election manifesto suggests that, while it may be long on what the state can – and should – do, it is rather short on what needs to be done to encourage the private sector to save or create jobs. The private sector remains the largest employer by far, yet not enough attention has been given to the environment in which the private sector can maximise the number of jobs created at any given growth rate. This is where future engagement between the private sector and a new government can help to fill the gap – and where several of the present essays can also contribute by helping to create a broader and more balanced agenda for growth and job creation.

This means that social dialogue through Nedlac, or other bilateral engagements with business and civil society, will remain important conduits for the policy responsiveness and flexibility that a changing economic environment will demand of decision-makers. 'Power', it has been said, 'is not a zero-sum game ... The alchemy of good relationships can turn base metal into gold.' By strengthening key relationships at different levels to mobilise additional power and influence, it is possible to boost the quality, speed and impact of appropriate policies and their implementation.

The latest Nedlac Annual Report (2007/8: 3) usefully reminds us of the benefits of 'robust' social dialogue, for example:

- 'consultation leads to the accommodation of the interests of key social partners which is likely to improve the quality of decisions;
- negotiation may build political bases of support for the proposed reforms. Representatives who act on the basis of proper mandates reach agreements that make the reforms more sustainable;
- social dialogue helps consolidate democracy in deeply divided societies by channelling discontent through institutions.'

One example of where consultation will prove valuable is around the key ANC–Cosatu–SACP proposals for the restructuring of government, including the possibility of a 'super-cabinet'. Business and other users of government services could make constructive input on how the possible reconfiguration of ministries could better serve their needs and promote closer cooperation between the public and private sectors. This could be an early priority of the new government.

What may be required is an upgrade, by both the public and private sectors, of the various institutions through which they interact with the government for maximum policy effectiveness and problem-solving. Key stakeholders in the economy and civil society need to enlarge their sphere of influence and the advice given should be professional, structured and coordinated as far as possible. A key test of the confidence of a government is its ability to receive – and respond to – criticism and to improve its systems and reactions in the light of such criticism in the national interest.

This is how someone experienced in the methods of advocacy and compromise expressed it colourfully some decades ago:

> I suggest [he said] that things get done gradually only between opposing forces. There is no such thing as self-restraint in people. What looks like it is indecision. ... It may be that truth is best

sought in the market of free speech, but the best decisions are neither bought nor sold. They are the result of disagreement, where the last word is not 'I admit you're right', but 'I've got to live with the son of a bitch, haven't I'. (Curtis, 1957: 112–13)

All this must *not* mean procrastination. Once consultative and related processes are complete, decisions must be taken and implemented with the necessary political will and expedition. Above all, over the next decade there must emerge, as a continuing element in the life of this country, a group of business, labour, civic, administrative and political leaders who can be relied upon to carry growth and development forward in dynamic ways. A developing society needs particularly to encourage this kind of leadership – leadership that can sensibly assess the long-term direction of events and demonstrate how these can best be shaped in the overall national interest.

The basic theme of the book therefore again affirms that, in the final analysis, *shared* economic prosperity remains the only secure guarantee of a democratic order in South Africa. While there are examples of countries that have flourished economically without democracy, it is difficult to find empirical evidence for the opposite. The search for a better tomorrow – sometimes called 'the procreant urge of the world' – remains at the heart of the economic, as well as the moral, challenge in South Africa. These essays are dedicated to that end.

References

Curtis, C. 1957. *A Commonplace Book*. New York, quoted in W.W. Rostow, *The Stages of Economic Growth*, Cambridge University Press, Cambridge, 1960, p. 151

Fairbanks, M. 2000. *Culture Matters: How Values Shape Human Progress*, ed. by Laurence E. Harrison and Samuel P. Huntington. Basic Books, New York

Greenspan, A. 2007. *The Age of Turbulence*. Allen Lane, London

PCAS. 2008. *South Africa Scenario 2025: The Future We Chose?* Coordination and Advisory Services, Pretoria

2

South Africa's economic performance since 1994: can we do better?

Charlotte du Toit and Johann van Tonder

South Africa's economic successes since 1994 are well known. The new government inherited an economy characterised by high levels of public debt, high inflation and poverty rates, as well as little social security protection for the most vulnerable. Stabilising an economy such as this was a daunting task. Given the successes of fiscal and monetary policy in achieving this stabilisation, the economy was able to share in flourishing international growth rates. Robust growth of 5% after 2004 did not, however, translate into meaningful lower poverty rates as government policies and their implementation were unable to resolve the unemployment and associated socio-economic problems in the economy.

Consequently the gap between the first and second economies in South Africa, with their opposing and unstable fundamentals, widened even further. The first economy is characterised by wealth creation, high levels of output growth, low fiscal debt, well-functioning financial markets and healthy cyclical consumption spending. In contrast the second economy is characterised by levels of extreme poverty stemming from high and structural unemployment as well as poor socio-economic conditions. The dualistic nature of the economy limits production ability and prevents the attainment of sustainable economic growth rates of 6% and higher, in which a larger part of the population should share. Indeed, the higher economic growth rates of the past four years have contributed to huge imbalances as the production capacity limitations were not able to keep up with growing demand. Consequently the economy is even more vulnerable to external shocks.

This chapter reviews the performance of the South African economy during this period of higher growth. It considers the structural impediments that have led to poor performance as well as the socio-economic conditions perpetuating these structural impediments. It concludes with a discussion of the potential lessons for policy-makers.

An unresponsive labour market

Economic growth rates after 2004 increased to levels of 5% after averaging 3% during the preceding ten years. Growth increased steadily to average 3.4% from 2000 to 2004, but jumped almost 50% during 2004–7 (SARB, 2008). Though economic growth was accompanied by an increase of 1.8 million jobs from 2004 to 2007, employment growth was not very high or stable (see Figure 1). In fact, the rate of total employment growth trended downwards from above 6% in 2004 to below 1% in 2007, compared to the upward-trending economic growth rate.

Moreover, the difference between employment growth in the formal and informal sectors is a fundamental problem in the economy. South Africa has relied primarily on faster employment growth in the informal sector, which is closely associated with the second economy, to reduce unemployment, as employment growth in the formal sector has lagged behind (see Figure 2). The inability of the formal sector to contribute meaningfully to job creation in times of higher economic growth is due to constraints in this sector. Indeed, growth in employment in the informal sector confirms the existence of these constraints, which limit or prevent job transmittance from the informal to the formal sector.

Uneven distribution of income and poverty

The high growth rates favouring wealth creation in the formal sector have contributed to an increasing Gini coefficient,[1] which reflects a more skewed distribution of income over this period. Research by the Bureau of Market Research at Unisa showed that South Africa's Gini coefficient increased from 0.57 in 1992 to almost 0.70 in 2008. From this one can infer that the more affluent part of society, including the black middle class (which in 2008 was estimated at 3 million), benefited more from the higher growth rates than the poor.

The increasing Gini coefficient and the high unemployment rate are clear indicators of the limited capacity of the economy to absorb more labour and reduce the skewed income distribution. Moreover, although

Figure 1: Economic growth outpaces employment growth

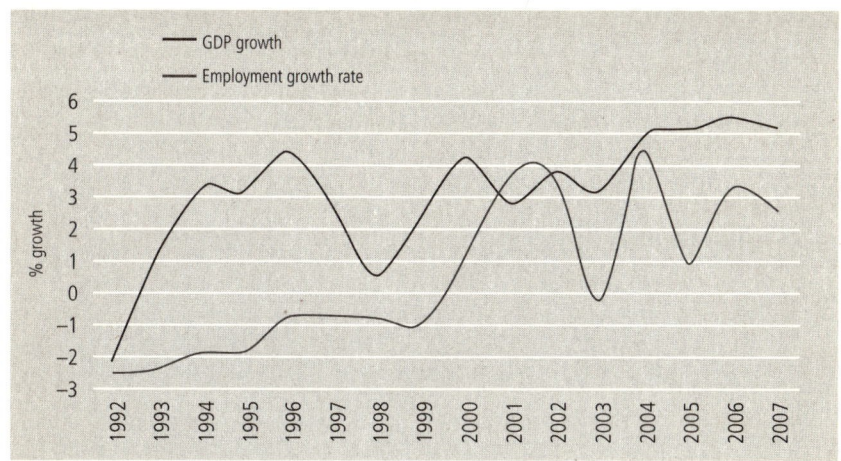

Sources: *SARB Quarterly Bulletin and BMR*

Figure 2: Reliance on employment growth in the informal sector to reduce unemployment

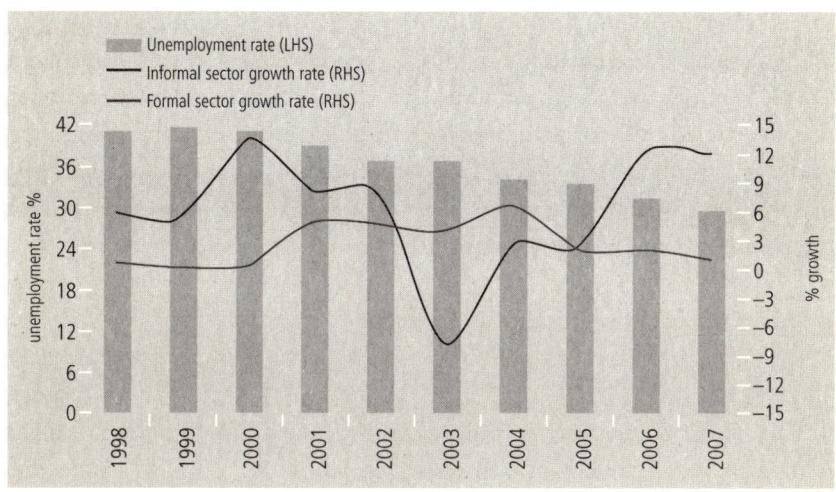

Source: *SARB Quarterly Bulletin and BMR*

the poverty rate as measured by the number of people subsisting below the minimum living level decreased during the period of high economic growth, the drop was in fact marginal – from 47.5% to 46.5% between 2004 and 2007 (see Figure 3).

Figure 3: High GDP growth does not reduce poverty

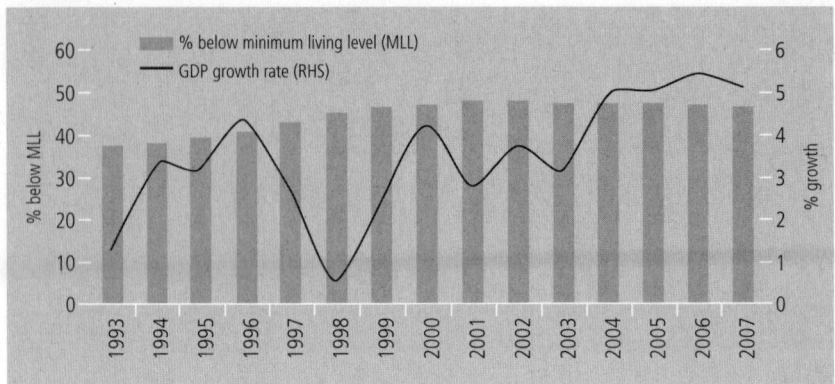

Source: SARB Quarterly Bulletin and BMR

Structural impediments

One reason why the unemployment rate stayed high is that a large part of the potential productive population has been immobilised and incapacitated. A number of structural rigidities prevent them from being employed or participating in any form of income-generating economic activity.

Structural unemployment may be crudely defined as that portion of unemployment that does not adjust with changes in wage rates and economic activity, and can be measured in terms of the non-accelerating wage rate of unemployment (NAWRU).[2] Structural employment is the product of socio-economic and economic factors especially in the supply side of the economy. The factors responsible for structural unemployment include the following.

- Mismatches between skills supplied and demanded;
- Insufficient access to effective education and skills development opportunities;
- Deterioration of skills and motivation of individual jobseekers caused by prolonged periods of unemployment;
- Insufficient opportunities for the unemployed to learn-by-doing or on-the-job training;
- Lack of mobility, exacerbated by high and increasing transport costs as well as the lack of infrastructure maintenance and development;
- Lack of sufficient social support services, resulting in high dependency rates and demand for social security grants.

Our own calculations show that structural unemployment in the South African economy is almost equal to the official unemployment rate as calculated by Statistics South Africa. Unemployment can thus be reduced by addressing the issues responsible for structural unemployment.

Transport

Limited access to transport as well as its cost deprives a large part of the population of the opportunity to work and to be more productive. According to the National Household Travel Survey (NHTS) in 2003 (DoT, 2003), some 38 million citizens lived in households without a car. This makes job-seeking difficult in an environment of poor public transport systems. As for the affordability of transport, some 10% of households (3.7 million) spend more than the maximum target of 10% of income on public transport. According to the NHTS, almost 50% of those earning R500 per month or less spend more than 20% of their earnings on transport.

At the same time, many households, especially the less affluent, live far from job opportunities, because of the history of residential segregation under apartheid. The NHTS found that between 87% and 98% of households do not have access to trains within 15–30 minutes' walking time from home, and between 43% and 52% have to walk longer than 15–30 minutes to buses. Furthermore, some 1.7 million commuters (18% of the total) spend more than an hour on getting to work (DoT, 2008).

These problems increase the cost of job-searching, making it almost impossible for those living on welfare grants. Coupled with the costs of poor public transport systems (many people have to make use of a train, bus and taxi for each trip to work), they make access to work unnecessarily challenging.

Education

Apartheid condemned the major portion of the population to a poor education, thereby contributing to the country's skills shortage. The current education system has not, unfortunately, alleviated the skills problem. As a result, a huge number of South Africans continue to be denied employment in a modern economy that requires skills.

Lack of money is not the problem. As Figure 4 clearly shows, South Africa in 2006 expended 5.4% of GDP on education compared to a weighted world average of 4.7%. Notwithstanding the money spent, South Africa

Figure 4: Public expenditure on education as a percentage of GDP, 2002–5 average

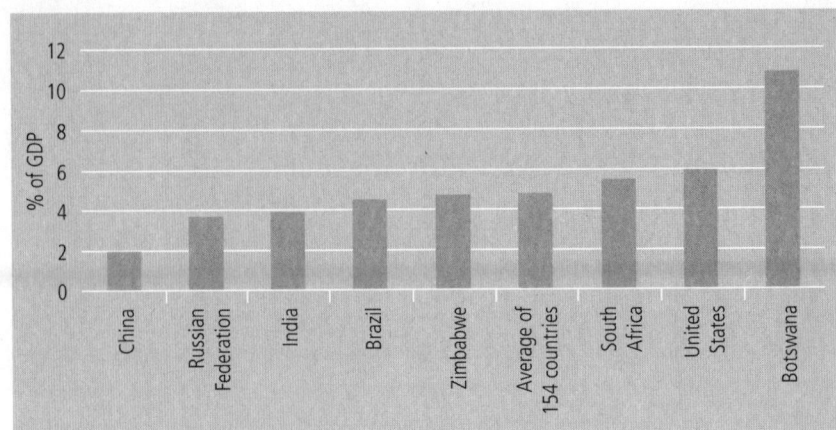

Source: *UNDP Human Development Report 2006*

still cannot produce pupils with basic numeracy and literacy skills. A survey released in 2008 showed a literacy rate of 36% and numeracy rate of 35% amongst Grade three children (Pandor, 2008). Only 10% of the children had scores above 70%. This confirmed the findings of the Progress in International Reading Literacy Study among Grade four pupils in 2006, in which South Africa finished last.

Moreover, pupils are not achieving the targets set by the Department of Education in acquiring mathematical and scientific skills. In 2006 only 13% of learners enrolled for Science and 9% for Mathematics at the higher-grade level.

As for tertiary education, public sector spending is much less compared to the average of 117 countries (see Figure 5). From this one can infer that the major portion of government funding flows to primary and secondary education and that affordability is becoming a stumbling block to tertiary education.

Skills development programmes

Many different initiatives and skills development programmes have been launched over the past decade to address the skills shortage. The life span of these programmes is normally very short as they are constantly replaced and superseded. The current programme of Sector Education and Training Authorities (Setas), which is funded by way of an additional payroll tax on companies, has yet to prove its worth. The preliminary results are mixed.

Figure 5: Current expenditure on tertiary education as a percentage of all levels, 2002–5 average

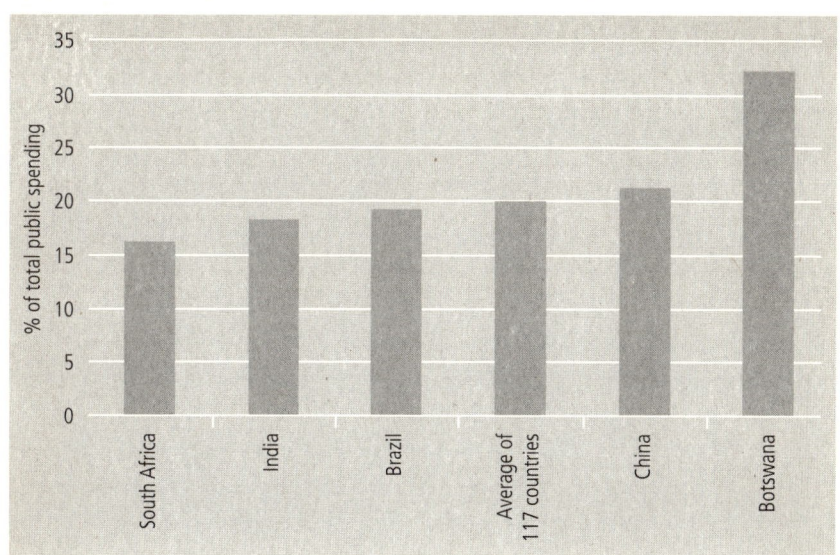

Source: UNDP Human Development Report 2006

Capacity problems have prevented Setas and the National Skills Fund from fully disbursing the taxes collected (DoL, 2008). During 2007/8 Setas managed to spend only R4.3 billion of the R5.1 billion received. Spending from the National Skills Fund was R1.066 billion compared to R1.257 billion received.

The training programmes did achieve some success. Some 101 924 unemployed people received training, of whom 75 431 were placed in jobs. Regarding the training of current workers in scarce and critical skills, 110 870 entered the training programme and 70 526 completed their courses. Of these the number of unemployed receiving training amounted to 56 344 whilst 39 240 completed their courses.

However, 15% of those enrolled in training programmes in 2006 terminated their studies prematurely. According to research by the Human Sciences Research Council (HSRC, 2008a), the respondents cited the poor quality of training as the main reason for not completing their studies. Another issue identified by the HSRC was that workers experience little change in their job status after their training. Promotions and salary increases were not forthcoming as expected by the respondents. Furthermore, as the Setas are not freely accessible to the structurally unemployed, their contribution to the alleviation of unemployment is limited.

Figure 6: Expenditure on health as a percentage of GDP, 2005

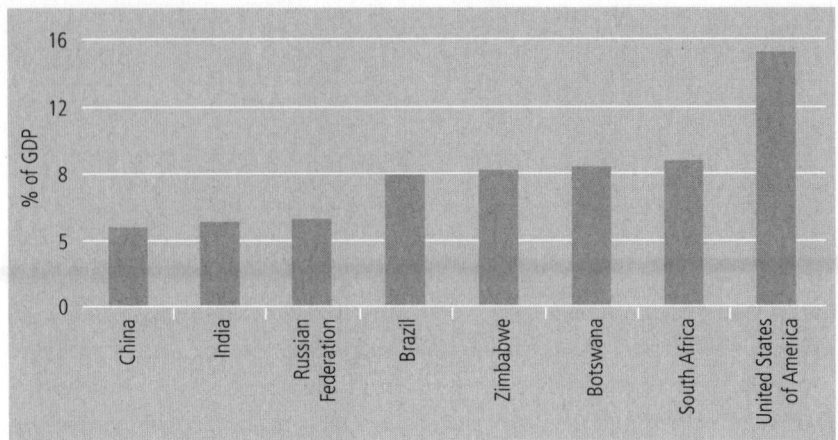

Source: *WHO, 2008*

Health

As with education, money does not seem to be the problem as far as health care is concerned. South Africa's spending on health compares favourably in international terms (see Figure 6). Despite these high spending rates, the country possesses one of the lowest life-expectancy rates.

Being sick and unable to work because of ill health is a serious structural obstacle in the way of skills acquirement, job-seeking and productivity on the job. In addition, the problem is exacerbated by the dwindling number of professional health personnel available to provide treatment.

There is a questionable perception that the healthcare problem can be partly attributed to the fact that the private healthcare sector receives a disproportionately larger piece of total healthcare spending whilst treating fewer patients. South African private healthcare spending compares favourably with that of other countries. In addition, the more affluent who can afford private health care are the same people who contribute most (through taxes) to public healthcare spending, though they do not use public facilities. That 58% of total healthcare spending accrues to the private sector points to a lack of confidence in the public system.

Services backlogs

Another constraint on employment, productivity and the ability to perform better at all levels of life is the huge backlog in the delivery of essential services. Though some inroads have been made, much more needs to be done. According to the Development Bank (DBSA, 2008), some 30% of households in 2008 lived in backyards or very informal structures. In the area of refuse removal almost 40% of households do not receive service; for access to water and electricity, the backlog is 20%.

Crime

According to the World Bank's Investment Climate Survey for 2005, the average cost of crime in South Africa for companies in the formal sector is 1.1% of sales, 3% of net value-added, and 5% of labour costs (World Bank, 2006). Apart from the negative effects on victims' productivity, security and other crime-related costs reduce profits. They also reduce the incentive to invest and thus diminish job-creation prospects. Though the research did not include the informal sector, the cost of crime is likely to be more severe for small and micro businesses in the second economy.

A study of the impact of crime on small businesses commissioned by the South African Presidency revealed that half of the respondents had experienced at least one crime incident in the past year (McDonald, 2008). These businesses were 20% less likely to have increased employment and 10% more likely to have decreased employment than other businesses. A quarter to a third of all respondents expressed unwillingness to expand or invest because of the threat of crime. Regarding the impact on costs, the smallest business can expect to lose 20% of turnover to crime. The study also found that a sizeable proportion of respondents identified the negative psychological impact of crime as significant. This confirms the finding of other research that crime is one of the major reasons for emigration by skilled South Africans.

Although crime did decrease in most categories, the level of severe crimes such as murder, rape and assault is still very high (see Figure 7). There is also a strong perception that corruption is increasing. A 2005 survey by PricewaterhouseCoopers reported increasing levels of corruption (PwC, 2005).

Public works programmes

Public works programmes can make a significant difference in alleviating unemployment and poverty. The first phase of South Africa's public works programme, which started in 2004, had as its goal one million work opportunities or 650 000 real jobs (equivalent to one year's full employment) achieved in five years. Again the results were mixed. The HSRC (Hemson, 2007) reported that while the main target was reached, only 19%

Figure 7: Cumulative change in some crime categories, 1995–2007

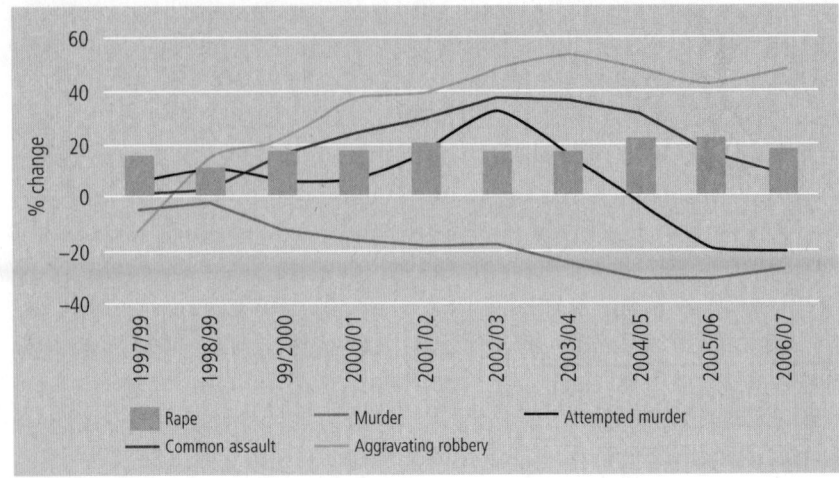

Source: SAPS, 2008

of the training target was met and only 59% of the funds allocated over three years was spent.

Institutional constraints
Information mismatches

What also contributes to unemployment is the lack of information on skills available and skills demanded. An asymmetry of information between employers wanting to fill vacancies and the workforce not knowing about the vacancies further aggravates the unemployment problem. The number of unfilled vacancies is estimated at about one million. Assuming these positions can all be filled by South Africans, the expanded unemployment rate would drop from 30% to 24.3%.

Though the Department of Labour is in the process of developing an integrated employment services system, it lacks accessibility and inclusiveness. The system only managed to place 5 578 people in formal employment despite registering 169 059 workseekers and 15 364 job opportunities. The creation of a national and provincial database of available vacancies and skills would go a long way in reducing the unemployment problem.

Cost of doing business

Appropriate regulations play a vital role in business. But inappropriate regulations can be a burden on society as they limit profitable opportunities and thereby hinder job creation and poverty alleviation.

Research done in 2004 estimated the regulatory compliance costs for the economy at R79 billion (SBP, 2005). Strikingly, the research found that even if all regulations were maintained, the costs could be halved by just simplifying the process of compliance, e.g. reducing the number of steps and forms to be completed. Companies identified difficult and rigid tax and labour regulations as their biggest constraints. The cost of doing business is also inflated by the high and increasing costs charged by state-owned enterprises such as Telkom and Transnet.

Equally important is the fact that regulation works against the objectives of government in job creation. Though tourism was identified as having the potential to create jobs, the compliance burden in this sector was almost three times higher than for the economy in general. While the average recurring compliance cost for businesses was R105 174 p.a. in 2004, in the tourism sector it was R323 286 (SBP, 2006).

Furthermore, confusing, complicated and inflexible procedures were identified by civil servants as a major stumbling block towards more efficient service delivery. According to an HSRC report, red tape in general, skills shortages, time wastage, lack of management and delivery information systems as well as some perverse incentives compound the problem (HSRC, 2008b).

All these problems are reflected by South Africa's standing in the International Finance Corporation's Ease of Doing Business Index for 2008 (World Bank, 2009). Though South Africa's ranking in 32nd place out of 181 economies does not seem bad, it is worse than that of Mauritius, which holds the first position in Africa. The country fares poorly in respect of labour and international trade. By relaxing some labour market regulations (especially difficulty of hiring and firing and rigidity of working hours), halving the time to import and export, and reducing the costs of importing and exporting containers, South Africa would jump to the 22nd position – above Mauritius and into the company of some of the world's top economies.

Factor productivity constraints
Technology

Most successful countries strive to improve international competitiveness as a means to increase production capacity and thus to generate jobs, skills and wealth. Technological improvement is one of the key measures for improving international competitiveness. South Africa has shown progress in this respect in various sectors but overall progress has been slow compared to other countries. As a result South Africa has lost several positions in international competitiveness rankings. South Africa slipped from 37th to 51st position in the 2007/8 Networked Readiness Index of the World Economic Forum (WEF, 2008). Table 1 provides an indication of South Africa's international strengths and weaknesses.

Research and development

As a way of improving the country's competitiveness, the government has sought to stimulate research and development (R&D). Various fiscal incentives exist for companies, universities and government agencies to invest more in R&D. However, according to the Organisation for Economic Cooperation and Development's latest research on R&D, South Africa is ranked 26th out of 39 countries in terms of total spending on R&D (OECD, 2007). Nevertheless, at 0.95% in 2006, South Africa approached its target of 1% for gross expenditure on research and development (Gerd) as a percentage of GDP. According to the Department of Science and Technology (DST, 2007), Gerd for the leading OECD countries is 3% of GDP.

Of concern is that South Africa has a huge lack of full-time researchers. The number of full-time researchers per 1000 of the population is 1.5, the same as for China but far behind Sweden's 12.6 and Japan's 11. As R&D output is significantly influenced by the number of researchers, major steps need to be taken to improve the situation.

The major recipients of research spending remained the same in 2006 and 2007. In 2006 the field of engineering sciences received 21% of total spending, followed by 20.3% for natural sciences, 15.1% for medical and health sciences and 14% for information, computer and communication technologies. What is of concern is that research spending on agriculture is not very high on the priority list even though the country is dependent on its agricultural sector for food provision.

International competitiveness

South Africa has more or less maintained its same position in the World Economic Forum's 2008/9 Global Competitiveness Index, which was released in October 2008. Its ranking out of 134 countries in 2008/9 was 45th, compared to 44th place out of 131 countries in 2007/8. Though it improved in most categories in its scores, other countries improved at a

Table 1: South Africa's international competitiveness

Strengths (SA economy's 10 best ranks)		Weaknesses (SA economy's 10 worst ranks)	
Variable name	Rank	Variable name	Rank
Prevalence of foreign technology licensing	11	Quality of maths and science education	125
Financial market sophistication	15	Quality of competition in the ISP sector	108
Number of procedures to enforce a contract	15	Quality of the educational system	101
Efficiency of legal framework	17	Availability of scientists and engineers	101
Effectiveness of law-making bodies	19	Burden of government regulation	98
Extent of staff training	21	Availability of new telephone lines	97
Property rights	22	Internet bandwidth	93
Quality of management schools	22	Tertiary enrolment	90
Judicial independence	23	Residential monthly telephone subscription	87
Intellectual property protection	24	Number of telephone lines	86

Source: *WEF, 2008*

faster rate. The major reasons cited for this failure to improve its international competitiveness are poor health and education delivery, and inefficient labour markets. Indeed, it is on account of these two areas that South Africa is constantly losing ranking positions. Compared to other African countries, South Africa is in the second position after Tunisia.

South Africa's performance is even poorer according to the Institute for Management Development's *World Competitiveness Yearbook*, which was released on 2 June 2008. In 2008 South Africa was ranked 53rd out of 55 countries compared to 50th position the previous year.

Macroeconomic constraints
Insufficient investment

In the absence of structural impediments, investment can be a powerful driver of sustainable and shared economic growth. Investment is well known to provide benefits through the accelerator-multiplier effects on economic growth and job creation, as well as its forward and backward linkages to other sectors of the economy.

However, despite the increase in net investment growth over the past few years, South Africa only reached the 4% growth mark in 2007 after a quarter of a century of low growth. The lack of larger investment growth was the product of a number of factors.

Lack of investment in infrastructure: Apartheid was responsible for the lack of sufficient economic and social investment until the early 1990s, and

Figure 8: Government spending on economic affairs is sacrificed to pay debt

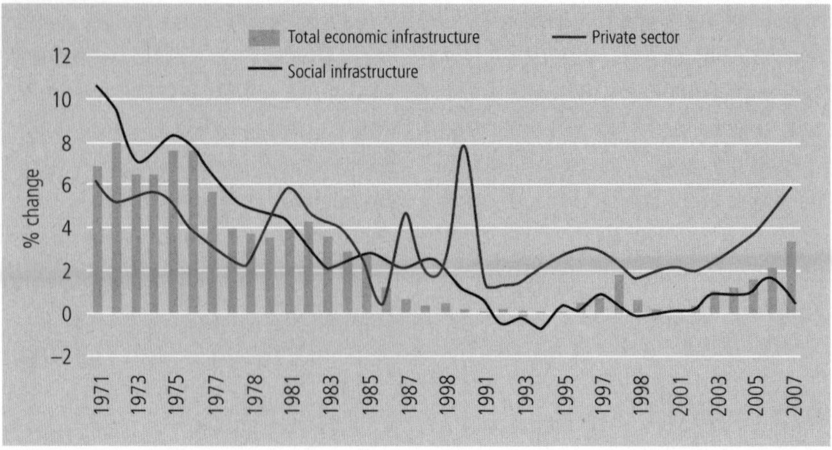

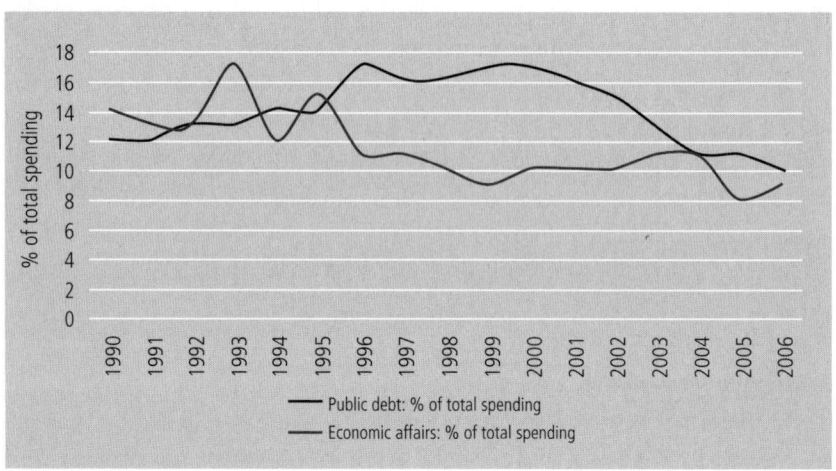

Source: SARB Quarterly Bulletins

Figure 9: Growth in infrastructure and private sector investment

Source: SARB Quarterly Bulletins

at the same time political uncertainty prohibited private sector investment. From the middle of the 1990s to 2002 the government decided to reduce public debt, but this happened at the expense of spending on economic and social infrastructure (see Figure 8). It was only from 2003 onwards that investment in infrastructure started increasing (see Figure 9).

Economic growth responded positively to the growth in infrastructure investment. Over the same period, private sector investment grew constantly at rates last observed in the 1970s. As a result, the expanded unemployment rate declined fairly rapidly from 37% in 2003 to 29% in 2007.

High interest rates a restriction on fixed investment growth: Also detrimental to investment growth was the effect of the high inflation rates and inflation targeting regime in increasing the cost of capital. The constant higher growth rates in investment experienced recently despite higher interest rates can be attributed to compulsory investment accruing from the state infrastructure programme (R482 billion till 2011), the Gautrain project and preparations for the 2010 World Soccer Cup tournament, which all stimulated private-sector investment as well.

Falling savings rate limits local financing pool: Investment growth was also hampered by low local savings. According to the Reserve Bank, the local savings rate declined steadily from more than 20% of GDP a few decades ago to 14% in 2007. In addition, not all local savings are available for investment financing as some are utilised to finance South African investment abroad. In 2007 only 56% of local savings were available for local investment financing needs. As a result, South Africa has to rely on foreign savings to finance its investment growth.

Foreign saving inflows not ideal: Unfortunately South Africa has not received a large portion of foreign direct investment (FDI) (see Figure 10). Though the figures indicate large FDI inflows in some years, they reflect a few large take-over transactions, mainly in the services sector. Through its failure to attract new green-field FDI, the country has had to rely on volatile, easily withdrawable, short-term capital flows to finance its investment needs.

Production growth lagging behind

In the primary sectors of mining and agriculture, the structural impediments discussed above have played a major role in preventing production from keeping up with spending growth. Growth rates in these subsectors varied considerably from high negative to very high positive growth rates. However, as the weights of the mining and agriculture subsectors are small, the sector as a whole was not able to contribute consistently to economic growth.

In contrast, growth in the secondary sector of construction accelerated markedly. Though growth in the manufacturing sector picked up pace from 2003 onward, it was not enough to outpace spending growth, which averaged 7% after 2003. As a result, South Africa has become increasingly

Figure 10: Foreign portfolio inflows are a major source of investment finance

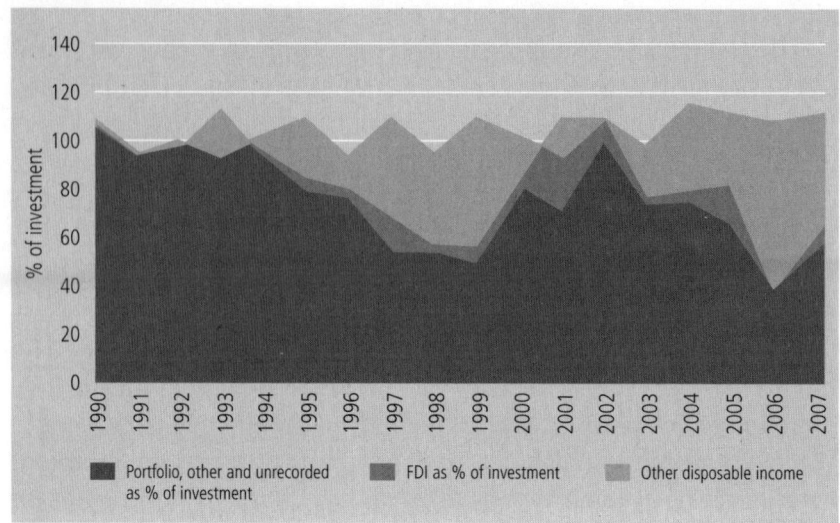

Source: SARB Quarterly Bulletins

more dependent on imports to satisfy consumer demand. As for electricity, the current lack of capacity shows in the rather low growth rates in this subsector.

The tertiary sector of services was to a larger extent able to provide for the needs created by the increase in spending growth. Constant increases in investments by the financial, trading, and transport and telecommunications subsectors were a major contributing reason for the ability of this sector to satisfy increasing demand. These subsectors managed to register growth rates of more than 5% after 2004.

Demand-side issues

Faster economic growth was mainly the result of demand-side-driven policies. Growth in spending by households (because of tax and interest rate cuts) and government, as well as an increase in investment spending, combined to produce some of the highest spending growth rates in the economy in decades. Growth in gross domestic expenditure increased by more than 9% in 2006 compared to rates barely higher than 4% in preceding decades. However, because of capacity constraints, local production did not keep pace with spending growth, and this created imbalances in the economy.

Figure 11: Tax relief boosts disposable income

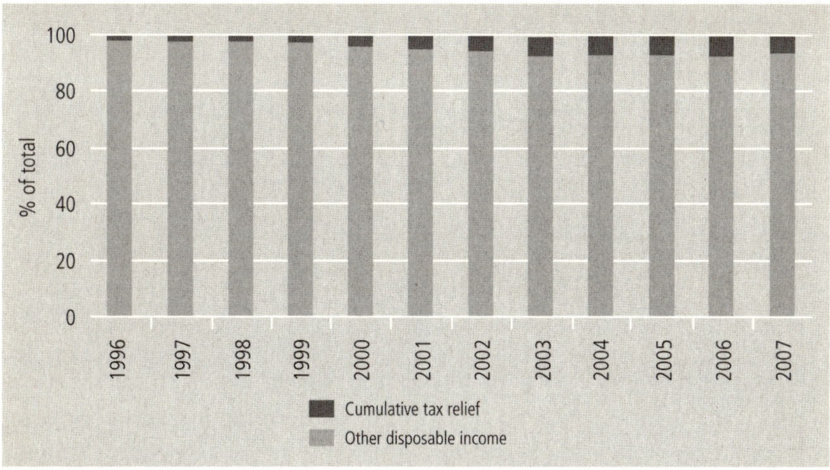

[Bar chart showing % of total from 1996 to 2007, with Cumulative tax relief and Other disposable income]

Source: *National Treasury Budget Review 1995–2008*

Fiscal policy

Fiscal policy was highly successful in stabilising the economy (by lowering state debt and the fiscal deficit) and then implementing policies for growth. Another success story was the reorganisation of state expenditure to address socio-economic needs and poverty alleviation. Furthermore, tax collection became more efficient as a result of various initiatives to increase the tax base. Almost 8.3 million taxpayers are currently registered – a long way from the 4 million of a decade ago.

After the initial phase of stabilisation, fiscal policy became expansionary from 2002 onwards, and spending growth rates of higher than 5% were registered. In addition, tax relief to individuals and others boosted disposable income (see Figure 11). The cumulative and compounded income tax relief to individuals since 1995 has amounted to more than R600 billion. Calculations show that the cumulative income tax relief comprises some 7% of household disposable income. After 2004 the boost in disposable income enabled households to increase their spending to rates above 7%, propelling annual economic growth rates to levels of 5%.

Monetary policy

South Africa employs inflation targeting to guide monetary policy decisions. In 2003 there was a major change in monetary policy and the repo rate was reduced by 5.5 percentage points within six months and twice during the next two years to 10.5%. This induced a massive credit uptake. According to the December 2008 *Quarterly Bulletin* of the South African Reserve Bank, credit growth outpaced income growth and as a result the ratio of household debt to disposable income increased to a high of 78.2% in the first quarter of 2008 from 52.6% in the last quarter of 2003. Companies reacted to the more profitable outlook and seized the opportunity to increase consumption and investment spending, thereby catapulting credit growth to even higher levels. This caused the rate of increase in gross domestic expenditure to reach a high of 9.2% in 2006. On the household side, it caused spending growth to exceed income growth by a growing margin (see Figure 12).

The imbalance between income and spending, which in a macroeconomic sense is most visible in the form of higher inflation and a growing current account deficit, eventually contributed to an increase in interest rates of 33% over a period of two years to June 2008. Together with the impact of high oil prices and the international credit crisis, the higher interest rates caused economic growth to slow in 2008.

Current account deficit (CAD)

The current account deficit, defined as the difference between gross domestic expenditure and gross national disposable income, or the difference between gross local savings and investment or between foreign payments and foreign receipts, has grown into a fully fledged structural problem. Though the structural nature of the CAD also contributed to the trade deficit increasing, the magnitude of the trade deficit is smaller than that of the services and income deficit combined. There are two reasons why the CAD became structural in nature. The first has to do with foreign transport service payments and the second with foreign exchange controls.

Although in 1970 South Africa had 50 vessels on the ship register, in 2005 there was only one left. As 80% to 95% of exports and imports are transported on freight ships, the country has had to turn to foreigners for this service. Taking other transportation services as a proxy for foreign payments and receipts for transporting exports and imports, South Africa's foreign receipts for transport services have been declining at a relatively fast pace since 1998. Expressed as a percentage of foreign payments for goods transport, foreign receipts declined from 40% in 1990 to about 6% in 2007. Given the lack of local freight transport ownership, South Africa has had to make an increasing amount of payments to foreign owners of

Figure 12: Household spending growth outpaces wage growth

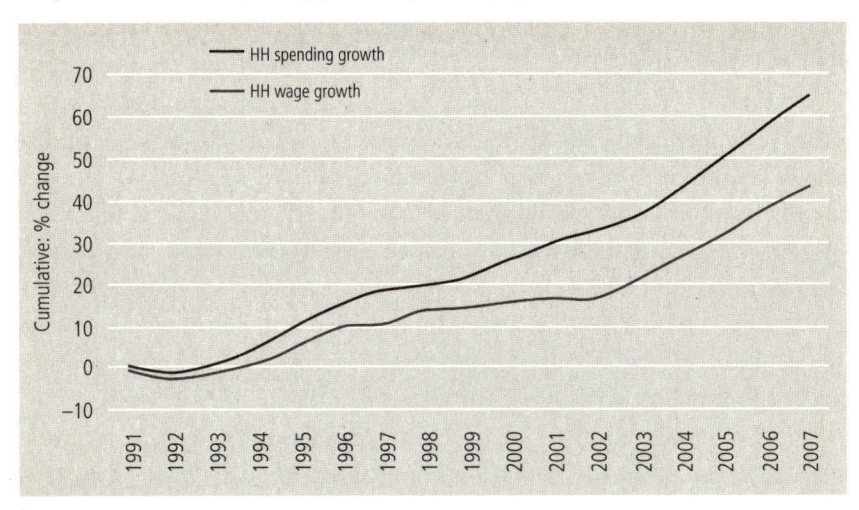

Source: SARB Quarterly Bulletins

Figure 13: Net foreign payments for transporting goods rises steeply

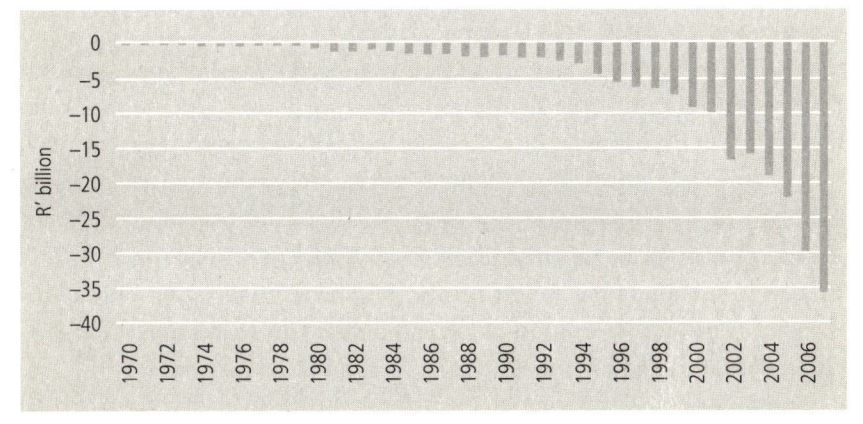

Source: SARB Quarterly Bulletins

vessels to transport the country's imports and exports. As Figure 13 shows, net foreign payments for transportation of goods increased from R6 billion in 1998 to R36 billion in 2007 and formed a substantial 25% of the CAD in 2007.

The second reason for the CAD becoming structural in nature has to do with foreign exchange controls. Though foreign exchange controls may have protected South Africa from the international credit crisis, they have also contributed to distortions in the economy. The biggest direct distortion is that they helped support an artificially high exchange rate, as two-way flows of money have been inhibited. As a result the rand exchange rate over the years has been kept at stronger levels, contributing to artificially lower inflation. This allowed interest rates to be reduced to levels that would otherwise not have been attained.

The artificially strong rand curbed South African exports and made imports cheaper, helping create a growing trade deficit and thus current account deficit. In this process the exporting manufacturing industry became especially uncompetitive, resulting in changing business models and the shedding of labour. The contribution of exports to total foreign receipts declined from almost 90% in the 1980s to less than 80% after 2004.

Furthermore, as South African companies were not able to invest freely in foreign countries, the country accumulated a net foreign income deficit. That dividends and interest payments to foreigners exceed dividend and interest income has become the biggest contributor to the increase in CAD. Net dividend and interest payments comprised 43% of the CAD in 2007, whereas the trade deficit was only 28%.

Even though the CAD had been growing because increases in production capacity were not able to keep up with spending, the shortfall was financed comfortably (see Figure 14). However, South Africa is unable to lure sufficient new foreign direct investment as a dominant source of CAD financing. In fact, most of the foreign direct investment received thus far has involved the take-over or purchase of interests in existing companies. Though these attract an initial inflow of capital, the long-run impact is negative as dividend payments to these companies will exceed the initial inflow – a case of selling the family silverware and then paying the purchaser for keeping it.

South Africa has thus to rely heavily on short-term portfolio capital to finance the CAD. This was not a problem as long as foreign investors had a risk appetite. However, in times of crisis, foreign investors normally withdraw their investments from emerging markets and this causes the currencies of these countries to tumble.

In addition, given the lack of foreign capital inflows, South Africa is using its foreign reserves to finance the CAD. Though the official foreign reserves held by the Reserve Bank have increased at a stable pace, the foreign currency reserves of South African banks are declining. Latest figures released by the Reserve Bank show that banks' foreign currency

Figure 14: Capital inflows sufficient to finance CAD

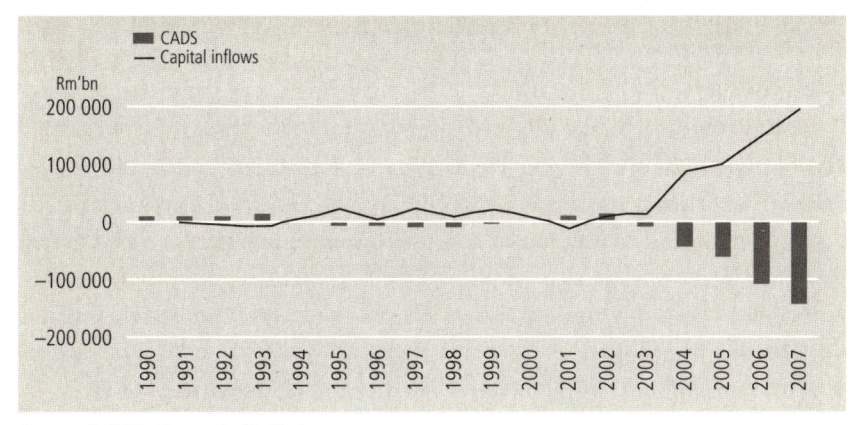

Source: SARB Quarterly Bulletins

Figure 15: South Africa's net foreign liabilities are increasing at an alarming rate

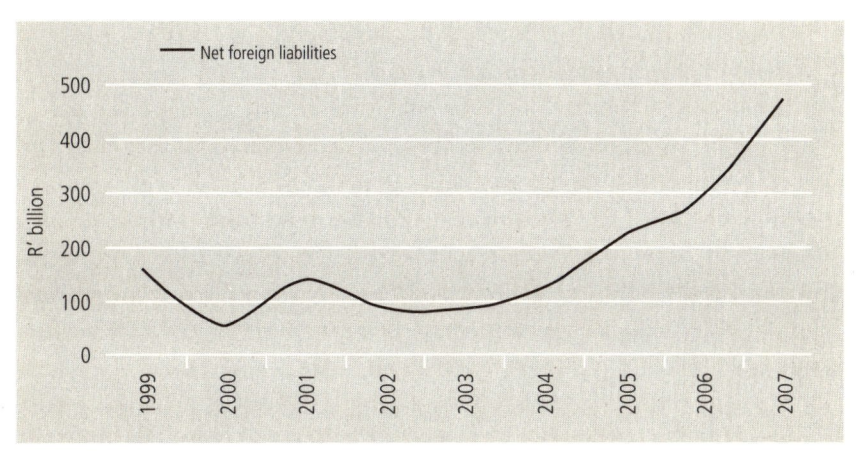

Source: SARB Quarterly Bulletins

reserves declined from R235 billion in August 2007 to R162 billion in July 2008.

Finally, South Africa's net foreign liabilities are increasing at an alarming rate (see Figure 15). This can be ascribed especially to the steep increase in dividend and interest payments to foreigners who invest in South Africa. Figure 15 shows that total net foreign liabilities (after deducting foreign assets) increased to R465 billion in 2007 from R80 billion in 2003. Of this amount, the net liabilities accruing from dividend and interest payments increased from R37 to R388 billion. This will add to the current strain on the rand if not corrected through prudent macroeconomic policies.

Conclusion

South Africa's average economic growth rate of 5% from 2004 to 2007 can be regarded as a blessing in disguise, as it revealed policy and implementation constraints limiting the economy's capacity to produce goods, absorb labour and reduce poverty. The following inferences can be drawn from our analysis:

- Higher economic growth rates from 2004 to 2007 were accompanied by higher employment.
- However, higher employment growth rates were primarily driven by employment growth in the informal sector of the economy.
- The formal sector is unable to absorb more labour.
- Much of the wealth creation following this growth was in the formal sector through increased asset and income growth.
- As a result the divergence between the poor and rich increased, as shown by the growing Gini coefficient.
- Moreover, the country's poverty rate as measured by the percentage of people below the minimum living level decreased only marginally despite four years of higher economic growth.

Impediments to higher employment growth come from both the supply and demand sides of the economy. Moreover, they are structural, institutional and cyclical in nature. Structural unemployment refers to structural rigidities preventing a large part of the potentially productive labour market from participating in any form of income-generating activities. Accordingly, adjustments in wage rates and economic activity will change little in the labour market. The factors responsible for structural unemployment include the following:

- Transportation and location constraints prevent a search for jobs.
- There is a mismatch between skills demanded and skills supply.
- There is insufficient access to educational and training opportunities to alleviate the skills shortage.
- Inadequate health facilities disable many seeking jobs.
- Poor housing and lack of access to other infrastructural services exacerbate poor conditions of living and limit the chance of productive opportunities.

Research has proved that ameliorating socio-economic conditions play an important part in improving the employability of the labour supply, including the structurally unemployed and discouraged workforce. At the same time, our analysis highlighted the policy and implementation constraints preventing an improvement in socio-economic conditions at the pace required to make a meaningful difference in the lives of the unemployed and of the population in general. These constraints include the following:
- Though South Africa is spending more on education than the world average, the quality of the output of this system is poor.
- Spending for the improvement of skills by means of the Sector Education and Training Authorities (Setas) and the National Skills Fund (NSF) continues to be hampered by institutional capacity, and its impact has been limited as a result.
- The Expanded Public Works Programme also produced mixed results.
- Spending on health care does not seem to be a problem but the country's life expectancy is one of the lowest in the world.
- The level of crime is another debilitating factor, decreasing employment opportunities especially in the small business sector.

A range of institutional factors not only prevents job creation, but also contributes to job vacancies not being filled.
- There is an asymmetry in information regarding job vacancies and available workers.
- The regulatory burden is not only increasing the cost of doing business, but also hampers more efficient service delivery by the government.
- Labour market rigidities and complicated tax regulations were identified as the most important problems for companies to deal with.
- The high cost of importing and exporting is another debilitating factor.

Though all of these factors have a direct and indirect impact on productivity, information technology and R&D are becoming increasingly important as incisive factors for improving competitiveness and economic progress. South Africa can do much more to improve its performance in these areas.

Though it is widely accepted and proven that investment is the most important driver of employment growth, many factors contribute to a lack of investment growth in the economy:

- Investment spending growth receded for decades and only recently picked up speed when government decided to increase infrastructure spending and the private sector saw profit opportunities.
- Investment spending was also hampered by high interest rates as South Africa struggled to reduce its inflation rate.
- The financing of investment was restricted by a lack of local savings available for investment.
- The country's reliance on foreign capital to finance its investment needs increased immensely from 2003 to 2007.
- However, the country failed to compete effectively for foreign direct investments, and the savings attracted were mostly foreign portfolio investments, which can be withdrawn overnight, making the economy vulnerable to and dependent on international developments.

With these and a myriad other factors hampering production, South Africa has had to rely especially on the services sector to propel its economic growth rate.

On the demand side the economy started boiling during the early to mid-2000s. Household and government consumption spending elevated company profits and contributed to investment spending growth in order to meet the higher demand. However, given the supply-side constraints, huge imbalances developed which have come to limit the economy's capacity to create new jobs and reduce the structural unemployment problem. These imbalances are manifested in the current account of the balance of payments, which is registering record deficits. Moreover, the current account deficit has developed into a structural problem. Although it has till now been comfortably financed by foreign inflows, the problem with the inflows is that they are of a volatile and short-term nature. The fragility of the current policy stance, which allows the deficit to grow and finances it with foreign portfolio flows, has been exposed by the international financial crisis that is now being experienced.

Notes

1   The Gini coefficient is a measure of inequality of income distribution or inequality of wealth distribution. It is expressed as a ratio with values between 0 and 1. A low Gini coefficient indicates more equal income or wealth distribution, while a high Gini coefficient indicates more unequal distribution. A value of 0 corresponds to perfect equality (everyone having exactly the same income) and 1 corresponds to perfect inequality (one person has all the income, while everyone else has zero income).

2   NAWRU or the non-accelerating wage rate of unemployment is a uniquely designed measure developed by Prof. Charlotte du Toit of the Department of Economics at the University of Pretoria. It states that workers will remain unemployed despite high increases in wage rates and increased economic activity. This is because these workers are structurally inhibited from participating in the labour market due to a number of factors.

References

DBSA. 2008. *Infrastructure Barometer. Economic and Social Infrastructure in South Africa: Scenarios for the Future.* DBSA, Pretoria

DoL. 2008. *Annual Report* (www.labour.gov.za)

DoT. 2003. *National Household Travel Survey 2003* (www.transport.gov.za)

DoT. 2008. *National Transport Master Plan 2050. Phase 1* (www.transport.gov.za)

DST. 2007. *National Survey of Research and Experimental Development 2006/07* (http://www.dst.gov.za)

Hemson, D. 2007. Expanded Public Works Programme: Hope for the Unemployed. *HSRC Review*, 6 (3), September 2008

HSRC. 2008a. The State of Skills in South Africa. *HSRC Review*, 6 (4), November 2008 (http://www.hsrc.ac.za)

HSRC. 2008b. Is There Value for Money in Public Sector Delivery? *HSRC Review*, 6 (2), June 2008 (http://www.hsrc.ac.za)

McDonald, K. 2008. *The Impact of Crime on Small Businesses in South Africa* (http://www.sbp.org.za)

OECD. 2007. Research Database

Pandor, N. 2008. Address at the Foundation Phase Conference, 30 September 2008 (http://www.search.gov.za)

PwC. 2005. Survey to Determine the Perception of Corruption in South Africa

SAPS. 2008. See http://www.saps.gov.za for crime statistics

SARB. 2008. *Quarterly Bulletin.* Pretoria

SBP. 2005. *Counting the Cost of red Tape for Business in South Africa*, ed. C. Darroll, L. Schlemmer, G. Bannock, L. Ahmed, D. Irvine and K. McDonald.

SBP. 2006. *Counting the Cost of Red Tape for Tourism in South Africa*, ed. C. Darroll, L. Schlemmer, S. Dagut, D. Irvine, K. McDonald and S. Meny-Gilbert.

UNDP. 2006. *Human Development Report* (http://hdr.undp.org)

WEF. 2008. *The Global Information Technology Report 2007–2008* (http://www.insead.edu)

WHO. 2008. *World Health Statistics Report 2008* (http://www.who.int)

World Bank. 2006. *South Africa: An Assessment of the Investment Climate.* Report 34907 (http://go.worldbank.org)

World Bank. 2009. *Doing Business in South Africa* (http://www.doingbusiness.org)

3

Economic policy: some lessons from Southeast Asia

Lefentse Nokaneng and Chris Harmse

During the 1960s the founder members of the Association of Southeast Asian Nations (ASEAN) – Indonesia, Malaysia, Thailand, the Philippines and Singapore – found themselves, like South Africa in 1994, in a critically important transitional phase, both politically and economically. None of them had fully recovered from the ravages of war or domestic violence; they were poor and almost no capital was available for investment. They all adopted the same approach to economic development: they opened their economies to greater international competition, and embarked upon a course of rapid industrialisation. This approach has since turned out to be a fruitful way of stimulating growth and development and a good example from which to draw at least guidelines for a successful economic policy.

Their policies were not developed separately from other governmental goals and planning strategies. In many cases a pragmatic approach was followed: governments were responsive, and able to react, to changes or challenges. Not only did they have to address issues of land reform, demographic change, education and health, labour and public administration, but at the same time absorb external shocks, above all the OPEC oil crisis of the early 1970s and the East Asian financial crisis of 1997–8. These external shocks contributed heavily to a deterioration in their terms of trade, a slowdown in foreign demand for their exports and growing external debt. Despite all these domestic and global challenges, the ASEAN countries nevertheless managed to maintain high real growth rates and to sustain general economic development by alleviating poverty, creating sustainable jobs and closing the gap between rich and poor.

More importantly, the experiences of the East Asian countries show clearly that peaceful political change can only take place on a foundation of stable and continuous economic development. Successful economic development since the 1960s has improved the standard of living of almost everyone in the East Asian region. Economic success in these countries has created a large middle class which has a vested interest in political stability. The golden thread running through the transition path of all these countries is the responsibility of government for maintaining a stable and peaceful political environment for economic development.

As the countries that embarked on outward-oriented adjustment policies in the early 1960s have invariably enjoyed considerable economic gains irrespective of their initial income levels, the question arises: what lessons can policy-makers in South Africa learn from them? Can we achieve similar growth, development, employment and poverty alleviation through greater participation in the world economy? Are there conditions and strategies which can be laid down for such a process to be successful and sustainable in the sense of producing growth and development over a long period?

Economic policy in Southeast Asia and South Africa

The economic achievements of the East Asian newly industrialised economies (NIEs) have been widely studied. There are obvious similarities in these economies, e.g. the drive to grow and develop through export expansion and productivity. Yet each has also had its own preconditions and approaches, varying as they do in the size of the economy, initial endowments and the role of government. A scrutiny of the vast literature on these countries indicates that necessary conditions for success do indeed exist. They can be summarised as the following: efficiency in production and welfare gains; socio-economic development policies; macroeconomic stability; a domestic policy mix consistent with overall fiscal constraint; and supply-side adjustment policies.

There has been intense controversy about the nature and implementation of structural adjustment programmes aimed at improving the growth and economic development of developing countries. Structural adjustment has two broad objectives, viz. establishing (and maintaining) macroeconomic stability, and improving microeconomic efficiency. There are extensive debates about the target and speed of macroeconomic adjustment and the timing and sequence of microeconomic measures for implementing the required policy and institutional reforms. However, the countries that undertook outward-orientation policies – which are associated with trade and investment liberalisation, a flexible and convertible currency, microeconomic reforms and macroeconomic stability – were not only successful with their adjustment processes, but were also able to absorb external shocks.

The policy objectives of the East Asian economies beginning in the 1960s were very similar to those of South Africa today. In general we can say that a stable macroeconomic environment was a prerequisite for successful economic development. The ASEAN countries targeted macroeconomic stability by
- containing budget deficits within a manageable range;
- containing inflation;
- responding promptly to macroeconomic shocks through adequate incentives for savings and investments and strengthening policies of outward-oriented trade and foreign direct investment; and
- directing social development policies in respect of health, education and infrastructure towards the reduction of inequality in order to stimulate growth.

South Africa's adjustment process during the post-apartheid era has been called 'getting the macroeconomic fundamentals correct'. Both the Growth, Employment and Redistribution strategy (Gear) and the Accelerated and Shared Growth Initiative for South Africa (Asgisa) explicitly targeted macroeconomic variables. Under the Gear programme an economic growth target of 6.0% by 2000 was the main target (the economy had failed to reach average real growth rates of more than 2.5% during the 1990s). Under the Asgisa strategy an average economic growth of 4.0% would have to be maintained until 2009, whereafter an increased target of 6.0% per annum was set until 2014; another target was to halve the unemployment rate of 25% to 12.5% by 2014.

The first thrust of strategy was to stabilise the economic environment, by achieving fiscal discipline: a budget surplus (down from the deficit of almost 8.0% at the beginning of the 1990s) was the aim in view. Government expenditure priorities were also shifted towards greater social development spending on education and health. This was accompanied by a substantial increase in government expenditure on social and economic investment. The second thrust of strategy involved monetary stabilisation: an inflation target band of between 3% and 6% was set. Inflation was to be managed by a monetary policy committee (MPC), using the repo rate (discount rate) as the main instrument.

Table 1: Key economic and development indicators for selected East Asian economies and South Africa

Country	Population		Life expectancy at birth (years)		Real GDP growth (average annual growth)		
	Total (mil) 2006	% growth 2000–6	Male 2005	Female 2005	1980–9	1990–9	2000–7
China	1312	0.6	70	74	8.0	8.8	8.7
Indonesia	223	1.3	66	70	5.9	4.1	4.6
Korea	48	0.5	74	81	7.0	5.6	4.9
Malaysia	26	1.9	71	76	5.5	6.5	4.9
Philippines	85	1.8	69	73	1.7	2.6	4.5
Singapore	4	1.5	78	82	6.9	6.8	5.0
Taiwan	023	0.6	75	8	8.2	6.5	3.8
Thailand	65	0.9	68	74	6.7	4.6	4.7
South Africa	47	1.2	47	49	2.1	1.3	4.0

*Negative current account to GDP values indicates a deficit on the current account.

Source: IMF Financial Statistics (various issues) and Daquila, 2007; World Bank

At the same time a comprehensive programme of trade liberalisation was introduced: a substantial number of quotas were abolished and replaced by lower tariffs. The dual exchange rate of the financial and commercial rand was scrapped and replaced by a flexible exchange rate. Exchange controls were lifted completely for foreigners and gradually for citizens. A fully fledged free-trade agreement between the 16 states of the Southern African Development Community (SADC) was introduced in 2008. A revised outcomes-based education system replaced previous systems, and provinces were given autonomy to manage their own economic development programmes.

As this analysis shows, the South African adjustment strategy after 1994 was not much out of line with that of the Asian economies of the 1970s–1990s. The main differences lie in the outcome of these policies. The Asian NIEs far outperformed South Africa's economy. Not only did they manage to keep their real economic growth rates high during times of severe downturn, but they continued to increase their share in world trade, create more jobs, develop capacity for even higher growth, attract more and more foreign direct investment, and enjoy balance of payments surpluses. Their per capita incomes more than doubled within two decades, whilst their distribution of income became more even. South Africa, on the other hand,

GDP per capita	Unemployment rate (%)				Adult literacy rate	Current account/GDP (%)		
% growth 2000–6	1984	1997–9	2002	2005	Ages 15 and older (%) 2000–5	1980–9	1990–9	2000–7
8.3	1.9	2.3	3.0	4.2	91	−0.3	1.7	6.1
3.8	6.8	3.9	5.9	10.3	90	−2.5	−1.0	3.0
3.9	3.8	4.0	3.8	3.7	87	−0.6	0.4	1.7
2.5	5.8	5.3	3.2	3.5	89	−2.9	−1.7	13.2
2.4	7.0	8.9	9.2	7.4	93	−1.9	−3.9	1.2
2.6	2.7	3.4	3.8	4.2	93	−1.8	14.22	20.2
3.6	2.5	4.2	3.3	2.8	90	9.2	3.5	7.5
4.0	4.8	2.4	1.9	1.3	93	−3.9	2.6	3.4
2.7	25.0	24.4	27.1	26.7	68	0.9	−0.05	−3.6

still struggles with ever-increasing poverty levels, high unemployment, lack of capacity and skills, and balance of payments deficits 14 years after the introduction of the new policy regime.

Economic performance

Traditionally, the progress or development of a country was mainly measured in terms of economic growth or an increase in income per capita. These approaches, while effective, do not give an indication of the improvement or deterioration of people's quality of life. For example, while an economy may record high income per capita levels, a significant part of the population may be subject to premature mortality, high unemployment, illiteracy, social exclusion and so forth (see Table 1). In analysing the performance of the Asian NIEs compared to South Africa we need therefore to focus both on economic and human development indicators.

A major achievement of the outward-oriented policies of the Asian NIEs was increased efficiency in production. From this followed eventual welfare gains in the form of higher per capita income and increased employment. The usual indicator of the performance of any economy is the growth in GDP. The Asian tigers have recorded impressive growth levels as a consequence of their outward-orientated economic and rapid industrialisation policies. The industrialisation policy depended on channelling foreign direct investment (FDI) first during the import-substitution industrialisation phase (1950s and 1960s), and thereafter towards exports during the export-oriented industrialisation phase. Indicative of the impact of this policy change, manufactured goods as a percentage of total exports rose from 18% to 79% between 1970 and 2001.

Table 2 shows trade and income per capita for five of the ASEAN countries for selected years. Although these countries went into a severe recession in the late 1990s, which decreased welfare per head of population, economic reforms and increased trade have led to a strong recovery in per capita income. All the countries increased their trade per capita by more than 100% between 1990 and 2003. At the same time their per capita gross national income (GNI) rose by more than 30%.

The final common element of the economic policies of these successful countries, which yielded production efficiency and consequent welfare gains, was a continuous and uncompromising application of their outward-oriented strategies. 'Economic growth has been most rapid in countries such as South Korea, Singapore and Taiwan which granted comparable incentives to exports and import substitution in manufacturing and ensured stability of the incentive over time' (Hiemenz and Langhammer, 1986: 25).

During 1970–2002, per capita income amongst the Southeast Asian economies increased by a weighted average of 8% p.a. (Daquila, 2007: 7). The continuous rapid increase in FDI and manufactured industrialisation created jobs and income for almost all the people of the region. As a result, these countries have been transformed within three decades from low-income levels to middle- and high-income levels. China has recorded the highest average annual growth rates in its GDP of over 9% between 1980 and 2007. The performance of the other Asian tigers has also been impressive, with only the Philippines recording mediocre growth. Over the same time period South Africa failed to record growth levels higher than 3% on average. It was during 2000–7 that the average annual growth climbed to 4%, still well under the set target of 6% (see Table 1). According to *The Economist* (2007: 28–9), four of the East Asian economies are ranked under the 55 highest per capita GDP countries in the world. They are Singapore (29th with $24 840), Hong Kong (30th with $22 960), South Korea (49th with $14 160) and Taiwan (51th with $13 450).

Through its Gear and Asgisa programmes post-apartheid South Africa has also attempted to increase growth through export promotion, foreign investment and a stable exchange rate. Unfortunately the higher growth achieved was the result of demand-side stimulus by lower interest rates that

Table 2: Trade per country and GNI of five ASEAN countries, 1970–2003

Year	Indonesia		Malaysia		Philippines		Singapore		Thailand	
	Trade*	GNI**	Trade*	GNI**	Trade*	GNI**	Trade*	GNI**	Trade	GNI**
1970	0.0017	80	0.028	400	0.006	230	0.193	950	0.005	210
1980	0.022	500	0.173	1830	0.029	690	1.79	4830	0.033	720
1985	0.017	530	0.176	1940	0.018	530	1.79	6850	0.031	810
1986	0.016	530	0.152	1890	0.018	560	1.75	7130	0.034	850
1987	0.017	520	0.184	1970	0.022	620	2.2	7940	0.046	970
1988	0.019	540	0.219	2140	0.027	680	2.92	9410	0.067	1190
1989	0.022	570	0.269	2240	0.031	720	3.21	10530	0.083	1350
1990	0.027	620	0.322	2380	0.035	740	3.72	11840	0.100	1520
1995	0.045	1010	0.735	4030	0.067	1040	6.88	23210	0.217	2760
1996	0.047	1120	0.742	1180	0.078	1190	6.98	25110	0.217	3010
1997	0.048	1120	0.728	4600	0.088	1240	6.78	27130	0.202	2770
1998	0.037	670	0.593	3630	0.083	1080	5.39	23500	0.162	2110
1999	0.035	590	0.657	3370	0.092	1040	5.71	22930	0.180	2000
2000	0.046	570	0.774	3390	0.100	1030	6.77	23000	0.215	2010
2003	0.043	810	0.732	3880	0.093	1080	6.4	21230	0.252	2190

*Trade per capita in percentage (export + import)/population (computed).
**GNI per capita in US$.

Source: World Bank DX database (2005)

led to excessive credit spending by consumers and progressive tax reliefs during the 2000s (R600 billion between 1996 and 2007). There was no increased efficiency in production and exports. As a consequence the current account went into a deficit reaching a level of more than 7% of GDP in 2008. It also became structural, which means that given the financing of the deficit through portfolio capital inflows, the resulting outflow of dividends and profits will create a chronically high current account deficit (CAD) in years to come. At the same time economic development has lagged behind, and welfare gains have been poor too. Although GDP per capita has increased substantially from 2000 compared to the negative rates recorded during the 1990s, the unemployment rate stayed above 25%. At the same time life expectancy came down considerably to less than 50 years and the adult literacy rate remained low (see Table 1).

Macroeconomic stability

If there is no economic stability, an outward-oriented programme will not bring about economic development. Of equal importance is the way in which a country attempts to achieve and maintain its stability. If it is done the wrong way grave instability may be the unintended result. 'Good macroeconomic management is associated with faster growth for a given rate of investment. It involves sound fiscal, monetary and exchange rate policies as well as good external debt management' (Daquila, 2007:21). These factors are crucial for attracting foreign direct investment. Macroeconomic stability and a high savings rate provide the secure environment necessary for private-sector investment and a certain return on these investments. Lastly, favourable foreign investment policies, including an increase in foreign equity participation, encourage the inflow of FDI as well as capital formation and economic growth.

External stability can be defined as balance of payments stability, including the real exchange rate. This requires both a decline in aggregate domestic expenditure and a redirection of expenditure and production from non-tradable to tradable. If domestic demand does not initially decrease and domestic production does not eventually adjust towards tradable or exportable import-replacement, the value of net imports will rise, followed by balance of payments instability in the form of structural deficits as well as exchange-rate deterioration and eventually increasing inflation.

In the case of Taiwan, foreign capital inflows and transfers constituted 40% of the source of funds for capital formation between 1956 and 1960. After US aid was terminated in 1961, there was a sharp decline in foreign capital inflows, which completely dried up by 1965 (Rong-I, 1987: 81). The same pattern repeated itself when speculation against the East Asian countries led to the Asian financial crisis in the late 1990s.

Despite these drawbacks, Southeast Asian Central Banks have been successful in bringing down inflation from their high levels in the 1970s. The ASEAN weighted average inflation rate came down from 13.7% for the decade 1971–80 to 8.3% for 1991–2002. However, aggregate domestic expenditure quickly adjusted as a result of an increase in domestic savings, which not only successfully filled the gap left by the loss of foreign capital inflows, but also helped to keep domestic capital formation at an increasing rate to support the switching process towards manufacturing production and exports (Rong-I, 1987: 79).

The Asian financial crisis of the late 1990s was a collective shock and incomparable event in the region's post-war economic history. That the crisis was felt so keenly owed much to the region's integration with the rest of the world due to trade, investment and financial liberalisation, but at the same time there was not the institutional strength to protect local currencies against speculative attack. For instance, Thailand's short-term debt was 78% of its foreign exchange reserves, as portfolio investment was nearly four times higher than long-term investment. The institutional deficiencies of the Asian region consisted of a pegged exchange regime, a weak banking system and highly leveraged borrowers. Once again opponents of the outward-oriented policy approach were proved wrong: the five ASEAN countries did not leave the outward-oriented path but rather strengthened their adjustment by implementing a wide range of regulatory and institutional reforms.

Many studies of trade-liberalisation strategies stress the need for a correct internal policy framework to assist trade policy: 'It is shown how the policy framework influences decision making at the firm level and that micro- and macroeconomic effects of a transition to a more outward-oriented trade regime crucially depend on the internal consistency of policy reform' (Hiemenz and Langhammer, 1986: 3). In order to promote savings and investment, excessive external borrowing and abrupt changes in policy measures should be avoided; policy measures should be coordinated and real interest rates should be positive. These should also be accompanied by supportive policies to create infrastructure and industrial capacity, develop skills, and extend industrial production capacity

In their effort to create a stable macroeconomic and social development environment, Southeast Asian governments exercised fiscal prudence, by quickly changing their deficits of the 1980s into surpluses. Even after the severe crisis of the late 1990s, when these economies began to use expanded fiscal stimulus measures, their deficits never went above 2.2% of GDP. In fact Singapore maintained a surplus of 7.6% over the crisis period (Daquila, 2007: 15).

One of the successful features of structural adjustment in South Africa was the speed with which internal price stability was reached. With the implementation of the RDP and Gear programmes in the mid-1990s, monetary discipline and fiscal stability were achieved quickly, by increasing interest rates, keeping exchange controls for citizens, and bringing down the fiscal deficit. The budget deficit was decreased from 10.1% in 1993/4 to 5.7% the next year and to 3% in 2000. In the same manner the inflation rate came down from a double-digit level to 8.9% in 1996. By 2001, CPI reached 5.4%. The same quick internal adjustment took place after 9/11, when speculation against the South African rand pushed domestic inflation rates quickly up again to average levels of more than 12% between August 2002 and January 2003. Once again, increased monetary discipline in the form of higher interest rates brought the inflation rate back to less than 6% by 2004.

Unfortunately, external balance could not be achieved after 1994. As South Africa's share in world trade declined, current account deficits worsened. Although the shortfall was financed comfortably, South Africa has been unable to lure sufficient new foreign direct investment as a dominant source of CAD financing. The deficit is being financed by portfolio flows. Though it attracts an initial inflow of capital, the long-run impact will be negative as dividend payments to companies will exceed the initial inflow.

Supply-side adjustment policies

All the East Asian NIEs applied a supply-side approach as part of their microeconomic adjustment towards industrialisation, trade, job creation and a more equitable income distribution. The first step was to introduce favourable agricultural policies and land reform in a move away from subsistence farming. Flexible labour policies led to an efficient allocation of labour. Joint ventures with foreign firms, leading to 'conglomerate-style' corporations, amplified success. The ASEAN countries had to address specific supply-side problems to improve the management capabilities of local companies, foster human resources related to the labour market, enhance technological capacity, improve distribution and information systems, develop infrastructure, and preserve the environment.

The first success of microeconomic reform in China was the introduction of a 'responsible agriculture' policy that allowed farm families to work a piece of land under contract and to keep whatever profits they earned. Thereafter China had to create market institutions and convert the economy from an administratively driven command economy to a price-driven market economy. Private property ownership encouraged small and medium-sized businesses. Joint ventures with foreign firms remain the main source of technology transfer. A low wage policy and high labour productivity help attract foreign investments and maintain high growth levels.

South Korea introduced land reforms to assist with the creation of industrialised parks. The adoption of an industrial policy based on promoting designated industries formed its unique production, export and development base – but at the expense of rent-seeking behaviour. Competition among industries for incentives or 'special treatment' by government became fierce. Business activities were protected by the government from labour movements and exchange rate fluctuations. Technology transfers and labour skills from Japanese companies also supported efficiency in production.

Taiwan started its industrialisation process through the privatisation of four public enterprises and awarding them to landlords as compensation for the land reform policy in the early 1950s. This initiative created a new group of successful entrepreneurs. Further incentives and privatisation policies were pursued during the 1960s and 1970s, leading to increased private investments and the development of new industries. Small and medium enterprises (SMEs) dominated Taiwan's manufacturing sector, with a share of 98% of all manufacturing firms. Government contributed by introducing tax incentives and subsidised credit to direct investments to certain industries. FDI became the cornerstone of microeconomic performance in Taiwan's economy during the 1980s, as 20% of the country's total exports were attributable to foreign firms; these generated between 15% and 17% of total employment in the manufacturing sector. Foreign firms operating in Taiwan during the 1980s and 1990s also used more capital-intensive technologies than domestic firms.

Policies regarding human resource development and utilisation also enhanced Taiwan's competitiveness. The shift from import-substitution to export-oriented production, as the way to add increased value to total output and thus to generate welfare domestically, caused an initial increase in the industrial demand for unskilled labour. Education and training programmes were gradually shifted during the 1980s to transform the industrial base and the export-processing zones into centres dependent on the application of advanced technology. By 1993 more than 48% of the workforce was employed in manufacturing, and Taiwan had a negligible unemployment rate of only 1.5% (Republic of China, 1995: 381–2).

In South Africa, the Gear and Asgisa strategies ushered in microeconomic and supply-side policies. An industrial policy framework was also a key part of both Gear and Asgisa, an approach confirmed at the 2007 Polokwane Conference. Unfortunately, the strategy was not carried through. Manufacturing as a proportion of total GDP declined from 21.4% in 1990 to 16.11% in 2007. The tertiary sector – wholesale and retail trade, catering and accommodation, transport and communications, real estate, business services and general government services – has increased rapidly to

58.03% in 2007, to accommodate the rapid increase in domestic demand. Meanwhile, training and skills development programmes have had limited success, while public works programmes have also had mixed results.

Economic development policies

The fundamental objective of economic development is to create an environment where people can enjoy long, healthy and productive lives. It is important therefore that we do not take a partial view of the impact of the policies of the Asian tigers and South Africa by just focusing on economic growth. We need to determine as well whether national income has benefited the intended beneficiaries by way of better nutrition and health services, greater access to education, more secure livelihoods, better working conditions and a sense of participating in the economy.

The best measure of human development is the Human Development Index (HDI). An HDI of above 0.8 indicates a country with high human development, an HDI of 0.5–0.8 medium human development, and an HDI below 0.5 low human development. It has three main components: longevity (life expectancy at birth), knowledge (adult literacy) and income (GDP per capita).

The Asian NIE countries have an HDI of above 0.7, with Singapore having the highest HDI of 0.9. South Africa still lags behind its Asian counterparts with an HDI of 0.6 (World Bank, 2007). South Africa has a very low life expectancy of 47 and 49 years for men and women respectively, whilst life expectancy amongst the Asian tigers ranges between 66 and 82 years for both genders. The Asian countries also have very high adult literacy rates of above 90%, whilst South Africa's is 82% (see Table 1).

Though the Asian countries have recorded impressive growth levels, the question is whether this has had an impact on the average member of society. Looking at GDP per capita growth since 2005–6, one can see that South Africa has not had any significant welfare gains – its GDP per capita growth was only 3.9% – whereas its Asian counterparts (with the exception of the Philippines) have recorded levels of more than 4.2%.

Another dimension to be considered is the distribution of income in the different countries. A Gini index of close to 100 represents inequitable income distribution. South Africa has a skewed income distribution with a Gini index of 66, which is also mirrored in the high unemployment levels that prevail in the country. The Asian countries have a Gini index of between 31.6 and 49.2, and have high employment levels (World Bank, 2007).

Lessons for South Africa

Although it seems on the face of it that the policy framework of Gear and Asgisa is similar to that of the Asian NIEs, its implementation has failed in South Africa. The following observations capture what we believe are the key lessons from the Asian experience.

- The Asian NIEs shifted from labour-intensive agricultural peasant production to small- and medium-scale manufacturing.
- They moved from import substitution to export-oriented industrialisation.
- Manufacturing production in the Asian NIEs was transformed by the inflow of FDI and the accompanying upgrading of industrial infrastructure. South Africa's share of FDI dwindled to less than 0.5 of total global FDI (IMF, 2007). A naturally beneficial cycle between investment and manufactured exports lies at the heart of industrial policy in the Asian NIEs.
- The success of Asian economic growth was underpinned by the relationship between increased demand and supply. Increased import demand for intermediate imports was matched by expanded exports and domestic production capacity creation. Current account deficits were quickly turned around into surpluses.
- Increased efficiency in production led to welfare gains in the form of higher per capita income, increased employment and equitable distribution of income.
- Favourable agricultural policies and land reform that moved away from subsistence farming helped ensure food security.
- Resource allocation through markets was introduced in the Asian NIEs. Flexible labour policies led to an efficient allocation of labour. Joint ventures with foreign firms, leading to so-called conglomerate-style corporations, enhanced the success of the Asian economies.

The ASEAN countries have had an impressive growth record because of the policies they have adopted to spur economic and human development. What is equally impressive is the impact they have had on the lives of their citizens through their social policies. South Africa has also made some strides albeit at a snail's pace. This does not augur well for the development of the country as a whole and has not so far led to significant welfare gains for the populace at large.

In part to remedy these deficiencies, a somewhat different policy approach was unveiled by the ANC at its Polokwane Conference in December 2007, which sought to refine the Asgisa strategy and inform it with four attributes of the 'developmental state'. The first of these is its strategic orientation: 'an approach premised on people-centred and people-driven change, and sustained development based on high growth rates, restructuring of the economy and socio-economic inclusion' (Yanagihara and Sambommatsu, 1997: 3). The second attribute is its capacity to lead in the national agenda and to mobilise the whole society to take part in its implementation. Such a state should have effective systems of interaction with all social partners, and exercise leadership informed by its popular mandate. The third attribute should be the state's organisational capacity; and the fourth attribute its technical capacity: the ability to translate broad objectives into programmes and projects and to ensure their implementation. This depends on the proper training, orientation and leadership of the public service, and on acquiring and retaining skilled personnel.

This approach is based on the premise that there is a central role for government in building a growing economy from which all South Africans can benefit. The resolution adopted at Polokwane clearly states the four pillars supporting the ANC's strategy for South Africa till 2014.

- Macroeconomic balance that supports sustainable growth and development.
- An industrial strategy, and a corresponding implementation programme, that addresses constraints on investment. A crucial element of this strategy will be a comprehensive programme of land and agrarian reform.
- Thirdly, a focus on creating decent jobs and ensuring an improved quality of life for workers. Government will implement programmes to eliminate economic dualism – first- and third-world economies within South Africa – and the exclusion of the majority of South Africans from the former. These include skills development, specific attention to industries that lend themselves to involvement by marginalised communities, access to micro-credit and small business assistance, land reform, public works projects, and the promotion of sustainable livelihoods at community and household levels.
- Lastly, intensified broad-based programmes to empower those previously excluded from mainstream economic activity, including women.

It remains to be seen whether this new approach will achieve what South Africa has so far failed to do.

References

Daquila, T.C. 2007. *The Transformation of the East Asian Economies*. Norva Publishers, California

Hiemenz, U. and Langhammer, R.J. 1986. Efficiency Pre-Conditions for Successful Integration of Developing Countries into the World Economy. *International Employment Policies, Working Paper no. 2*. Institute for World Economics, Kiel

IMF. 2007. *International Financial Statistics*. Washington

Republic of China. 1985. *The Republic of China Yearbook*

Rong-I Wu. 1987. The Strategy of Industrialization in East Asia. IDC, Johannesburg

The Economist. 2007. *Pocket World in Figures*. Profile Books, London

World Bank. 2007. *World Development Report*. Oxford University Press, Washington

Yanagihara, Y. and Sambommatsu, S. 2007. *East Asian Development Experience, Economic System Approach and Its Applicability*. Institute for Developing Economies, Tokyo

4

Inflation targeting: a pillar of post-Polokwane prosperity

Stan du Plessis

At the time of writing – November 2008 – an international financial crisis of almost unprecedented intensity was casting a long shadow over the prospects for the South African economy. It has even become fashionable to compare present events with the Great Crash of October 1929, which contributed so much to the subsequent Great Depression. But economists know that the stock market crash of 1929 did not lead inexorably to the Great Depression; rather, Central Banks, especially the Federal Reserve Board in America, pushed their economies downward on the path to depression with an unhappy combination of bad judgement and worse luck (Friedman and Schwartz, 1963).

Sweden's economy and its Central Bank were straining from the same crisis in September 1931, but their policy response differed, as did the resulting experience. It was the month that Britain moved off the gold standard, and the Swedish krona was cast adrift from its former mooring to gold via sterling. Facing massive currency speculation, the government of Sweden turned to the country's leading economists, who proposed a price-level target. It was duly implemented and is a forerunner of the inflation targeting regimes of a more modern vintage. Even under the tremendous stresses of the thirties Sweden's price-level target functioned remarkably well to deliver zero inflation while avoiding the worst economic growth declines.

Yet the Swedes abandoned their price-level target in 1937, in an episode rich with lessons for our present policy debate. Although the mechanism was reviewed favourably, a group of younger Swedish economists, including Ohlin and Myrdal, argued that something more ambitious might well be tried. More specifically, and under the Keynesian influence of that era, they asked: might not the tools of monetary policy be employed in the service of growing the economy? The attempt to extend the goals of monetary policy in this direction was, unfortunately, a failure. Not only did the Swedish economy fail to achieve the additional growth it sought, but it also experienced the sustained inflation it had been so successful in avoiding before (Berg and Jonung, 1998).

The debate over the appropriate goals for monetary policy is just as heated today in South Africa, as is clear from the following extract from the Declaration of the ANC–Cosatu–SACP Alliance Economic Summit in October 2008: 'Both exchange rates and interest rates need to be calibrated to take account of industrial policy imperatives. This will require, among others, a discussion on the mandate and practices of the SARB [South African Reserve Bank] to include considerations of employment and economic growth in addition to the mandate on price stability' (ANC, 2008: 2). Similar sentiments have been common fare from senior ANC Alliance figures over the last year, including Jeremy Cronin and Gwede Mantashe. They indicate that today in South Africa, as in the Sweden of 1937, a potentially significant shift has taken place in the social and political support for low and stable inflation as the appropriate goal for monetary policy. In its own terms, however, inflation targeting has been a success in South Africa, as elsewhere, though this assessment needs clearer articulation and is a major motivation for this chapter. Maintaining social and political support for the current policy regime will require more than this demonstration of success for inflation targeting, though; it is also necessary to demonstrate that more ambitious goals lack theoretical or historical support. Here, luckily, the evidence is clear: these goals have led to monetary instability and inflation, with no gain in output to balance the scales. This has been true not just in Sweden post-1937 but wherever these ambitious monetary policies have been tried.

Inflation targeting under pressure

Inflation targeting has attracted considerable controversy in South Africa since its formal adoption in February 2000. But critics have become more vocal in recent months and some of them, including leaders of the ANC's alliance partners, have moved from the fringes of the political landscape to its centre, adding new political weight to their views on monetary policy. And they were no doubt greatly encouraged to read controversial Economics Nobel Laureate Joseph Stiglitz's widely circulated broadside against inflation targeting during May 2008, in which one finds the following unambiguous rejection of inflation targeting:

> He opened with the claim that 'Today, inflation targeting is being put to the test – and it will almost certainly fail' to which he added that '… inflation in these countries is, for the most part, imported' which means, so he argued, that '… unless taken to an intolerable level, these measures [raising interest rates] by themselves cannot bring inflation down to the targeted levels' and he concluded with the remedy as he saw it, namely that 'Most importantly, both developing and developed countries need to abandon inflation targeting' (Stiglitz, 2008).

Both Stiglitz's criticism and the South African debate revolve around three lines of attack on inflation targeting. Firstly, there is the charge that the SARB has been inflexible in its implementation of inflation targeting with negative consequences for the growth of the South African economy. Secondly, inflation targeting has not worked, i.e. it has not been effective in its main task of controlling inflation. Thirdly, inflation targeting implies the wrong mandate for monetary authorities in a developing country with various other social and economic challenges. These three lines often overlap. For example, the first and third lines overlap when the suggestion of a broader mandate for the Central Bank is made as a step towards a more flexible monetary policy. It is for this reason that the first and third lines of attack will be discussed together in the next section on flexibility and the mandate of the SARB. Consideration of the effectiveness of monetary policy follows subsequently.

Is the SARB an 'inflation nutter'?

The mandate of the SARB, as formulated in section 13.224(1) of the South African Constitution, reads: 'The primary object of the South African Reserve Bank is to protect the value of the currency in the interest of balanced and sustainable economic growth in the Republic.' At stake is whether the SARB has interpreted its mandate very narrowly, at the expense of the Constitution's inclusion of reference to the 'interest of balanced and sustainable economic growth'.

In the jargon of monetary policy an 'inflation nutter' is a central banker who disregards all other issues in the dogged pursuit of low and stable inflation (King, 1997). But the inflation nutter is a mythical creature and we have no record of any sightings in the real world. On this, central bankers such as Mervyn King (1997), academic proponents of inflation targeting such as Lars Svensson (1999) and mild sceptics of inflation targeting such as Alan Blinder (1998) all agree. Governor Mboweni (1999) of the SARB has said the same: 'it is important that the public does not get the impression that the Central Bank is dogmatic about the containment of inflation and does not care about other critical issues of importance to the economy'.

There is therefore widespread agreement that inflation-targeting Central Banks are not 'inflation nutters' but 'flexible inflation targeters', as Svensson called them. In practice this means that the Central Bank has at least two objectives, the first to keep inflation close to the numerical inflation target (or within the band of 3–6% as in the South African case), and the second to keep the economy growing at or near its potential growth rate (as determined by the expansion of capital and labour and the rate at which productivity is expanding).

The SARB's operating procedure is as follows: the monetary policy committee (MPC) of the SARB considers the present and expected future development of the economy over roughly a two-year horizon and uses it to assess the appropriateness of the stance of monetary policy. Specifically, the MPC compares the forecasted inflation rate with the inflation target at a horizon of 18–24 months; if forecasted inflation exceeds the target at that horizon, the MPC uses formal econometric models and additional knowledge of the economy to calculate by how much the policy interest rate (repo rate in South Africa) has to be raised to ensure consistency between the forecasted inflation rate and the target at the appropriate horizon.[1] Since the inflation target is symmetrical, the opposite steps are taken when forecasted inflation falls below the target band.

This procedure is not mechanistic, though.[2] The MPC exercises considerable judgement about the appropriate path that forecasted inflation should follow to return to the target band, or to remain within the target band. If, for example, the forecasted inflation rate exceeds the target, then the MPC needs to decide on an appropriate upward adjustment for interest rates. That is, it has to decide on the expected path for interest rates: a steeper and higher trajectory for the repo rate will lead to more rapid disinflation, but at greater cost in terms of output relative to its potential, while a more modest and gentler rise of the repo rate will be less disruptive to production but also less powerful as a disinflationary influence.

This trade-off between the speed of inflationary adjustment and disruption of output is central to the inflation-targeting Central Bank's problem, and it is in the resolution of this trade-off that we see the flexibility of the policy framework. The 'inflation nutter' mentioned above is, in this scheme, simply a Central Bank that gives no weight to output fluctuations in its deliberation. But this has never been observed in the real world of central banking. Instead, the practical question for inflation-targeting Central Banks is how much weight to give to inflation and how much to output. Too much weight on inflation exacts an unbearable cost in terms of output volatility, while an overemphasis on output undermines the credibility of the Central Bank's commitment to low and stable inflation.

Criticism of the MPC's flexibility in South Africa needs to be seen against this backdrop. For example, the charge by the chief economist of the Industrial Development Corporation (IDC), Lumkile Mondi (2007), that 'unfortunately for South Africans, flexibility in times of market volatility does not exist in our Reserve Bank's vocabulary' amounts to a claim that the MPC gives zero weight to output in its policy deliberations. Let us consider the evidence.

There are two ways to measure the weight given to output in the inflation-targeting procedure (Kahn, 2008). The first is direct measurement of the weight given to output in the policy procedure, which can be done by creating an econometric model of the MPC's response to changes in forecasted inflation and forecasted output relative to its potential. If the monetary authorities truly did not care about output fluctuations, then the estimated weight on this factor in the model would be very small. In the South African literature there are two direct estimates of this weight, one by Woglom (2003) and the other by Ortiz and Sturzenegger (2007). Both of these measure significant positive weight on output in the procedure of the MPC. Woglom finds an increased response to output since the adoption of inflation targeting in South Africa while Ortiz and Sturzenegger find a weight on output that is high in a class of similar estimates for a peer group of emerging markets.

The second method of measuring the flexibility of the MPC is to consider the horizon at which it aims to keep the forecasted inflation rate consistent with the target rate. For an inflation-targeting Central Bank a shorter horizon over which forecasted inflation must match the target range means less discretion for the Bank to decide amongst alternative paths of forecasted inflation and, in effect, a diminished ability to consider the consequences for economic growth of the chosen monetary policy stance. Bearing in mind that in a flexible monetary policy regime policy-makers are able to consider the consequences of their decisions for economic growth and not only for inflation, it follows that the shorter this horizon, the less flexible is the MPC, while a longer horizon indicates more flexibility. In South Africa the MPC uses a horizon of about 18–24 months, which suggests substantial flexibility. Almost any of the Monetary Policy Statements released by the MPC after its regular policy meetings reveal this flexibility. For example, the June 2007 Monetary Policy Statement reflected on the fact that inflation, as measured by the CPIX index, had breached the upper end of the 3–6% target band in April of that year, and though the MPC did not ignore this unpleasant event, its response was measured and flexible, as can be seen from this extract:

> CPIX inflation breached the upper end of the inflation target range in April 2007 for the first time since August 2003 ... The breach of the target is in the past and there is nothing that monetary policy can do about past inflation. Nevertheless the Monetary Policy Committee cannot ignore the possible impact of this breach on inflation expectations and the public's understanding of the monetary policy process. Monetary policy acts with a lag, and the focus of the MPC will remain, as always, on the medium-term inflation outlook which is the period over which monetary policy can be effective ... The Monetary Policy Committee has decided that in view of the further deterioration in the inflation outlook, the monetary policy stance needs to be adjusted to ensure that CPIX inflation returns to within the inflation target range over time. (MPC, 2007)

There is no hint here of a narrow-minded focus on inflation alone; rather we see a concern for the deteriorating outlook on inflation and an awareness that tools of monetary policy work only gradually and should be used to return forecasted inflation to the target range over time. The international evidence suggests that other inflation-targeting Central Banks have also implemented their targets with considerable flexibility. For example, internationally the observed inflation rates are outside their target bands by roughly 30% of the time, to which the Central Banks respond neither with draconian interest rate rises, nor by abandoning the targeting regimes (Roger and Stone, 2005). Instead they use their policy instruments flexibly to manage forecasted inflation back to their respective target ranges in a manner comparable to the South African example.

In some cases the lengthening of the target horizon by an inflation-targeting Central Bank is accompanied by the use of a formal 'escape clause'. This is an institutional device that the Central Bank can invoke when exceptional circumstances, e.g. large supply shocks such as a rise in the international oil price, would require unduly disruptive policy adjustments to meet the target. Using such a clause in a forward-looking manner, as described here, implies an effective lengthening of the horizon over which forecasted inflation is compared with the target range; it is usually accompanied by some formal public announcement.

The escape clause becomes, in essence, a communication device which enables the Central Bank to explain its policy stance in a forward-looking manner to the public, without undermining its anti-inflation credibility. Bernanke et al. (1999) have interpreted the auspicious implementation of money growth targets during the 1970s and 1980s by the Bundesbank and the Swiss National Bank as analogous to this forward-looking use of an escape clause. Both Central Banks used the forecasts for monetary growth as a way of explaining their policy stance, focusing on the long-run inflation impact, while cognisant of real economic developments in the shorter run. Posen (1997) has summarised the consequent flexibility of the Bundesbank's targeting regime:

> The Bundesbank consciously used these targets as a framework for signalling its intent and explaining its policies to its constituent public. In consequence, these targets actually granted the German central bank *greater* flexibility in responding to the problems of monetary control ... the use of monetary targets in Germany has conferred greater transparency on the Bundesbank's monetary policy stances, enhancing flexibility without obvious cost to its independence.

However, neither the Swiss National Bank nor the Bundesbank employed a formal escape clause. Indeed, it seems as if a sufficiently open communication strategy can substitute for a formal escape clause. The SARB resorted to just such a strategy for the formal escape clause following the inflationary consequences of the rand's rapid depreciation in 2001, and this has since become known as the 'explanation clause' (Kahn, 2008). Ironically, this clause, part of the open communication strategy of the MPC, has been the source of much misunderstanding of monetary policy in recent times. Some economists and other commentators have criticised the MPC since 2007 for failing to invoke the explanation clause. For example, Garrow (2007: 11) argued in December 2007 that 'Food price movements as they have arisen from volatile weather conditions and the impact of geopolitical risk on international crude oil prices have pressured price, but not to the extent that the monetary policy committee (MPC) has felt it necessary to invoke the explanation clause'. A few months later, the editor of the *Financial Mail* (2008) argued that Governor Mboweni has 'consistently refused to make use of the explanation clause in the inflation targeting regime'. Yet by that time the MPC had long since invoked the escape clause.

How did the MPC respond to the events of 2007 when, as mentioned above, inflation as measured by the CPIX moved above the target range? It responded by (i) identifying the nature of the price shock, (ii) explaining the expected impact on inflation as it saw it and (iii) explaining how its policy stance needed to be adjusted to ensure long-run consistency between forecasted inflation and the target range. To take these steps *is* to invoke the explanation clause, and it follows precisely those examples from Germany and Switzerland which inspired this part of the institutional design (Kahn, 2008).

A final piece of evidence that attests to the practical flexibility of inflation targeting is the remarkable durability of the monetary policy framework encompassing inflation targeting with a floating exchange rate and openness to international capital flows. In this respect the critical observation, made recently by Andrew Rose (2006), is the striking contrast between the longevity of the inflation-targeting regimes internationally and the short-lived nature of almost all the alternatives in the modern era.

In the 18 years since New Zealand started the modern experiment with inflation targeting, no inflation-targeting Central Bank has abandoned the system other than Finland and Spain. In South Africa we have now had 8 years of experience with inflation targeting. Both 18 years in New Zealand and 8 years in South Africa might sound short, but they are in fact remarkably long given the fragility of monetary policy regimes in the modern era. By comparison, the Bretton Woods system fell short of 13 years, starting in

January 1959 when European currencies restored their convertibility and ending in August 1971. Rose considered the evidence from all inflation-targeting countries and a large control group of 42 countries. He calculated that the probability of a monetary policy regime lasting for even the 8 years of the South African inflation target has been less than 30% (Rose, 2006: 9). The combined observations that inflation targets are often missed – about a third of the time in the international experience – and that countries nevertheless stick with these regimes with remarkable fortitude suggest that their implementation has been highly flexible.

Contrary to the claims of its critics, the evidence reported here supports the interpretation of South Africa's inflation target as a highly flexible monetary policy regime in which the forecasted development of output and that of inflation are both considered in the operating procedure followed by the MPC. Given this flexible approach, any attempt to widen the mandate of the SARB to include output with inflation would have little practical impact on the way that it currently implements monetary policy.

Does inflation targeting actually work?

The second main line of criticism in the recent South African debate is the argument that inflation targeting has not facilitated an effective monetary policy response to the price shocks that have pushed headline inflation rates higher since late 2006. Interest rates are a 'blunt tool' for combating supply-side shocks, such as the oil price and food prices, so this argument runs, and not only will the MPC's attempts to combat such inflation with interest rate adjustments fail, but they will also cause pro-cyclical monetary policy, i.e. monetary policy that exacerbates (as opposed to stabilising) the economic cycle.

Before we examine the evidence for this claim, it is necessary to do some housekeeping on the concepts of inflation, prices and the cost of living. Inflation is a process that erodes the value of money over time. When this process takes root, the price of everything else rises in terms of money. Since the relative prices of other goods, services and factors of production do not change with inflation, it does not lead us to change our consumption and production decisions. Rather, inflation erodes the value of income and assets that are fixed in nominal rand amounts (like government pensions), it weakens the exchange rate, distorts taxes and causes us to rebalance our asset portfolios. Ultimately the causes of inflation are the failure by the MPC to control the money supply and to anchor inflation expectations, both of which are sensitive to interest rate adjustments (Woodford, 2003).

Unlike other prices in the economy, though, inflation itself is unobservable. In practice we use various price indices such as the consumer price index (CPI), producer price index (PPI) and the GDP deflator, to measure inflation approximately. For example, the CPI is a price index composed of the weighted prices of various goods and services combined to reflect the consumption basket of an 'average' household in South Africa. We can say that the CPI measures the average cost of living in South Africa. The value of this index changes from month to month when the value of money declines relative to all goods, i.e. as a result of inflation. But the index also changes when the relative prices of goods and services change. Under normal circumstances these relative price movements are comparatively small, and rising relative prices in one area of the basket (say food) is often balanced by relative declines in other areas (say electronics), leaving the aggregate movement in the index as a fairly good approximation of the change in the value of money relative to all goods and services. Normally changes in the CPI approximate inflation accurately.

But all approximations have their limits. CPI works well as an inflation proxy when its components are not subject to large relative price movements. But that is exactly what we have experienced since 2006: energy and food prices (two large components of the CPI basket) have risen dramatically in relative terms, pushing up the CPI and, consequently, the observed 'inflation' rate to more than 13% at the time of writing. Is this an accurate measure of inflation given the circumstances? And does the MPC fail to understand (as we read in the press) that inflation is driven by factors beyond its control? The answer to both questions is clearly no.

It is precisely because of the large, externally driven relative price movements in food and energy that CPI has, for the time being, become a poor measure of the process of inflation. These relative rises in prices drive up the cost of living, but they do not represent a decline in the value of money *relative to all goods*; i.e. this is not inflation. Nor is the MPC trying to reverse their effect. On the contrary, it wants us to respond as consumers and producers to the critically important information in these relative price movements. As consumers the MPC wants us to economise on our use of energy and to rationalise our food consumption baskets, and as producers the MPC wants us to consider alternative energy sources and the expansion of agriculture relative to other land uses. These would be some of the appropriate supply and demand responses to the information carried by the relative price signals that have been driving up our cost of living. Alternative policies, such as price control, or import and export quotas, will not solve the underlying forces at work either. Price controls on food will not raise its supply; instead it is likely to lead to outright shortages of food and a black market, as often happens with attempts to lower prices through regulation.

The MPC in South Africa is thoroughly sensitive to the conceptual and practical differences between movements in relative prices and in the value of money. Its concern is with preventing relative price shocks from raising higher inflation expectations, which would ultimately feed the process of inflation, or what the MPC calls the 'second-round effects' of relative price shocks. Governor Mboweni gave a particularly clear explanation of this line of reasoning at the conference of the Bureau for Economic Research (BER) in May 2008:

> The nature of the original cost pressures that are facing the economy is well known. These pressures – food and energy – do not appear to be cyclical ... We are facing a significant and probably a permanent change in relative prices globally. We also have to be concerned about pricing and unit labour cost responses to these relative price changes ... if we allow this process to take effect, inflation expectations will deteriorate and generalised inflation will accelerate. (Mboweni, 2008)

The MPC wants to rein in the process of inflation and has turned its attention to other approximations of inflation that are more robust in the present environment, including the 'core' CPI (CPI less energy and food prices) and surveys of inflation expectations. This interpretation of the MPC's decisions not only is consistent with its own narrative but also fits the decisions taken by the MPC better than the 'blunt instrument' proposition.

It will be helpful to consider the responses of the MPC to the most recent increases in energy and food prices that have occurred since mid-2006. The MPC started to raise the repo rate in June 2006. To gauge the stance of monetary policy we need to calculate the real interest rate,[3] i.e. the difference between the nominal interest rate and a measure of expected inflation. More specifically, the real repo rate is the difference between the nominal repo rate and a measure of expected inflation. For the purpose of

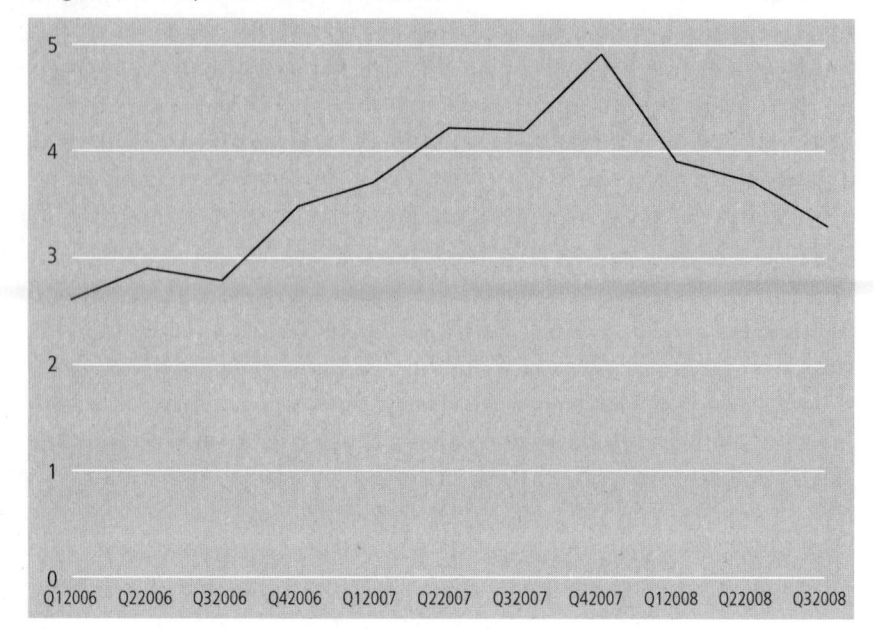

Figure 1: Real repo rate in South Africa since 2006

The real interest rate was calculated as the difference between the nominal repo rate and expected inflation (for the next year) measured as the average of the three surveys conducted quarterly by the BER.

this exercise, let us use the survey of inflation expectations gathered on a quarterly basis by the BER at the University of Stellenbosch and used by the MPC in its policy deliberation. The result is shown in Figure 1.

From mid-2006 to the time of writing the CPIX proxy for inflation rose from 4.5% to 13%, or 850 basis points. How did the MPC respond? It raised the nominal repo rate by 500 basis points in total and the resultant pattern for the real interest rate can be seen in Figure 1. In 2006 the real interest rate was tightened by just more than 50 basis points, with a further tightening of about 100 basis points maintained through 2007. During 2008, as economic activity seemed to be slowing, the MPC allowed the real rate to ease very moderately. In total it raised the nominal repo rate by 500 basis points while this proxy of inflation (closer to core inflation) went up by 370 basis points. Though this cycle of interest-rate tightening was real, it was also undoubtedly modest, just enough to maintain the Taylor principle of a real tightening,[4] which was necessary to combat the danger of inflation feeding off rises in inflation expectations.

This interpretation of the MPC's behaviour suggests that it has not been using interest rates as a 'blunt tool' in a quixotic struggle with relative price shocks. On the contrary, the MPC has accommodated the relative price shocks in the headline indices of inflation, while positioning monetary policy to combat the second-round effects created by inflation expectations. This response is consistent with the flexible interpretation given to inflation targeting above, and also illustrates why inflation targeting is not pro-cyclical (destabilising) in the manner feared by some of its academic critics.

The so-called Harvard Group of local and international economists who advised government on aspects of policy raised a theoretical concern with inflation targeting. According to the argument, inflation targeting would lead the Central Bank to take pro-cyclical policy decisions under circumstances such as we have faced since 2006. On this argument, a positive shock to expenditure, e.g. household consumption, leads to both higher output relative to its potential and higher inflation. But a relative price shock, e.g. a sharp rise in the oil price, decreases actual (and potential) output, while it raises inflation. While a monetary policy aimed at keeping inflation low and stable would, therefore, also stabilise output under the first scenario, it would destabilise output in the second (Frankel, Smit and Sturzenegger, 2007: 61).

The theoretical possibility that so troubled the Harvard Group is not, however, of much practical concern for the SARB or any other inflation-targeting Central Bank. The theoretical concern assumes the SARB would be an 'inflation nutter', but we have already seen that this is a poor description of inflation targeting – especially in South Africa.

The concern about destabilising monetary policy can also be investigated directly, and a number of studies have done so in the South African literature. The starting point for such a discussion is the recognition that the South African economy has become remarkably more stable since the 1980s. In the course of twenty years the South African economy has stabilised not just relative to its own past, but also against the performance of other emerging market economies. Furthermore, this stabilisation occurred around a rising growth trend for the economy (Du Plessis and Smit, 2007).

The real question therefore is whether monetary policy helped or hindered this remarkable stabilisation around a higher growth trend. A number of papers have addressed this question directly using different methods, but the results are largely consistent. Most recently Burger (2008) and also Du Plessis et al. (2007) as well as Du Plessis and Smit (2003) found evidence of monetary policy stabilising over the period of the inflation target (but not limited to that period).

Since there is no evidence that the SARB is an inflation 'nutter' or that its implementation of inflation targeting has destabilised output, the only remaining question about the impact of inflation targeting on output relates to the long-run growth trajectory of the economy. Would a higher growth path have been possible for South Africa under an alternative policy regime?

There are two ways to investigate this question. The first is to examine the factors that contribute to economic growth in South Africa and that might suggest a role for monetary policy in raising the long-run growth path. This rather large literature was recently summarised by Du Plessis and Smit (2007); they found no evidence to suggest that a more relaxed monetary policy would boost the long-run growth rate of the economy. On the contrary, one of their clearest results was that the improved macroeconomic stability of the post-1994 period has been a decisively positive factor in the improved growth trajectory of the same period. Prudent monetary policy, especially inflation targeting, played a central part in achieving that stability.

A second approach is to examine what economists call the Phillips curve, a relationship in two dimensions between unemployment and inflation or, alternatively, between real output and inflation. When first discovered as a purely statistical relationship in the late 1950s, this curve suggested a long-run trade-off between inflation and unemployment, offering a menu of policy choices ranging from high unemployment and low inflation on one side to low unemployment and high inflation on the other.

An enormous amount of energy has been spent in the subsequent investigation of this relationship and at least three Nobel Prizes in Economics have been won for work directly related to this research.[5] The happy result is that this is one area of macroeconomic research where the effort of decades has brought us to a consensus: in the short run the Central Bank can boost economic growth, or lower unemployment, by lowering interest rates, but in the longer run there is no positive growth and employment effect for such a policy, only higher inflation. For the renowned American macroeconomist John Taylor (2000), these results are two of the 'five things we know for sure' in macroeconomics.

But we need not be satisfied with international evidence only, since there is a substantial South African literature on the topic, of which two papers are highlighted here. First, Hodge (2002) found little association between unemployment and inflation, but he did find evidence of a short-run trade-off between growth and inflation. More recently, Burger and Marinkov (2006) found even weaker evidence of the Phillips curve in South Africa. It is reasonable to conclude from the international and local literature that while monetary policy has undoubted short-run implications for economic growth, there is no evidence that monetary policy can raise the long-run growth rate of the economy in any way other than by contributing to a stable macroeconomic environment.

The message of this section is clear: monetary policy under inflation targeting in South Africa has not destabilised the economy – indeed the evidence suggests the opposite: it has contributed importantly to the significant stabilisation of the economy. This is also the most important contribution that monetary policy has made and could have made to economic growth, since here, as elsewhere, there is no evidence for a long-run trade-off between inflation and economic growth. But we have learnt something more unsettling too, which is a source of grave difficulties for any Central Bank in a democratic society and which is the topic of the next section.

Operating a Central Bank in a democratic society

The consensus on the Phillips curve mentioned in the previous section was not only about the long-run inability of monetary policy to raise the growth rate of the economy, but also about the very real consequences of monetary policy for economic growth over shorter horizons. This tension between the short- and the long-run consequences lies at the heart of the monetary policy problem. This problem is acute when the Central Bank has to operate in a democratic society in which public institutions have to maintain the confidence of the electorate. Central bankers have long since been aware of the problem, but its exact nature and solution were not clearly understood until the late 1970s.

About thirty years ago Arthur Burns – then recently retired as the chairperson of the Federal Reserve Board – spoke memorably of a paradox he had experienced as a central banker: 'Why … have central bankers, whose main business one might suppose is to fight inflation, been so ineffective in dealing with the worldwide problem? … despite their antipathy to inflation and powerful weapons they could wield against it, central bankers have failed so utterly in this mission in recent years. In this paradox lies the anguish of central banking.' The causes of his anguish were institutional, or so he saw it, and associated with what he called 'the philosophical and political currents that have been transforming economic life in the United States' (Burns, 1979: 9). Milton Friedman (1977) had said something similar in his Nobel acceptance lecture a few years earlier. But the clearest analysis of the problem was given by Kydland and Prescott (1977) in a seminal contribution that helped them win the Nobel Prize in Economics in 2004. They identified the problem experienced, for example, by a Central Bank when it tries to make a credible commitment to using monetary policy to deliver low and stable inflation in the service of high and sustainable economic growth.

In the light of the relationship between inflation and economic growth summarised above, it is preferable for a Central Bank to commit to low and stable inflation as the socially appropriate goal for monetary policy. If the public believes this to be a credible commitment and acts accordingly, moderating inflation expectations and hence wage and price expectations, inflation will be low too. But once the private sector has acted on the Central Bank's initial commitment, an incentive arises for the Central Bank to renege on its commitment to low and stable inflation and to use the short-run trade-off between inflation and unemployment to pursue slightly higher employment. In fact, reneging on its prior commitment is optimal in the light of the private sector response to the initial commitment, and at least temporarily everybody will benefit from the changed course at the Central Bank. But soon inflation will rise as the private sector responds to the Central Bank's new path, and as inflation expectations rise it will become ever harder for the Central Bank to generate a growth benefit, even in the short run. The attempt at stimulating growth becomes self-defeating in this way, and ultimately output is left no higher than before, but with socially costly higher inflation.

With this argument Kydland and Prescott demonstrated that the Central Bank's prior commitment to low and stable inflation is not consistent over time. In fact, since the private sector can figure out that the Central Bank has an incentive to renege on such a commitment, the private sector will not respond to the initial commitment as described, but will raise its inflation expectations in anticipation of the Central Bank's reversal of position. We can say that the Central Bank's prior commitment lacked credibility. This theoretical problem, a lack of credibility due to inconsistent policy commitments, provides a compelling explanation for the anguish experienced by Arthur Burns.

The solution to this problem and the rise of inflation targeting are intimately connected. A numerical inflation target, which allows the public to monitor the Central Bank's commitment, provides a constraint on discretion at the Bank and a disincentive for reneging on its commitment to low and stable inflation. It is only by limiting its own discretion that the Central Bank can anchor the public's inflation expectations. But these limits are not sufficient to build credibility for monetary policy; long experience has taught us that a track record of honesty, of persistently fighting inflation pressure, and maintaining independence for monetary policy decisions is even more important than constraining discretion (Blinder, 2000).

Building a track record of honesty requires, however, an extensive communication strategy, since the public can only evaluate honesty in the context of commitments explicitly made. Recent scholarship − for example, Bernanke et al. (1999) − has attributed a central role to the communication strategy during the 1970s at the Bundesbank when it maintained its famed credibility at a time when other Central Banks suffered the anguish spoken of by Arthur Burns. Central Banks around the world have since adopted extensive communication strategies in a move towards unprecedented transparency by monetary authorities, with inflation-targeting Central Banks in the vanguard.

The SARB has joined this trend towards greater transparency, especially since the adoption of inflation targeting in 2000. Aron and Muellbauer (2007) measured the SARB's progress in transparency with the widely used Eijffinger and Geraats index and recorded a sharp improvement from the mid-1990s until 2004, leaving the SARB with the same score as the Reserve Bank of Australia. Further empirical research has lately shown how these improvements in transparency, in combination with the adoption of the more coherent inflation-targeting framework, have improved the credibility of the SARB: Aron and Muellbauer have demonstrated how inflation expectations at a one-year horizon have converged on the SARB's target range, and Reid (2008) has shown that longer-term inflation expectations have also become well anchored in South Africa, as in other inflation-targeting countries; Aron and Muellbauer also showed evidence of declining forecast errors in private sector forecasts of interest-rate decisions by the SARB, and Rigobon (2007) demonstrated that the pass-through of exchange-rate shocks to domestic prices has declined sharply since the inception of inflation targeting.

But these successes are not enough to persuade critics concerned with the degree of autonomy given to the Central Bank under inflation targeting. The 'democratic deficit' of an independent Central Bank refers to the problem of handing control of a powerful policy instrument to a group of unelected technocrats at the Central Bank. The standard solution to the democratic deficit requires a distinction between two levels of Central Bank independence: goal independence occurs when the monetary authorities can set their goals, while instrument independence occurs when the monetary authorities can pursue the given goals, without interference, using the instruments of monetary policy. There is widespread consensus that a goal-dependent but instrument-independent Central Bank solves the democratic deficit, as long as the Central Bank is held effectively accountable to Parliament and (by extension) to the citizens. The existing institutional design of inflation targeting in South Africa solves the democratic deficit to a large extent along these lines: our political leaders set the target for monetary policy, and though the SARB enjoys instrument independence in the pursuit of those targets, it is held accountable to the political agents and to the public for the stance of monetary policy.

However, the standard solution to the democratic deficit risks reintroducing political control over monetary policy through the power of politicians to set the goals of monetary policy. This is not just a theoretical possibility in South Africa where the Minister of Finance has already once (on 29 October 2002) changed the target range, and post-Polokwane it has become increasingly likely that this power will be used again. The only secure safeguard against undermining monetary policy credibility by manipulating the goals or mandate of the SARB is to remove those goals from the scope of short-term politics. In a democratic society these policy goals require democratic support, but that support can be expressed in, for example, the Reserve Bank Act, requiring far greater political effort to change the goals under short-term political pressure.

Should inflation targeting be revisited after Polokwane?

During the Polokwane conference of December 2007 the Alliance partners of the ANC gained in influence relative to the faction of the ANC associated with Thabo Mbeki, the sponsor of the Gear framework for macroeconomic policy, within which inflation targeting was so seamlessly accommodated. Since the conference critics of inflation targeting in the ANC Alliance have, therefore, gained in prominence and power, and though they have been circumspect in their criticism, the Alliance leaders have flagged their intention to review and debate both the implementation and the goal of monetary policy in the Declaration of the Economic Summit held in October 2008.

This debate might have been more salutary if it wasn't so ill informed. The opponents of inflation targeting, whether internationally or locally, often simply ignore the very extensive empirical support for the beneficial impact of inflation targeting in both developed and, especially, developing countries. Inflation targeting has helped to deliver low and stable inflation, without sacrificing economic growth. In South Africa, too, the flexibility of the inflation-targeting procedure has helped to stabilise output and, very likely, has helped to improve the trajectory of growth as well. Meanwhile, the extensive communication strategy pioneered by inflation-targeting Central Banks has helped to improve credibility for the SARB as measured in the predictability of interest rates, the pass-through of international shocks to the economy and the anchoring of inflation expectations.

Ultimately the sustainability of all monetary policy regimes depends on social and political support. In 1937 Sweden abandoned its successful price-level target, not because of demonstrable problems, but because political and social support had been mobilised for a more ambitious monetary policy, one which would in fact see Sweden suffer decades of inflation until it became a leading exponent of inflation targeting in the 1990s. Towards the end of the 1970s Arthur Burns attributed the anguish of central bankers to 'the philosophical and political currents that have been transforming economic life in the United States'. Central bankers have since lost their anguish, but not only for purely technical reasons such as more coherent policy, increased transparency and rising credibility. There has been considerable political space for the Central Bank to use the instruments of monetary policy independently and flexibly to keep inflation low and stable. This political space may now be under threat in South Africa and, like Sweden in the decades after the 1930s, we might be served with a bill of higher inflation and no gain in growth, a bill which the relatively poor will pay in diminished welfare more than the relatively rich.

Notes
1   The focus is on 'forecasted' inflation because the Central Bank has no control over real-time inflation. Instead the Central Bank can influence expected future inflation by adjusting its policy interest rate, which will have an impact on future inflation as it works through the economy along the various channels of the

monetary policy transmission mechanism. These channels include the impact of interest rates on planned investment and consumption, on the asset markets, on the exchange rate, on the balance sheets of corporations and banks, and so on. The impact of monetary policy along these channels occurs with what Milton Friedman (1968) famously called 'long and variable' lags.

2. Inflation targeting is appropriately described as an intermediate position – Bernanke and Mishkin (1997) – requiring 'constrained discretion' – between a rigid rule on the one hand and limitless discretion for the monetary authorities on the other.

3. It is the real interest rate that reflects the time value of money in an economy in which expected inflation is non-zero; it measures the opportunity cost of investing as opposed to saving resources in a monetary economy and is hence the more relevant gauge of the stance of monetary policy.

4. The 'Taylor principle' states that the interest rate should respond more than one-for-one with changes in inflation, both to stabilise inflation and to ensure determinacy of the policy model (Taylor, 1999).

5. Milton Friedman (1976), Robert Lucas (1995) and Edmund Phelps (2006)

References

ANC. 2008. Declaration of the Alliance Economic Summit. Retrieved 4 November 2008, from http://www.anc.org.za/ancdocs/pr/2008/pr1019.html

Aron, J. and J. Muellbauer. 2007. Review of Monetary Policy in South Africa since 1994. *Journal of African Economies*, 16 (5): 705–744

Berg, C. and L. Jonung. 1998. Pioneering Price Level Targeting: The Swedish Experience 1931–1937. SSW/EFI Working Paper Series in Economics and Finance No. 290, Stockholm

Bernanke, B., T. Laubach, F.S. Mishkin and A.S. Posen. 1999. *Inflation Targeting. Lessons from the International Experience.* Princeton, Princeton University Press

Bernanke, B. and F.S. Mishkin. 1997. Inflation Targeting: A New Framework for Monetary Policy? *Journal of Economic Perspectives*, 11 (2): 97–116

Blinder, A.S. 1998. *Central Banking in Theory and Practise.* Cambridge, Ma., The MIT Press

Blinder, A.S. 2000. Central Bank Credibility: Why Do We Care? How Do We Build It? *American Economic Review*, 90 (5): 1421–1431

Burger, P. 2008. The Changing Volatility of the South African Economy. *South African Journal of Economics*, 76 (3): 335–355

Burger, P. and M. Marinkov. 2006. The South African Phillips Curve: How Applicable Is the Gordon Model? *South African Journal of Economics*, 74 (2): 172–189

Burns, A.F. 1979. The Anguish of Central Banking. *The 1979 Per Jacobsson Lecture.* M. Cirovic and J. J. Polak. Belgrade, The Per Jacobsson Foundation

Du Plessis, S.A. and B.W. Smit. 2003. Stabilisation Policy in South Africa. Paper presented at the 8th annual conference for econometric modelling in Africa, held in Stellenbosch during July 2003

Du Plessis, S.A. and B.W. Smit. 2007. South Africa's Growth Revival after 1994. *Journal of African Economies*, 16 (5): 668–704

Du Plessis, S.A., B.W. Smit and F. Sturzenegger. 2007. The Cyclicality of Monetary and Fiscal Policy in South Africa since 1994. *South African Journal of Economics*, 75 (3): 391–411

Ensor, L. 2008. Mantashe Vows ANC will Keep Inflation Targeting. *Business Day*, 17 July 2008: 1

Financial Mail. 2008. Monetary Flexibility Needed. 18 April 2008: 1

Frankel, J., B.W. Smit and F. Sturzenegger. 2007. South Africa: Macroeconomic Challenges after a Decade of Success. CID Working Paper no. 133, April 2007, Cambridge, Ma.

Friedman, M. 1968. The Role of Monetary Policy. *American Economic Review*, 58 (1): 1–17

Friedman, M. 1977. Nobel Lecture: Inflation and Unemployment. *Journal of Political Economy*, 85 (3): 451–472

Friedman, M. and A.J. Schwartz. 1963. *A Monetary History of the United States 1867 to 1960*. Princeton, Princeton University Press

Garrow, C. 2007. Why Reflex Inflation Targeting Could Shoot SA in the Foot. *Business Day*, 5 December 2007:11

Hodge, D. 2002. Inflation versus Unemployment in South Africa: Is There a Trade-off? *South African Journal of Economics*, 70 (3), 417–443

Kahn, B. 2008. Challenges of Inflation Targeting for Emerging Market Economies: The South African Case. Paper delivered at the SARB conference, 29–31 October 2008, Pretoria

King, M.A. 1997. 'Changes in UK Monetary Policy: Rules and Discretion in Practise. *Journal of Monetary Economics*, 39 (June): 81–97

Kydland, F.E. and E.C. Prescott. 1977. Rules Rather than Discretion: The Inconsistency of Optimal Plans. *Journal of Political Economy*, 85 (1): 473–491

Mboweni, T.T. 2008. Monetary Policy, Inflation Targeting and Inflation Pressures: Address to the Bureau for Economic Research Annual Conference, Johannesburg, 22 May 2008. Retrieved 5 November 2008, from www.reservebank.co.za

Mondi, L. 2007. We Need a Flexible Inflation Target. *City Press*, 5

MPC. 2007. Statement of the Monetary Policy Committee, 7 June 2007. Retrieved 5 November 2008, from http://www.reservebank.co.za/

Ortiz, A. and F. Sturzenegger. 2007. Estimating SARB's Policy Reaction Function. *South African Journal of Economics*, 75 (4): 659–680

Posen, A.S. 1997. Lessons from the Bundesbank on the Occasion of its 40th Birthday. Institute of International Economics Working Paper, 97-4, Washington

Reid, M. 2008. The Sensitivity of South African Inflation Expectations to Surprises. Department of Economics, University of Stellenbosch MComm

Rigobon, R. 2007. Through the Pass-Through: Measuring Central Bank Credibility. CID Working Paper no. 143, March 2007, Boston

Roger, S. and M.R. Stone. 2005. On Target? The International Experience with

Achieving Inflation Targets. IMF Working Paper, WP/05/163, Washington

Rose, A.K. 2006. A Stable International Monetary System Emerges: Inflation Targeting Is Bretton Woods, Reversed. NBER Working Paper 12711, Boston

Stiglitz, J.E. 2008. The Failure of Inflation Targeting. Retrieved 5 November 2008, from http://www.project-syndicate.org/commentary/stiglitz99

Svendsen, I., O. Roisland and K. Olsen. 2004. Trade-offs in Monetary Policy. *Norges Bank Economic Bulletin*, 2004 (Quarter 2): 1–2

Svensson, L.E.O. 1999. Inflation Targeting as a Monetary Policy Rule. *Journal of Monetary Economics*, 43: 607–654

Taylor, J.B. 1999. A Historical Analysis of Monetary Policy Rules. In J.B. Taylor (ed.), *Monetary Policy Rules*. University of Chicago Press and NBER, Chicago

Taylor, J.B. 2000. Five Things We Know for Sure. *Hoover Digest*, 1998 (3)

Woglom, G. 2003. How Has Inflation Targeting Affected Monetary Policy in South Africa? *South African Journal of Economics*, 71 (2): 380–406

Woodford, M. 2003. *Interest and Prices: Foundations of a Theory of Monetary Policy*. Princeton University Press, Princeton

5

Fiscal policy beyond 2008: prospects, risks and opportunities

Iraj Abedian and Tania Ajam

A combination of rapid economic contraction, and imminent change in political leadership in South Africa, has opened up an interesting new vista for South Africa's fiscal policy prospects. Key macroeconomic policies underpinning fiscal structures are under review. Whilst no specific policy framework has been confirmed, and indeed cannot be confirmed until the 2009 elections are conducted, it is nonetheless safe to assume that the ruling ANC-led Alliance (ANC, SACP and Cosatu) will win the election. As such, the Alliance's recent pronouncements about possible macroeconomic policy changes have caused much concern locally and internationally. The rating agencies have placed the country's sovereign risk rating under constant watch, and South Africa's prospects have been downgraded from 'stable' to 'negative'. Meanwhile, as a result of global financial and economic meltdown, domestic economic growth has declined from its high of 5.7% in 2007 to a meagre 0.2% in the third quarter of 2008 and is projected to remain in the doldrums for a while.

Given the rising threat of global recession at the time of writing, one thing that is very likely is a fall in the country's fiscal revenues over the next few years. Meanwhile, the ANC Alliance has mooted the adoption of a fairly ambitious fiscal project for the future. Many of the proposed fiscal programmes are welfarist and some developmental. The welfarist and populist elements of the proposed policies are known to create medium- to long-term fiscal liabilities that are hard to escape from. Developmental fiscal undertakings require a well-known set of technical prerequisites that are lacking within the public sector at present. At the time of writing, not much has been said about the infirmities and fault-lines within the fiscal management institutional structures.

It is against this backdrop that this essay examines the fiscal policy prospects in South Africa beyond 2008. To this end, we begin by reviewing the background to the current fiscal status dating back to 1994 – the dawn of the new democratic dispensation and the start of the fiscal reform initiatives. The purpose of the review is to highlight the considerable gains made, and the challenges remaining in the path of fiscal reform and modernisation. The next section analyses the key risks facing the country's fiscal management in the next few years. These vary from global to local, from institutional to managerial. Yet their collective threat to the country's fiscal integrity is real and needs consistent political management. Failure in this regard is more than likely to reverse the remarkable achievements made over the past ten years. This is particularly important given the global financial and economic circumstances that are likely to prevail over the next decade. The last section outlines some key fiscal opportunities that provide constructive options for public sector interventions over the next period. In our view, here lies the scope for the next generation of fiscal reform and modernisation. Admittedly, some of these reforms are complex, require time and call for consistent leadership of the political economy arena. Our concluding remarks attempt to underline some salient points emerging from the essay's analysis.

Review of fiscal reform, 1994–2008
Pre-1994 fiscal conditions

Any review of fiscal policy must start with the developmental and macroeconomic conditions prevailing in 1994. Probably the most striking and alarming features of the start of the post-apartheid era were the extent of poverty and deprivation, and the degree of racially skewed inequality in income, wealth and opportunity which characterised South African society. The new democratic dispensation faced a host of developmental, governance and fiscal policy problems.

Fiscal conditions at the time of the transition to a democratic order were daunting. While there had been previous attempts to broaden the tax base, aggregate fiscal discipline was weak. Burgeoning debt fuelled by increasing government expenditures, themselves accompanied by weak revenue collections, raised serious concerns about sustainability and the spectre of a debt trap. Levels of interest expenditure were high and rising.

A further disconcerting trend in the economic composition of general government expenditure was the secular increase in current expenditures with concomitant declines in capital expenditures, creating an environment of government dis-saving in an economy characterised by low household savings rates.

Fiscal discipline was lacking, with government departments frequently overspending their budget allocations, resulting in the 'annual ubiquitous Part Appropriation Bill' (Abedian and Standish, 1992). Budgeting was a highly secretive process with minimal transparency or effective accountability to Parliament. There was very little detailed, credible and timely information on the budget, expenditure and service delivery outputs available to Parliament or to civil society. Thus few informed conclusions on operational efficiency trends could be made. The financial situation of local authorities was also precarious, and consolidated, credible information on their financial condition was virtually non-existent.

Fiscal policy objectives of the ANC government

Faced with the legitimate expectations of a newly enfranchised electorate, the new government experienced considerable uncertainty about its ability to resist populist spending pressures. Its fiscal reform initiatives were first articulated through government macroeconomic programmes, the Reconstruction and Development Programme (RDP), launched in January 1994, and the Growth, Employment and Redistribution (Gear) strategy of June 1996. Even then these programmes were hotly contested policy terrains.

As the ANC's election manifesto agreed upon by the Tripartite Alliance, the RDP was not a macroeconomic policy per se, but rather a broad policy framework aimed at promoting sustainable human development and accelerating service delivery to the poor. It concentrated on meeting basic needs, developing human resources, building the economy, and democratising state and society. In order to avoid negative inflationary and balance of payments consequences, the RDP aimed to redirect government spending, rather than increasing it as a proportion of GDP.

The RDP also called for an end to unnecessary secrecy around the making of the budget, more effective parliamentary oversight, the merging of the departments of Finance and State Expenditure, and the use of multi-year budgeting. A Ministry for the RDP was created in the Office of the Presidency in 1994, and the RDP White Paper in 1994 incorporated the programme into the official policy stance of government.

Besides deficit reduction, the importance of reprioritisation of expenditures and improved tax collection was also stressed. Even prior to the adoption of Gear, the goals of fiscal policy had been expressed as 'The reduction of the overall budget deficit and the level of government dissaving; the avoidance of permanent increases in the tax burden; reducing consumption expenditure by general government relative to GDP which translates into the containment of non-interest recurrent expenditure in real terms; keeping overall wage and salary increases within inflation limits; and strengthening the general government contribution to gross domestic fixed investment' (Department of Finance, 1995: 2.3).

On 14 June 1996, in the wake of severe currency depreciation and volatility, the Minister of Finance, Trevor Manuel, tabled the Gear strategy in Parliament, announcing that the parameters of the policy 'were not up for negotiation at this stage'. Gear aimed to attain a growth rate of 6% per annum and the creation of 400 000 jobs per annum by the year 2000.

While drawing widespread support from business, both the substance of the macroeconomic strategy and the process by which it was compiled drew criticism from the labour movement (Cosatu), the Communist Party (SACP) and NGOs (like the South African Council of Churches). Although government claimed that there had been no major shift in macroeconomic policy and that the Gear policy had actually underpinned the development goals of the RDP, it was widely regarded as a turnabout in economic policy – 'neoliberalism' triumphant over the more activist, developmental state-oriented approaches of the RDP.

Labour opposed the basic thrust of the Gear strategy, creating tensions in the Alliance (Gomomo, 1997). Cosatu argued that decreases in budget deficits would be inimical to economic growth and job creation. Proposals for reductions in current government expenditure were seen as weakening government's commitment to reducing the social backlogs identified in the RDP. Cosatu's People's Budget identified 'the current macroeconomic policy as a major obstacle to development' and aimed to 'counter the deep budget cuts on public spending', arguing that budget cuts had compromised service delivery and the satisfaction of basic needs (Cosatu, 2000).

The divergence of views on fiscal policy held by government and business, on the one hand, and labour and the NGOs, on the other, stemmed from fundamentally different underlying growth models and paradigms of growth and development. While government essentially argued that the causality should run from disciplined, sustainable fiscal policy to economic growth and then enabling sustainable development, labour contended that the causality would run in the opposite direction. Since then, the tensions within the Alliance seem to have subsided somewhat.

The fiscal reform programme

South Africa's fiscal reform since 1994 has been extensive and one of the most successful in developing countries. In what follows we briefly assess three of the key areas of fiscal policy modernisation, viz. tax reform, enhancing public management, and fiscal oversight reforms.[1]

Tax reform: Tax policy and administration reforms have greatly contributed to broadening the tax base and enhancing revenue collection efficiency. Foremost was the creation of an autonomous revenue service entity known as the South African Revenue Service (SARS) with improved audit capability through the introduction of computerised systems, enhanced capacity to investigate and prosecute tax evaders, and better debt recovery procedures. At the same time discriminatory tax legislation was reviewed to eliminate gender and racial discrimination and ensure compliance with other constitutional provisions for the right to privacy and administrative justice.

Enhancing public management: One of the major reforms at national and provincial level has been the improvement in the quality and comprehensiveness of data since 1994. Other reforms include greater political input into the budget through MinComBud,[2] tabling the budget before the start of the financial year, introducing an annual Medium Term Budget Policy Statement (MTBPS) which announces government's broad fiscal intentions for the following year's budget, improved debt and cash management strategies, and a move towards budgeting over a three-year horizon by means of a Medium Term Expenditure Framework (MTEF). The link between budget reform and the roll-out of the intergovernmental fiscal system was clearly articulated: 'The introduction of three year budgets and their consolidation into resource envelopes is an important step in the evolution of the institutional framework for intergovernmental policy making and budget planning. The intergovernmental forums of the spending departments will, for the first time, have expenditure projections within which to develop and refine the norms and standards for service delivery' (Department of Finance, 1997b: 5).

The Public Finance Management Act (PFMA) of 1999 gave effect to

Section 216 of the Constitution, and began the move from a highly centralised input-oriented expenditure control system towards a more performance-oriented system that would 'allow managers to manage but hold them accountable'. The PFMA also formally established the National Treasury, as envisaged by the Constitution, amalgamating the former departments of Finance and State Expenditure. In 2003 the Municipal Finance Management Act (MFMA) was passed to extend budget reforms to municipalities. In 2004 a new budget and reporting format, aligned with international standards, was introduced, based on a new standard chart of accounts.

While the initial focus in implementing the PFMA was primarily on improving financial reporting and financial management systems and procedures, this has gradually expanded to include efficiency and effectiveness analysis, which requires non-financial service delivery information. In addition to annual budgets in Parliament and the provincial legislatures, ministers and MECs have to table strategic plans or annual performance plans for scrutiny and approval. The linking of output measures (in measurable objectives) to the resource allocation in budget programmes and sub-programmes is crucial for creating an orientation towards value for money. These plans and budgets lay the foundation for in-year monthly financial reporting and quarterly performance reporting, as well as year-end annual reports and audited financial statements. Each of these instruments is crucial for effective oversight of the execution of the budget.

Since 2003, the National Treasury has engaged extensively with provincial government departments to put in place a system of standardised five-year strategic plans, annual performance plans and quarterly performance reports, which monitor progress of actual service delivery achievement and spending against plans. In May 2007, the Treasury published its Framework for Managing Programme Performance Information, which aimed to clarify the standards and definitions for performance information in support of audits of non-financial information.

Fiscal oversight reforms: Unlike in many other countries, the ideals of good fiscal governance are constitutionally entrenched in South Africa. Sections 215–17 of the Constitution require that budget processes of all three spheres of government promote transparency, accountability and effective financial management, using uniform classifications. These imperatives were eventually given substance by legislation like the PFMA of 1999 and the MFMA of 2003, as described above.

The PFMA and its regulations, together with the intergovernmental

Table 1: Main budget revenue and expenditure

R billions		Revenue	Expenditure	Cost of debt service	Non-interest expenditure	Contingency reserve	Budget balance
1995/6	Actual outcome	126.0	151.4	29.3	122.1		−25.4
1996/7		146.5	175.5	33.2	142.3		−29.0
1997/8		163.2	189.9	38.8	151.1		−26.6
1998/9		183.2	201.4	42.7	158.7		−17.4
1999/2000		198.0	214.7	44.3	170.5		−16.6
2000/1		215.4	233.9	46.3	187.6		−18.3
2001/2		248.2	262.9	47.6	215.3		−14.6
2002/3		278.1	291.5	46.8	244.7		−13.0
2003/4		298.7	328.7	46.3	282.4		−29.2
2004/5		347.2	368.5	48.9	319.6		−20.6
2005/6		410.8	416.7	50.9	365.8		−4.9
2006/7	Preliminary outcome	479.4	470.2	52.2	418.0		11.0
2007/8		559.8	541.5	52.9	488.6		18.3
2008/9	Revised estimate	626.5	635.5	53.9	581.6		−9.0
2009/10	MTBPS estimate	682.9	735.0	52.7	678.3	4.0	−52.1
2010/11		751.1	792.5	55.1	717.4	12.0	−41.4
2011/12		833.4	844.6	56.7	787.9	20.0	−11.2

fiscal legislative framework, thus provide Parliament and the provincial legislatures with timely and credible oversight tools. Prior to PFMA implementation, credible in-year financial reporting was virtually non-existent. This meant that there was no 'early warning system' for Parliament and the legislatures to enable them to detect over- or underspending within the fiscal year and to respond accordingly. This clearly undermined effective in-year oversight of budget execution. Furthermore, there was often a lag of up to two years before audited financial statements were available to public accounts committees, which undermined the notion of fiscal accountability. The PFMA requires that financial statements be produced no later than three months following the end of the financial year, and that these be audited by no later than seven months after year-end.

During the apartheid era, Parliament acted as a mere 'rubber stamp' of the budget. The Constitution of 1996 enhanced Parliament's oversight role of budget formulation and implementation (sections 55 and 77). It even provided for Parliament to amend money bills (i.e. budgets). In 1998 a draft

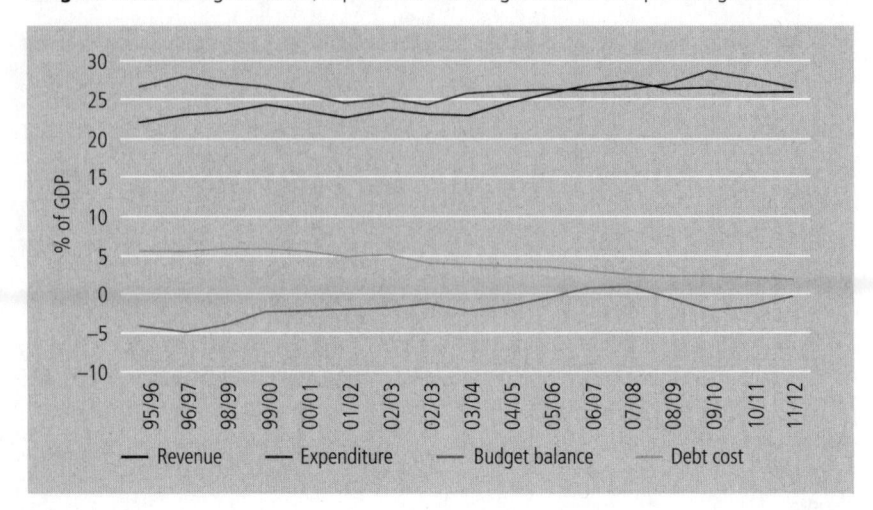

Figure 1: Main budget revenue, expenditure and budget balance as a percentage of GDP

bill called the Money Bills Amendment Procedure Bill was approved by Cabinet and sent to Parliament, but was never enacted because, as it stood, it was not deemed consonant with the Constitution. In 2008, a revised version of this bill was tabled which envisaged a much more active role for Parliament in amending budgets.

Fiscal policy outcomes

Table 1 shows actual trends in fiscal aggregates over the last decade as well as budgeted estimates for the current fiscal year and the next two years, as reflected in the 2008 MTBPS. The size of these figures relative to the size of the economy (as measured by GDP) is shown in Figure 1.

Main budget revenue increased gradually in 1995/6 to a peak in 2008, but is expected to decline in 2011/12. Expenditure remained fairly constant at around 26.3% of GDP, dipping below this only in 1999/2000 and 2004/5. As a result, budget deficits declined in 1995/96 to 2005/6. The main budget balance then moved into surplus in 2006/7 and 2007/8. A marginal deficit is projected for the 2008/9 fiscal year. The 2008 MTBPS projected budget deficits of 2.0%, 2.4% and 0.4% of GDP for 2009/10, 2010/11 and 2011/12 respectively, driven by growth forecasts which had been revised downwards in line with deteriorating growth prospects in the wake of the global financial crisis.

Over the medium term, expenditure levels are expected to remain stable while tax revenue will likely decline in line with lower expected

Table 2: Main budget revenue sources

	Persons & individuals	Companies	STC	Tax on retirement fund[1]	Taxes on property[2]	VAT[3]	Taxes on international trade and transactions[4]	Fuel levy[5]	Other[6]
Average percent contribution of revenue sources to total main budget tax revenue									
1988/9–1992/3	32.6	18.1	0.0	–	1.5	28.5	4.4	6.3	8.5
1993/4–1997/8	40.1	12.4	0.0	–	1.7	25.2	7.4	4.7	8.6
1998/9–2002/3	38.6	14.5	1.7	2.0	1.8	24.3	6.5	3.4	7.2
2003/4–2007/8	30.4	21.9	2.7	0.9	2.3	26.9	4.9	4.1	5.8
2008/9–2010/11	30.2	24.1	3.1	–	2.2	26.0	3.9	5.0	5.4
Average annual nominal growth rates of revenue source as percentages									
1988/9–1992/3	22.7	3.9	–	–	3.5	–7.3	127.7	–1.3	–7.6
1993/4–1997/8	15.1	10.3	–	–	17.1	18.0	11.3	4.0	19.0
1998/9–2002/3	6.7	21.1	–	–	14.2	11.8	4.9	11.3	4.2
2003/4–2007/8	12.3	20.5	26.1	–53.0	20.1	15.9	9.4	22.9	10.1
2008/9–2010/11	12.6	9.6	6.9	–	10.7	11.0	6.5	12.5	10.9

Source: Calculations based on National Treasury, Budget Review 2008 and other Budget Reviews.

Note: Figures prior to 1995/6 include collections by the former TBVC states and self-governing territories.

1 Average annual growth rates for retirement funds tax introduced in 1996/7, covers period from 1996/7 to 1999/2000.
2 Taxes on property includes donations tax, estate duty, marketable securities tax and transfer duties.
3 Including sales duty, replaced by general sales tax in July 1978, and value added tax in September 1991.
4 Includes customs duties, import surcharges, diamond export duties, miscellaneous customs and excise income, as well as ordinary levy collections.
5 Including the former fuel levy directed to Regional Services Councils and the levy allocated to the National Road Fund for the period 1983/4 to 1986/7.
6 Including various levies, mining leases and ownership, cinematographic tax and other special levies, the skills development levy, specific and ad valorem taxes, and stamp duties and fees.

corporate profitability. Also conspicuous is the trend of steadily declining cost-of-debt service. This has freed up more resources for discretionary non-interest expenditures, particularly for social services.

The tax reforms have markedly improved the efficiency of tax collection and revenue sources have diversified (see Table 2). The broadening of the tax base has permitted considerable tax relief since 1995, of which roughly 85% comprised personal income tax relief.

As can be seen from Table 3, 'social services' jointly consume more than half of consolidated national and provincial expenditure. While education expenditure has fallen as a percentage of total consolidated expenditure

Table 3: Consolidated national and provincial expenditure by functional classification

	1997/8	1998/9	1999/2000	2000/1	2002/3
	Percentage of consolidated				
General govt services & unallocatable expenditure	8.3	5.9	6.0	6.2	6.5
Protection services	15.3	16.2	16.0	16.7	17.5
Defence and intelligence	5.9	5.7	5.4	6.3	6.4
Police	6.3	6.8	6.8	6.7	7.0
Prisons	1.9	2.5	2.4	2.4	2.5
Justice	1.1	1.2	1.4	1.3	1.6
Social services	48.5	49.2	48.5	48.1	47.3
Education	22.0	21.6	21.3	21.1	20.4
Health	11.3	11.8	11.4	11.6	11.3
Social security and welfare	11.6	12.1	11.9	11.8	11.8
Housing	3.4	3.1	1.7	1.7	1.6
Community development & other social	0.3	0.6	2.1	2.0	2.2
Economic services	8.9	9.1	9.6	9.9	11.3
Water schemes and related services	1.2	1.4	1.3	1.4	1.4
Fuel and energy	0.2	0.1	0.2	0.3	0.5
Agriculture, forestry and fishing	1.8	1.9	1.8	1.7	1.8
Mining, manufacturing and construction	0.5	0.6	0.5	0.5	0.4
Transport and communication	3.6	3.7	3.9	3.8	4.3
Other economic services	1.5	1.3	2.0	2.2	2.9
Contingency reserve	0.0	0.0	0.0	0.0	0.0
Interest	19.0	20.2	19.9	19.0	17.4
Total consolidated expenditure	100.0	100.5	100.0	100.0	100.0

Source: National Treasury, Budget Review 2006 and other Budget Reviews

between 1995/6 and 2007/8, social welfare expenditure, which includes means-tested child support grants, disability grants and universal old-age grants, has been increasing from 11.6% of total consolidated expenditure in 1995/6 to 16.4% in 2007/8. This makes social grant expenditure the second largest category after education spending.

Social security grant beneficiaries have increased rapidly, from 5.8 million in 2003 to 12.4 million in 2008 (National Treasury, 2008). While old-age pension beneficiaries have only increased at an average annual rate of 2%, the safety net for children beneficiaries under 14 years old has been progressively widened over this period. Child-support grant beneficiaries

2002/3	2003/4	2004/5	2005/6	2006/7	2007/8	2008/9	2009/10	2010/11
national and provincial expenditure								
6.2	6.4	6.4	6.0	6.0	6.1	6.1	6.2	6.0
17.7	17.1	16.4	16.5	15.4	15.0	14.7	14.5	14.7
6.8	6.5	5.6	5.7	5.0	4.8	4.6	4.4	4.3
6.9	6.8	7.0	7.1	7.0	6.8	6.6	6.7	6.7
2.5	2.3	2.4	2.3	1.9	1.9	1.9	1.8	2.0
1.6	1.5	1.5	1.5	1.5	1.5	1.6	1.6	1.6
48.8	50.9	51.8	52.5	53.5	53.7	54.3	54.6	55.0
19.9	20.1	19.7	19.2	18.7	18.4	18.8	18.7	18.8
11.1	11.1	11.3	11.5	11.6	11.5	11.3	11.4	11.5
13.6	14.9	15.8	16.6	16.4	16.1	16.4	16.3	16.2
1.8	1.7	1.7	1.7	1.9	1.9	2.1	2.2	2.4
2.4	3.0	3.2	3.5	5.0	5.7	5.8	5.9	6.1
12.3	12.3	12.7	13.3	14.5	15.9	15.9	15.9	15.1
1.5	1.5	1.5	1.4	1.4	1.6	1.7	1.8	1.8
0.6	0.5	0.6	1.1	1.0	1.2	0.8	0.9	0.6
1.7	1.8	1.9	2.0	2.1	2.4	2.2	2.0	2.0
0.4	0.4	0.3	0.4	0.4	0.4	0.4	0.3	0.3
4.6	4.5	4.7	4.8	5.9	6.2	6.5	6.6	6.4
3.6	3.6	3.6	3.4	3.6	4.1	4.2	4.2	4.0
0.0	0.0	0.0	0.0	0.0	0.0	0.9	1.7	2.6
15.0	13.3	12.8	11.7	10.6	9.3	8.0	7.2	6.6
100.0	100.0	100.0	100.0	100.0	100.0	100.0	100.0	100.0

rose from 2.6 million in 2003 to 7.8 million in 2007, with an annual average rate of 31.6%. The foster-care grant and the care-dependency grant grew annually at an average rate of 28.7% and 15.6% respectively (National Treasury, 2007). The recent relaxation of the means test requirements and the proposed extension of the child support grant to the 14–18 age group would create further take-up over the medium term. The HIV/AIDS epidemic has also created pressure within the disability grant.

Research has indicated that this unprecedented expansion in income support has been well targeted. For instance, Agüero et al. (2007) have found robust evidence that these targeted unconditional payments have bolstered early childhood nutrition as measured by child height-for-age, and also present evidence for the likely beneficial long-term raised earnings based on these short-term transfers. However, large increases in entitlement spending may tend to create fiscal rigidities, be politically irreversible and reduce fiscal discretion during business cycle downturns.

The government has committed itself to further social security and retirement financing reform. Currently under consideration is a mandatory contributory earnings-related savings and social insurance framework, accompanied by a wage subsidy for those with incomes below the personal income tax threshold (National Treasury, 2007). This would provide basic retirement, death and disability benefits, and would bridge the existing gap between social assistance grant arrangements, which cater for the poorest of the poor, and the tax-incentivised private pensions sector, catering for formal sector employees.

Key fiscal risks

On the eve of its fourth election, South Africa faces sobering fiscal prospects. There is renewed tension within the ANC-led Alliance, and indeed within society at large. These tensions re-emerged strongly at the December 2007 ANC Policy Conference in Polokwane, followed by the ANC-led Alliance Economic Summit in October 2008. This was a period of turbulent political realignment: a change of political leadership within the ANC, the recall of President Mbeki in September 2008, the accession of President Motlanthe, and the formation of a new political party, the Congress of the People (Cope) from within the ANC.

In the run-up to the MTBPS in October 2008, uncertainty persisted about the future trajectory of fiscal policy. In the wake of the worsening global credit crisis, conflicting reports on the future direction of macroeconomic and fiscal policy were widespread. Clearly, South Africa's fiscal risks have risen. In what follows we itemise these risks and provide a brief analysis of each to illustrate the nature of the risk involved.

Declining growth due to global contraction

By the end of 2008, it became evident that the global economy had entered into a recession characterised by financial market volatility and rising uncertainty. What began in the USA as a housing market financial problem, commonly known as the sub-prime crisis, rapidly spread across the globe. A tightening of credit in financial markets and large-scale write-offs within the global financial system followed. A worldwide credit crunch engulfed the global economy, adversely impacting on economic output albeit with differing effects on various regions. With unprecedented rapidity, the financial and credit crises soon led to considerable slow-down in growth prospects for the world economy.

The sum total of these developments has been a considerable reduction in actual and expected economic growth rates. Whereas the global GDP was expected to grow at over 6% per annum at the start of 2008, by the middle of the year growth had been revised to approximately 4%. By December 2008, global GDP projections had dwindled to a mere 2% and were declining. Whilst the South African financial system did not suffer any major direct losses, the indirect effects proved inescapable. Slowly but surely the bad debt of the banking system rose, commodity exports dried up rapidly, and at the same time commodity prices collapsed sharply. Consequently, GDP registered a mere 0.2% growth in the third quarter of 2008. Projections for the last quarter, and indeed the following year, are not promising either. Driven by the global meltdown and exacerbated by relatively high domestic interest rates, the South African economy is in the throes of rapid contraction. This poses serious revenue dilemmas for the fiscus in the next few years.

Policy shift, political economy risk and threat to sovereign rating

As 2008 drew to a close, the policy intentions expressed by the ANC-led Alliance and the rising global risk aversion combined to place the country's credit rating at risk. Nearly all global rating agencies have expressed serious concerns and have issued statements that change the country's prospects from 'stable' to 'negative' or have placed the country under review. This is in the context of a decade of steady improvement in the country's sovereign risk ratings.

With rising creditworthiness and considerably improved macroeconomic and fiscal conditions, the country's sovereign risk premium (as measured by the additional yield over and above the benchmark US Treasury bonds) has declined considerably. As a result, the cost of borrowing in the global capital market declined steadily for both the public and private sectors. This was an explicit and considerable reduction in South Africa's implicit risk premium. Since 2006 a series of local and global factors has contributed to a rising sovereign risk premium, yet at levels substantially lower than a decade ago.

Against this backdrop, the prevailing concerns around the growing uncertainty emanating from policy shifts towards populism within the ANC-led Alliance impart immediate fiscal risks with regard to the rising cost of borrowing. This is particularly relevant because global and national trends suggest an increasing public-sector borrowing requirement. At a time of rising public debt, any increase in the price at which borrowing is effected results in a growing debt service charge. This in turn entails a rising trade-off between allocation to 'debt service' and that to other socio-economic needs. This fiscal trend eventuates in mounting government debt and revisions in the country's credit rating. To undermine the country's sovereign credit rating is tantamount to a self-imposed 'structural adjustment', with massive social consequences for the poor and the vulnerable.

Rising debt and macro crowding-out effect

With rising public-sector borrowing, the threat of a macroeconomic 'crowding-out' effect has emerged once again. The 'crowding-out' effect becomes binding particularly in times of limited credit availability in the capital market. It is interesting that some contributors to the present policy debate have argued the case for the relevance of 'crowding-in' at a time when the global and local economies are contracting. The theoretical debate between the 'crowding-in' and 'crowding-out' paradigms has been raging for decades. There is no doubt that both outcomes are possible. The issue can only be resolved empirically.

In effect, what needs to be carefully considered is the conditions under which either outcome will obtain. The conditions for crowding-out may be summarised as follows:

- Public spending with low multiplier effect, i.e. multipliers equal to or less than 1. Welfare spending is a typical case in point.
- Rising public-sector investment or expenditure when public management is ineffective, owing to poor planning, low management capacity, weak implementation, corruption and institutional infirmities, which eventuate in expenditure overruns and low expenditure efficiency.
- Low national saving levels, which lead to low levels of loanable funds. In such cases, the sheer volume of national savings cannot support concurrent high levels of private and public investment. Consequently, as public borrowing increases, the cost of borrowing rises commensurately and thereby places private-sector investments at risk, and in particular marginal projects become unbankable.

- Periods of low economic growth or recession leading to low investor confidence, hence the probability of 'crowding-out' is relatively high. In such times, expected returns on investments are lower, as any marginal increase in the actual or expected cost of borrowing tends to discourage private-sector investment.

It is interesting that all these conditions obtain concurrently in South Africa. The intended shift towards populist welfarism appears to coincide with the widely recognised poor managerial capacity within the state. Add to this the low national savings that have characterised the economy, and we have the near-perfect conditions for a creeping private-sector investment 'crowding-out', given the prevailing global and domestic contractionary economic conditions.

Infrastructure investment vs welfare trade-offs

In times of economic contraction, one of the key elements of economic policy is a ramp-up of infrastructure investment, primarily spearheaded by the public sector. Provided the infrastructure planning is properly done, and its implementation is professional, such investments tend to have maximum multiplier effects on economic recovery. In such cases, the probability of 'crowding-in' is at its peak.

At the allocative level, fiscal resources are traded among competing ends. For example, the ANC Alliance's policy of extending the child grant to the age of 18 is estimated to put another 4 million beneficiaries on the government's monthly welfare payroll. The medium-term social consequences of such a policy aside, its immediate fiscal implication is a reduction in infrastructure investment, be it 'social' or 'economic'. This trade-off has considerable socio-economic consequences. In general, populist fiscal policy may be seen to have a short-term political gain, but its socio-economic effects are destructive. Over time, such policies constitute a major fiscal risk that takes decades to expunge from the system.

It is worth noting that while social security is supposed to cushion the most vulnerable, it is generally acknowledged that this is a short-term measure. Over the medium to long term, the education system should help build human capital and provide a springboard for economic and social mobility. Retrospectively, it is now evident that the inability to improve the quality of the education system over 1994–2008 has deepened the skills mismatch in the economy. Instead of addressing the underlying institutional and structural issues of the education system, and that of human resource development more generally, the response has been to propose the expansion of welfare payments to the youth in the 18–25 age bracket.

Implementation capacity and rising public investment risk

That the South African public sector lacks competent implementation capacity is not in dispute. This is possibly the most vivid, and potentially devastating, risk in the fiscal landscape, capable of undermining the much-needed public-sector investment programme. Over the past decade, this lack of competent capacity has led to the neglect of some vital infrastructure planning such as sustainable energy, water resources and human resource development. Most commonly, the country's ageing urban infrastructure has been largely ignored. Even the key metropolitan centres suffer from basic symptoms of decay in their urban utilities, poor institutional performance and weak financial management capability. More generally, the local government institutional infrastructure has been left to falter.

To indicate the severity of the problem, it suffices to note that according to a Municipal Demarcation Board (MDB) study in 2008, 23% of the municipal chief financial officers only had Grade 12 certificates, 64% of technical services managers had less than four years of experience and 46% of municipal managers had been in their position for less than one year. In addition, the level of skills mismatch and vacancies in local municipalities was as high as 40%. The implications of such infrastructural deficiencies for local economic development, social welfare and economic competitiveness are considerable.

Closely linked to poor infrastructural planning has been a pervasive and damaging 'coordination and integration failure' within and between government departments. This is true for inter-departmental relations within each sphere of government, for intra-spheres of government, as well as within state-owned entities. Furthermore, operationally the public sector lacks efficiency and systemic dynamism, despite initiatives such as Batho Pele, the new Public Service Act and the PFMA.

In this light, the more complex the public investment programme, the more likely it will entail rising fiscal risks. As such, the much-desired 'developmental state', requiring complex public-sector planning and coordination, and driven by fiscal resource, faces an insurmountable start-up obstacle.

SARS's falling marginal efficiency

The efficacy of SARS over the past decade has been a central and critical factor in South Africa's fiscal policy success. SARS's rising efficiency coincided with a period of rising economic growth to generate much-needed fiscal revenues and so facilitate tax breaks in excess of R110 billion over the period 1999–2007. Over 70% of this tax concession accrued to lower-income households, and to a lesser extent to small enterprises. Going forward, however, SARS faces two binding constraints. First, as is to be expected, its efficiency at the margin is waning and is bound to stop yielding any additional fiscal revenues. Secondly, and more importantly, declining GDP growth rates imply lower expected tax revenues over the next MTEF period.

Falling tax revenues will entail rising public-sector borrowing. It is therefore to be expected that budget deficits will rise, and public debt–GDP ratios will increase. Whilst there is no inherent risk in rising budget deficits or public debt, the uses to which such public funds are put could well constitute short- to medium-term fiscal risks. At one extreme, injudicious application of public debt in inefficient and populist expenditure could lead to a variation of 'debt trap' over time. A gradual fall in the marginal efficiency of public borrowings could also lead to a slow but creeping decline in macroeconomic performance.

Political economy challenges and policy sustainability

Pervasive poverty and systemic unemployment are the two obstinate political economy challenges facing South Africa. The legacies of apartheid, compounded by key 'government failures' since then, have culminated in intractable socio-economic problems. At the forefront of the failures has been human resource development. At present the single most obstinate factor hindering economic growth, development and welfare is the prevailing inadequacy of our education and training system. Widespread shortage of skills within the society is but one of its manifestations.

It is a fact that the modernisation and technological upgrading of the economy during the past decade have increased the economy's skills intensity sharply. This in turn has accentuated the systemic unemployment problem. Meanwhile, the country's human capital accumulation has proved wanting. Whilst much has been achieved in promoting access to the public schooling system, little has been achieved with regard to improving the quality of the education offered. 'Unemployability', widespread vacancies and the huge skills gap have emerged concurrently. As a result, the income and wealth inequalities within society have been exacerbated.

Furthermore, intra-racial inequalities have also increased as shown in Table 4.

■ **Table 4:** Inequality shifts by race: Gini coefficients for 1995 and 2005

Race	1995	2005
African	0.55	0.56
Coloured	0.49	0.58
Asian	0.45	0.53
White	0.39	0.45
Total	0.64	0.69

Source: Bhorat & Van der Westhuizen, 2008

1. The changes in the values of the Gini coefficients between 1995 and 2005 are statistically significant at the 95% level, with the exception of Africans.
2. The population in 1995 has been weighted by population weights according to the 1996 Census. Population weights are not available for the 2005 dataset and the population has been weighted by the household weight multiplied by the household size. The 2005 weights are based on the 2001 Census.

Beyond 2009, South Africa's political leadership has to create the will to transform the operational fiscal framework beyond the customary rhetoric. It is imperative to lay the foundation for an effective and accelerated normalisation of the political economy landscape by focusing on the micro-institutional foundations of sustainable growth. In this context, the effectiveness of fiscal operations has a central role to play. As stated before, it is the government's task to put in place redistributive and corrective measures to rectify maldistributions caused by free market operations. To this end, the fiscal micro-institutional fault-lines need urgent and consistent remedial interventions. Throwing fiscal resources in the form of welfarist redistribution at structural poverty and systemic unemployability would only prolong the social inequities and would prove financially unsustainable.

As with macro and fiscal policy reforms during the mid-1990s, the next generation of fiscal policy reforms requires clear, focused and committed leadership, both politically and technically. Whilst it is tempting to muddle through these critical and thorny issues, the political leadership has to rise to the occasion, create a vision, carve out the roadmap, and stay the course until the issues are tackled conclusively. For a glimpse of what is required, the contemporary experience of India, South Korea and Vietnam offers much to emulate.

Fiscal opportunities

In the light of our analysis, it is important to underscore the central role that fiscal policy and operations will assume over the next decade. Both from a political economy perspective, and for reasons of short-term economic stimulation of the economy – given the cyclical downturn – fiscal policy has to fulfil a two-fold objective. Firstly, its operations have to become a great deal more efficient so as to be able to 'do more with less'. Secondly, it has to undergo a tectonic shift to be able to plan and implement a well-coordinated public-sector investment programme with a view to expanding productive capacity and stimulating economic performance. To unpack the key elements of fiscal opportunities over the next period, we briefly analyse three critical components of the fiscal sphere. Whilst our analyses are not exhaustive, they nonetheless indicate the nature of fiscal opportunities and the direction in which leadership focus needs to be pointed.

National and urban infrastructure investment backlog

Empirical evidence has found that infrastructure in South Africa has influenced growth positively, with electricity capacity having the greatest and most robust impact. Yet there has been a long-term decline in infrastructure investment and capital stock, with real investment per capita falling by 72% from 1976 to 2002 (Bogetic and Fedderke, 2006). Electricity shortages due to under-investment in the electricity grid remain a risk to economic growth, and need to be carefully managed. The availability of water has also become a recent focus of concern. Public transport has long been recognised as an area of under-investment.

Public investment in infrastructure to remedy this situation constitutes an opportunity to improve economic productivity, provide a platform for sustained economic growth and create employment. Public capital constraints have begun to receive extensive policy attention (e.g. significant expansions have been planned in successive budgets since 2005). The needs of the 2010 Soccer World Cup have also provided increased stimulus for infrastructural investment. The global credit crunch, which will increase the cost of capital, may result in such plans being deferred or cancelled.

It is critical to recognise that the existence of infrastructural backlogs provides an opportunity to introduce meaningful fiscal interventions only if the planning, coordination and implementation of such projects and programmes happen effectively and professionally.

Socio-economic infrastructure

In certain provinces and municipalities, there is a backlog of hospitals, schools and clinics. In addition, the existing social infrastructure stock needs to be maintained. However, Van der Berg (2007) cautions that the problem in respect of schooling is not one of budgets, infrastructure or other teaching resources alone, but also of improving school management. He contends that the problem seems to be operational inefficiency, rather than allocative inefficiency per se, since increased resources devoted to education have not, by and large, improved educational performance at black schools. Similarly, with regard to health spending, it is not the quantum of fiscal allocations, but rather the inefficiency of management, that has caused poor health outcomes within society.

That our social infrastructure needs radical upgrading is beyond debate. Communities have even taken to the streets to demonstrate their displeasure, anger and frustration at endless procrastination in service delivery or the gradual degeneration of service quality. Going forward, therefore, what is required is not so much 'analysis of needs', but rather the meaningful overhaul of the political and managerial structures and inefficiencies that have beset the operational systems within the state machinery controlling such services. Therein lies a great fiscal opportunity that may not necessarily require more fiscal resources; indeed it may even save some.

Expunging x-inefficiencies and raising public-sector productivity

Generally, x-inefficiency takes numerous forms and appears in diverse guises within both private and public organisations. For example, in the private sector once upon a time it was common practice to have excessive spending on 'corporate jets', 'chairman's dining rooms' and the like. In short, x-efficiencies arise out of those expenditures that have no or little impact on 'the production or service delivery processes'. In extreme cases, x-inefficiencies may have counterproductive results within the working environment too.

X-inefficiencies are common in public-sector organisations and government departments. Operationally, public service delivery is inherently labour-intensive, and labour-intensive production processes more readily lend themselves to the systemic x-inefficiency syndrome. Such processes are typically far more management-intensive and system-intensive and require ongoing performance assessment. Yet these are the very attributes that our public-sector organisations lack.

Furthermore, it is a fact that since 1994, the social imperative for black economic empowerment has deepened the politicisation of the public service. This is not to say that prior to 1994 the public service was not politicised; indeed it was heavily populated by the protégés of the ruling National Party. The political change since 1994 transformed the racial composition of the public service but did not transform the managerial culture of its operations. It is not surprising that the same abuses of public resources that existed in the dying years of apartheid have continued. Managerial ineptitude, misapplication of public resources, and corruption are rife right across the three spheres of government. It is this managerial culture that generates inordinate amounts of wasteful x-inefficiency. The welfare loss resulting from such inefficiencies is likely to be considerable.

It has become common cause that it is not the quantum of expenditure in health, education, police services and other public arenas which is the main constraint on achieving service-delivery outcomes. There is instead growing recognition that the binding constraint is management capacity or management culture. So, for instance, while there have been significant budget allocations for infrastructure in the past five years, there has also been considerable under-spending due to inadequate planning and project execution. Annual financial reviews of the Auditor-General on the majority of government departments bear testimony to the existence of a wide range of x-inefficiencies within the state operations. These dysfunctions noted by the Auditor-General recur year after year, with little evidence of proactive managerial response.

The elimination of fiscal x-inefficiencies offers a ready and meaningful opportunity in the near future. In general, when times are tough, money-saving measures become a necessity. Given that public-sector expenditure constitutes more than 40% of GDP, significant improvements in public-sector productivity would translate into increased productivity for the entire economy. This in turn would have a positive indirect effect on the overall resource availability envelope as well.

Last but not least, it should be noted that the expunging of x-inefficiencies is never an easy task. It is not easy in the private sector, and it is even more complex in the public sector. Moreover, it will not happen quickly.

Changing the operational culture of a complex and varied organisation such as the public service takes time and perseverance. At the same time, in the absence of such a cultural transformation, the promise of better public service delivery or cost-effective fiscal management of the country is bound to remain a mere slogan.

Concluding remarks

South Africa's fiscal indicators at the end of 2008 compared favourably with those of many of its peer countries. This was, to a large extent, the outcome of a consistent and ambitious fiscal reform programme over the 1994–2007 period. Given the precarious point of departure back in 1994, South Africa's fiscal policy reform has achieved a great deal at the macrofinancial level. This helped underpin the country's much-needed macroeconomic stabilisation goal during the critical period following the birth of the country's democratic era. Not only were inflation and interest rates brought down, but there was also a considerable reallocation of resources in favour of the poor and the lower-income households. Thanks to the consistent success of SARS in improving its collection capability and restoring tax morality, the additional fiscal resources enabled both reallocation to the poorer segments within the society and a lowering of personal income taxes and company taxes, particularly for small and medium enterprises. Over the same period, the democratic government invested a great deal of political and technical capital in the modernisation and systemic design of the new fiscal architecture. The fiscal reform programme and government's political leadership were further enhanced by the rising local and domestic economic performance.

Whilst the fiscal policies of the last decade achieved remarkable success at macro level by reducing budget deficit and government debt ratios, their success at micro-institutional levels was limited. The operational efficiency of state departments and their micro-financial management left much to be desired. Weak fiscal and financial management at departmental level, be it in the national or sub-national spheres, perpetuated a culture of poor management of public resources. Consequently, public service delivery has suffered. In particular, the quality of public services such as health, education and policing has led to much concern. Allocation of more resources to these sectors without addressing the chronic underlying managerial and institutional dysfunctions is likely to perpetuate inefficient and ineffective service delivery outcomes. The experience of the last decade is that government failure has been more in implementation rather than in formulation of policy. The temptation should be resisted to seek the solution for government failure in the realm of policy development or in organisational reconfiguration, simply because these are more politically visible and effected more quickly and expediently, rather than grappling with the fundamental but more intractable problems of improving managerial and technical skills and other institutional capabilities for effective service delivery implementation.

From a public finance and macroeconomic perspective, judicious fiscal policy in the past has bought South Africa some 'fiscal space' in the short term. This is fortuitous, given that the sudden global financial and economic meltdown in 2008 has brought much instability to the world's socio-economic arena. Private and public finances have been shaken to the core, and nearly all governments are in search of remedial policies.

However, with deteriorating prospects for the world economy, growing adverse effects on the domestic growth trajectory, a limited tax base and spending pressures from existing social entitlements, South Africa's 'fiscal space' is likely to shrink further very soon. Going forward, extreme caution should be exercised in the creation of further social entitlements which create fiscal rigidities, and hence fiscal risk, in an increasingly volatile and deteriorating economic climate. Even without any additional expansion in welfare entitlements, at present the number of beneficiaries is over 12 million and increasing at a rate much faster than the number of taxpayers. With SARS hitting diminishing returns in ensuring compliance from existing tax bases, the only other way to increase the yield in future would be to grow the number of taxpayers. This is the overarching challenge of fiscal policy if it is to deliver sustainable resources for social upliftment.

Fiscal and macroeconomic policies more broadly need to focus on interventions that rectify structural dysfunctions within the economy, and more specifically within the fiscal management framework. Instead of continuing the trend of spending more on social concerns but achieving little impact and value for money, concerted managerial action is required to ensure that the quality of education, health and other services is dramatically improved. Our analysis in this chapter has presented specific opportunities that exist for productive investments which fiscal policy should consider. At the same time, we caution against creating a populist and welfarist fiscal framework that is detrimental to the sustainable upliftment of the poor within the society and inimical to the performance of the economy.

Notes

1. This section draws heavily on Ajam and Aron, 2007.
2. A Cabinet subcommittee called the Minister's Committee on the Budget, chaired by the Minister of Finance.

References

Abedian, I. and B. Standish. 1992. The South African Economy: An Historic Overview. In I. Abedian and B. Standish (eds.), *Economic Growth in South Africa: Selected Policy Issues*. Oxford University Press, Cape Town

Agüero, J.M., M.R. Carter and I. Woolard. 2007. The Impact of Unconditional Cash Transfers on Nutrition: The South African Child Support Grant. International Poverty Centre, Working Paper no. 39, September 2007

Ajam, T. and J. Aron. 2007. Fiscal Renaissance in a Democratic South Africa. *Journal of African Economies*, 23 August 2007

Bhorat, H. and C. van der Westhuizen. 2008. Economic Growth, Poverty and Inequality in South Africa: The First Decade of Democracy. Paper prepared for the Presidency 15-Year Review Process. Development Policy Research Unit, University of Cape Town

Bogetic, Z. and J.W. Fedderke. 2006. Forecasting Investment Needs In South Africa's Electricity and Telecom Sectors. *South African Journal of Economics*, 74 (3): 557–574

Cosatu. 1997. Sharpening Budget Reform for Effective Delivery of the RDP. Paper produced for the ANC Policy Conference, Gallagher Estate, Midrand, 1–2 November 1997

Cosatu. 2000. Towards a People's Budget: COSATU Comments on the Medium-term Budget Policy Statement

Department of Finance. 1995. *Budget Review 1995*. Pretoria

Department of Finance. 1996. *Budget Review 1996*. Pretoria

Department of Finance. 1997a. *Budget Review 1997*. Pretoria

Department of Finance. 1997b. *Medium Term Budget Policy Statement 1997*. Pretoria

Gomomo, J. 1997. Labour Opposed to the Basic Thrust of GEAR. *Mayibuye*, October 1997

National Treasury. 2007. *Budget*

National Treasury. 2008. *Budget*

Van der Berg, S. 2001. Trends in Racial Fiscal Incidence in South Africa. *South African Journal of Economics*, 69 (2), 243–268

Van der Berg, S. 2007. Apartheid's Enduring Legacy: Inequalities in Education. *Journal of African Economies*, 16 (5): 849–880

6

Trade, industrial and competition policy

Riaan de Lange and Reyno Seymore

The customs, excise and international trade environment has had a clear and robust impact on South Africa since 1994. After the advent of democracy, South Africa was welcomed back into the international trade fold – but it was one that had substantially changed from that which South Africa had left many years before. This chapter reflects on the road travelled since 1994 in the areas of trade, industrial and competition policy, considers the trials and tribulations endured, gazes into the crystal ball, and concludes by summarising what we believe the direction of policy ideally should be.

Membership of an international rules-based system

Contrary to popular belief, the customs, excise and international trade environment in which we operate today is one based on rules. As with any system, it provides its participants with both rights and obligations (or responsibilities). However, it is not always certain whether participants are even aware of their rights and responsibilities. As a consequence, some simply do not have an effective understanding of the rules. If you do not understand the rules of the game, how are you able to have a realistic chance of winning?

To show why an understanding of rules is so important for customs, excise and international trade, we need to take a brief journey. Firstly, South Africa introduced the Harmonised Customs and Excise System, also known as the HS System, on 1 January 1988. The HS System was devised by the World Customs Organisation (WCO), of which South Africa is a member, to ensure consistency in the classification of imported and exported products among all countries trading with one another.

Secondly, South Africa is also a founding member of the General Agreement on Tariffs and Trade (GATT) and a founding member of the World Trade Organisation (WTO). By way of a reminder, the distinction between GATT and the WTO is that countries who are signatories of GATT can decide to which of the GATT agreements they are willing to commit, whereas members of the WTO are contracting parties to all the WTO agreements. Through membership of the WCO and the WTO, South Africa is by definition a contracting party to the customs, excise and international trade rule-based system. This means that it is not what you know about the WCO and the WTO that matters, but rather what you know about the agreements they administer. In addition, you need to know and understand your rights and, more importantly, your responsibilities and obligations. In essence, being competitive (and ultimately successful) in the customs, excise and international trade environment is all about knowing and understanding your rights, obligations and responsibilities.

South Africa's re-emergence on the international trade scene

The year 1994 was without the shadow of a doubt a watershed year for South Africa domestically. The same year also saw the conclusion of the Uruguay Round of Trade Negotiations, the GATT Negotiations, which led to the establishment of the WTO on 1 January 1995 and resulted in what many commentators saw as the completion of the trinity of Bretton Woods institutions – the other two being the World Bank and the IMF.

Given all the developments on the domestic front at the time, not everyone recognised the importance of South Africa's re-entry into the international trade fold. Although South Africa has a history of international trade dating back to at least the early 16th century, by the late 20th century it had become an effectively closed economy because of economic sanctions and political isolation during the apartheid years. Especially in the 1980s, the economic policies of the day were inward-focused, consisting of import-replacing strategies associated with inward industrialisation. Accordingly South Africa built up a number of industries in which it had no comparative advantage in the production of products.

On coming to power in 1994 the new democratic government realised that if South Africa was to re-enter the international trade arena, the tariff dispensation had to be liberalised for it to become internationally competitive. During the Uruguay Round of Trade Negotiations, South Africa negotiated a tariff phase-down schedule for customs duties (also known as import tariffs, tariffs, or import duties) in accordance with the HS System. What this meant was that the rate of customs duty on a product, depending on its tariff classification, had to be phased down over a five- or eight-year period. Consequently, domestic manufacturers that had been accustomed to protection by very high customs duties now had to account for the reduction, and in some instances a very significant reduction, in the rate of customs duties over this period.

However, the Minister of Trade and Industry of the day, Trevor Manuel, believed that the only way for South African manufacturers to become internationally competitive was to reduce the rate of customs duties *faster* than the commitments required under the WTO Agreement. This of course resulted in protests by South African manufacturers, and one prominent businessperson accused the government of being 'holier than GATT' (*Sunday Times*, 13 August 1995).

At the time, South Africa's tariff and trade policy dictated that in the interest of fostering domestic manufacture, tariff protection should be afforded the industry and structural adjustment programmes (SAPs) should be developed and implemented. In South Africa today, two of the old SAPs still exist: the Motor Industry Development Programme (MIDP), which is to be renamed the Motor Development Programme (MDP), and the Textile and Clothing Industry Development Programme (TCIDP), previously known as the Duty Credit Certificate Scheme (DCCS). The third SAP, which disappeared along the way, was the Television Receiving Set Programme, covering the electronics industry.

With the phased reductions in the rates of customs duties (at a pace faster than that of the country's WTO commitments), a number of domestic manufacturers simply could not compete with the imported product, and either closed their businesses or became distributors of imported goods. However, the full impact of South Africa's tariff phase-down was not initially felt, and it may even have been severely cushioned by the depreciation, at the time, of the South African rand against major currencies. Depreciation of the rand effectively results in increased protection for domestic manufacturers. This can be termed natural protection. To illustrate, assume imported goods are transported or shipped to South Africa, for which payment is denominated in US dollars. In addition, the imported products are acquired in dollars or European currencies. All this of course results in a higher landed cost, which equates to natural protection. Natural protection as well as the additional protection afforded by the imposition of customs duties provides an ideal climate for the practice of import parity pricing whereby local producers set their prices at the world price and add the tariffs and transport costs that would be faced by the customer. Although the government has acted against such practice by removing the rate of customs duty in its totality in certain areas, it has not necessarily eradicated it because natural protection still remains.

South Africa's revealed comparative advantage

The South African government, through various policies and incentive schemes, aims to stimulate exports to its main trading partners. At the same time these policies attempt to promote the industrialisation of the local economy. How successful have these policies been?

In evaluating this issue, it is important to consider South Africa's revealed comparative advantage (RCA), calculated for the first three-quarters of 2008. The RCA is the ratio between the weighted exports and imports for the different industries. In other words, if South Africa exports relatively more than it imports in a specific industry, the country has revealed an advantage for specialisation within that industry. In analysing the table, bear in mind that a number greater than 1 represents an RCA for South Africa, while a number smaller than 1 represents a revealed comparative disadvantage. What is obvious from the table is that South Africa is structurally still an agricultural and resource economy, with some success in the production of transport equipment and works of art.

The main industrial development policies, which have a history dating back to the old SAPs, are the MIDP/MDP and the TCIDP. These programmes are supported by means of tariff protection (customs duties, excise duties, and permit systems) combined with industrial incentives and tariff measures such as rebate items. It is evident from the table that the Textiles and Clothing sectors, and the Motor Vehicle Industry sector both have a negative RCA.

But what about the RCA of the four lead sectors identified by the National Industrial Policy Framework (NIPF), viz. Capital or Transport Equipment and Metals Fabrication; Automotive and Components; Chemicals, Plastics Fabrication and Pharmaceuticals; and Forestry, Pulp, Paper and Furniture? Only Wood, Paper and Pulp, Base Metals, and Transport Equipment have an RCA.

Table 1: South Africa's revealed comparative advantage for various industries, 2008

	Product sections	Exports	% exports	Imports	% imports	RCA
1	Live Animals	4 092.29	0.83%	3 541.36	0.64%	1.30
2	Vegetable Products	17 503.83	3.57%	8 805.81	1.60%	2.23
3	Oils & Fats	846.57	0.17%	5 098.21	0.92%	−0.18
4	Foodstuffs & Beverages	12 578.32	2.57%	10 312.19	1.87%	1.37
5	Mineral Products	87 672.65	17.88%	133 045.63	24.10%	0.74
6	Chemical	30 123.51	6.14%	48 349.69	8.76%	−0.70
7	Hides, Skins & Leather	7 919.65	1.62%	17 910.68	3.24%	−0.50
8	Plastics & Rubber	1 277.28	0.26%	1 719.33	0.31%	−0.84
9	Wood	2 510.59	0.51%	2 328.71	0.42%	1.21
10	Pulp and Paper	8 391.85	1.71%	7 842.35	1.42%	1.20
11	Textiles & Clothing	4 055.38	0.83%	12 321.31	2.23%	−0.37
12	Footwear	254.50	0.05%	3 781.91	0.69%	0.07
13	Stone & Plaster	1 641.04	0.33%	6 502.92	1.18%	−0.30
14	Precious Stones	117 028.43	23.87%	15 209.82	2.76%	8.65
15	Base Metals	89 702.87	18.29%	27 042.49	4.90%	3.73
16	Machinery & Appliances	48 840.90	9.96%	135 262.27	24.50%	−0.41
17	Transport Equipment	47 560.31	9.70%	53 060.77	9.61%	1.01
18	Optical, Photographical	2 749.27	0.56%	13 510.94	2.45%	−0.23
19	Misc. Manufactures	3 930.62	0.80%	7 147.35	1.29%	0.62
20	Works of Art	611.80	0.12%	194.49	0.04%	3.00
21	Other Unclassified	1 019.03	0.21%	615.08	0.11%	1.91
22	Special Provisions	33.99	0.01%	38 379.51	6.95%	
	Total	**490 344.68**	**100.00%**	**551 982.82**	**100.00%**	

Source: *SARS, Global Insight, Tariff & Trade Intelligence*

These data call into question the focus of South African industrial policy and suggest that the country is attempting to create or stimulate industries that will not be sustainable without continued protection. It is our contention that industrial policy should rather focus on sectors that exhibit the potential to be internationally competitive and therefore offer growth opportunities as well as possible job creation. On the basis of RCA, which sectors meet these criteria?

The sectors with the largest RCA scores are all resource-based, with the best-performing sectors being Precious Stones, Base Metals, Works of Art and Vegetable Products. This is unfortunate as it implies that South Africa has not yet industrialised to an internationally competitive level. The country exports raw materials and then imports the refined goods produced from its own raw materials. The only other product sections with RCA are Live Animals, Foodstuffs and Beverages, and Other Unclassified.

As South Africa is still an agricultural resource-based economy, raw material beneficiation is an important issue. Why is it that none of the four lead sectors is related to agriculture or agri-processing? These production sections clearly have an RCA, and their beneficiation and downstream transformation must surely be of significance to the South African economy as a whole.

It is our contention that the critical focus of the NIPF should be on transforming the economy from a resource-based one, which it has remained now for many years. Note should also be made of the country's RCAs and use made of them as a starting point for true industrialisation. This could be done through a thorough analysis of downstream potential.

The NIPF: defining South Africa's tariff and trade policy?

South Africa does not have a stated tariff and trade policy. It has an industrial policy, which incorporates tariff and trade policy. In our view this is not an adequate basis for developing and implementing an effective tariff and trade policy.

In considering how this came about, we need to dwell on the recent history of industrial policy. After more than eight and a half years the Department of Trade and Industry (DTI) finally released its National Industrial Policy Framework (NIPF) and the Implementation of Government's National Industrial Policy Framework: Industrial Policy Action Plan on 3 August 2007. As far as tariff and trade policy is concerned, the NIPF does identify four lead sectors that require special attention. These are:
- Capital or transport equipment and metals fabrication;
- Automotive and components;
- Chemicals, plastics fabrication and pharmaceuticals;
- Forestry, pulp, paper and furniture.

At face value, these four lead sectors may well imply a focused intervention. However, in determining whether it is focused or not, one needs to examine the four lead sectors in the context of the 98 tariff chapters of the South African Harmonised Customs and Excise Tariff schedule. The relevant chapters of the four lead sectors are indicated in brackets.
- Capital or transport equipment (84) and metals fabrication (72–81);
- Automotive and components (98);

- Chemicals (28 to 38), plastics fabrication (39), and pharmaceuticals (28–38); and
- Forestry (44), pulp (47), paper (48), and furniture (44).

In total, the four lead sectors account for 27 tariff chapters. If one considers that 16 of the remaining tariff chapters have a customs duty rate of 0% (or free), then 43 of the 98 tariff chapters are affected. If the chapters for the TCIDP are added, the total is 57. As the 25 tariff chapters for agricultural products have also been included in the NIPF, this brings the total to 81 tariff chapters falling under this policy framework. Only 17 of the total number of 98 chapters are thus not affected by the NIPF (excluding the TCIDP ones).

The question that remains is whether the four lead sectors can really be considered to constitute a sufficiently focused approach from a trade policy point of view. Since there are no distinct tariffs and trade policy interventions formalised for the four lead sectors identified in the NIPF, this seems to be a case of one size fits all. Surely this cannot be considered an adequate basis for South Africa's tariff and trade policy?

In line with the NIPF, the International Trade Administration Commission (ITAC), which deals with trade and tariff policy within the DTI, has already published a number of tariff review investigations, some even before the publication of the NIPF. The tariff review in respect of capital and transport equipment was closed for comment only a few days after the publication of the NIPF. Tariff reviews were also published in respect of aluminium products, upstream chemicals, and textiles and clothing. Of concern is the fact that, at the time of writing, no tariff reviews had been published for comment in respect of metals fabrication, automotive and components, plastics fabrication, pharmaceuticals, forestry, pulp, and furniture. Moreover, according to the NIPF, the responsible authorities were supposed 'to finalise a comprehensive review ... by March 2008' in line with the Industrial Policy Action Plan of August 2007. It is not certain whether this meant that the reviews only had to be completed by this date, or whether the findings of such reviews were to be instituted by then. The obvious fact is that the deadlines have been missed, and no new deadlines have been set. This is a major concern, for in a fast-paced world, none of our competitors will wait for us.

Accounting for competition policy

The Competition Commission of South Africa has in recent months become prominent in the news, in part because of the high-profile companies against which it has successfully launched a number of investigations. The government's emphasis on competition policy can be attributed to what it perceives to be a historical legacy of excessive economic concentration and ownership, collusive practices and the abuse of economic power by firms in dominant positions. Linked to this, the government also recognises the fact that the South African economy and society are in a state of transition, in view of the broader restructuring of the economy, the effects of globalisation and trade liberalisation, and the need to redress past inequality and non-participation in the national economy. As a consequence, according to the Competition Commission's website, the government believes that the fundamental principle of competition policy and law in South Africa is the need to balance economic efficiency with socio-economic equity and development.

The Competition Act of 1989 is designed to promote and maintain competition in South Africa. It has the following stated objectives:
- To promote the efficiency, adaptability and development of the economy;
- To provide consumers with competitive prices and product choices;
- To promote employment and advance the social and economic welfare of South Africans;
- To expand opportunities for South African participation in world markets and recognise the role of foreign competition in South Africa;
- To ensure that small and medium-sized enterprises have an equitable opportunity to participate in the economy; and
- To promote a greater spread of ownership, in particular to increase the ownership stakes of historically disadvantaged persons.

One major problem is that whilst the competition policy considers economic concentration and its redress, the NIPF deals with support to specific industrial sections and as a result may at times be in potential conflict with the goals and implementation of competition policy.

It is evident that industry sectors in South Africa are to a large extent still dominated by a few big players, a situation which developed over years of protection. As a consequence there are very high barriers to entry, which effectively limit opportunities for new firms to enter the market. In addition, because South Africa is considered a long-haul destination (being far removed from its trading partners), local manufacturers are also provided with natural protection against imported products.

Although the Competition Commission has dealt with the issue of import parity pricing, in essence by having the rate of customs duty on imported products reduced to zero, it has not dealt with the natural protection offered by the depreciation of the exchange rate. Though the rate of customs duty contributes to the practice of import parity pricing, the practice is still quite possible even if the rate of customs duty is free, in part because the movement of products is charged for in US dollars.

Export parity pricing also prevails, yet it is not dealt with with the same vigour as import parity pricing. To clarify, import parity pricing applies when a company sells its products locally at a price that its customers would pay if they were to import the same product from another country. Export parity pricing applies when a domestic manufacturer of a product bases its domestic price on the price it can derive by selling the same product on the export market. Consumers are then faced with the option of either purchasing the domestic manufactured product at the export price, or importing the product themselves; by doing so, they have to contend with the effect of natural protection afforded the domestically manufactured product.

In our view competition policy should take account both of the practice of import parity pricing, whether a rate of customs duty is applicable or not, and of export parity pricing. In addition, the Competition Commission should take account of the tariff applications and consider whether any form of protection is justified, considering its own aims and objectives.

Banking on the weakness of the rand

In October 2008, the South African rand depreciated sharply against the currencies of its main trading partners. The traditional argument about the benefits of this scenario goes like this: As the currency weakens, so exporters earn more rands for their exports. In addition, they should be able to export more as they become more internationally competitive.

Unfortunately, the truth is not so simple. As economists, we look at policies and circumstances that maximise the welfare of society, and a depreciating currency is not one of them. Why? If we boost our exports based on a depreciating currency, we implicitly assume that a weaker rand is our comparative advantage in world trade. The problem is that this source of comparative advantage is not a sustainable source of advantage. There are several reasons for this.

Firstly, the rand is a floating currency and the level is determined by supply and demand. This, together with the international tradability of the rand, makes the value of the rand volatile. In other words, the advantage can disappear once the world favours the rand again. Therefore, the advantage of a weak rand may be short-lived for exporters. This type of advantage is not going to attract either long-term quality exporters to establish themselves in South Africa or the investment in local companies that are internationally competitive at the new, depreciated exchange rate. This is not going to create sustainable jobs and stimulate economic growth.

Secondly, the rand has depreciated because of international weaknesses. If the world is heading for a recession, who is going to buy our exports?

Thirdly, many of the products that we export consist to a large extent of imported goods and services. Alternatively, imported capital goods are required to produce these goods. A weaker rand will increase the production cost of exports, forcing exporters to increase the rand price of their products, and thereby decreasing our competitiveness.

Finally, a weaker currency creates inflationary pressure, leading to either higher interest rates or a delay in possible interest rate cuts. As interest rates represent the opportunity cost of physical investment, this can delay further investment.

The true comparative advantage of South Africa will only surface once the currency stabilises and the government creates a conducive environment for exporters. A depreciating currency should not be seen as a source of comparative advantage. Rather, what is desirable is a stable currency, as this will create an environment in which exporters can plan for the future and in the process create sustainable jobs and stimulate economic growth.

Tariff and trade policy: a back to basics approach

Whenever the topic of tariff and trade policy is raised, the usual response is to solicit a number of academic studies in which extremely complicated economic models are formulated to assess the impact of any changes and amendments to the policy. While these have their place, we believe a 'back to basics' review will provide a useful perspective.

In the first place, the South African Harmonised Customs and Excise Tariff requires a major overall. The mere size of the Tariff Book is shocking enough (and once it has been opened this impression is confirmed). An extremely common problem in dealing with the Tariff Book is that the majority of those with detailed knowledge of its contents are not inclined to share it. This creates a significant barrier to entry for importers and exporters.

The simplification of the Tariff Book has been a constant recommendation in a number of recent studies, and was again recently emphasised by the Harvard Group of international development economists. They recommended the simplification of the tariff system, with low or no tariffs on imports, to stimulate exports. But the simplification of the tariff regime requires much more than creating low or no tariffs on imports. Rather, we need to get back to the Tariff Book, and its 98 tariff chapters and 10 schedules. We need to start here, since dealing with the reduction of the rates of duty implies that the Tariff Book in its current form is acceptable. This is not the case.

The Tariff Book has seen a number of *ad hoc* amendments effected to it over recent years. First there was the introduction of the Uruguay Round bound rate phase-down (1 January 1995), then the 2002 HS System amendments (1 January 2002), and the subsequent amendment of the HS System in January 2007. In addition, there were a number of tariff amendments introduced as a result of tariff investigations initiated by ITAC. Finally, the South African Revenue Service (SARS), in an effort to simplify the Tariff Book, merged a number of tariff subheadings.

The only solution is to review the Tariff Book in its entirety. A good way to start is by defining three product categories:
- Category 1 – Primary products
- Category 2 – Secondary products (further processed)
- Category 3 – Final products (end products)

In defining these product categories, consideration should be given to the rate of customs duty that should apply in respect of each category of product. In other words, a band rate must be defined for each of the product categories. For instance, for primary products a duty band of 0–5% could be considered, for secondary products 6–10%, and for final products 11–15%.

Once the tariff bands have been decided on, these need to be applied to each tariff heading and tariff subheading in the Tariff Book. Thereafter the rates of customs duties need to be compared with the applied rates of duty (also known as the prevailing or current rates of duty). Such an exercise should result in the amendment of the applied rates of duty.

The adjustment of the rates of customs duty will impact on the other schedules of the Tariff Book. The more important of these are the manufacturing rebate provisions, which in certain instances would no longer be applicable. Their removal would also assist in the simplification of the Tariff Book.

Conclusion

When considering trade, industrial and competition policy in the same chapter, the perception might well be that we are dealing with three distinct and exclusive policies. But this is not the case. The NIPF includes trade policy as part of industrial policy where it is not treated as a separate policy. Competition policy is considered exclusively, though it should not be, as its operation is directly affected by the decisions taken with the design and implementation of the other two. When considering the liberalisation of South Africa's tariff policy, the interaction between tariff, industrial and competition policy should be explicitly considered.

The identification of four lead sectors in the NIPF raised a number of questions. Why these four sectors? What about other sectors? What exactly will be achieved in prioritising these sectors? The fact that South Africa has a revealed comparative disadvantage for the majority of these product sections calls into question the sustainable effectiveness of these choices. We argue for a focus more aligned with our existing revealed comparative advantage, for example agriculture or agri-processing.

As far as reforming tariff policy is concerned, we suggest a back to basics approach. The simplification of the South African Harmonised Tariff Book should be the starting point. The tariff headings and tariff subheadings should be classified in accordance with three categories, for primary products, secondary products and final products. Once this has been done, the rate of customs duty for the respective categories should be considered and should be applied to each. In other words, a band rate must be defined for each of the product categories. This approach will have the added benefit of resulting in the deletion or removal of a number of rebate provisions.

The final step should be to compare the applied (or current) rates to the bound (or highest or ceiling) rates. In those instances where the applied rates are below the bound rates, the question should be asked why they exist and whether they should not be adjusted. Quite simply, if this situation exists, it implies that South Africa has reduced its rate of customs duty to a level lower than its commitment to the WTO. The significance of this is that all trade negotiations commence with the applied rate, and not the bound rate. Why would any country be prepared to start negotiating from a higher rate of customs duty, if the lower rate of duty already applies? If you are a domestic manufacturer, then the further reduction or phase-down in the rate of customs duty on your product ought to be of significance.

Finally, any proposed amendments to the South African Harmonised Customs and Excise Tariff need to take notice of competition policy. The adjustment in the tariff dispensation could well influence competition in the domestic market. Although the Competition Commission has made concerted efforts to deal with import parity pricing, it should arguably be just as vigilant in respect of export parity pricing

7

Industrial policy and national competitiveness: the spatial dimension

Glen Robbins

Since the Polokwane Conference of 2007 the president of the ANC, Jacob Zuma, has consistently used the terms 'continuity' and 'change' to represent the likely approach of the party to government policy in the next few years. One area that could undoubtedly do with a mixture of the two, and arguably more of the latter, is the field of industrial policy.

South Africa has, to date, trodden a relatively ambiguous route in both the content and form of industrial policy focused on state support to improve industrial output, productivity and competitiveness. On the one hand the government has committed substantial resources behind ambitious industry-specific programmes such as the Motor Industry Development Plan (MIDP), which has involved an effective subsidy to automotive firms to retain and grow significant scales of original equipment production in South Africa. On the other hand it has also demonstrated a tendency towards a less assertive role, for example in facilitating the collaboration of key national sectoral stakeholders to remove obstacles to exporting.

However, what is noticeable about the character of both types of intervention is that the accompanying policy frameworks have been largely silent on the matter of space in the sense of geographically influenced inter-relationships. This essay suggests that any new administration must seek to understand and embrace the possibilities that would come with incorporating a spatial dimension to such policies. Excessively centralised programmes of any sort, whether they be interventionist or more market-oriented, are likely to miss many of the complexities and opportunities offered by unique local configurations of economic relationships and processes. Rather, policy must be informed by sensitivity to an economic fabric that is substantially heterogeneous across space. What is needed is a new framework for industrial policy focused on how best both state and non-state actors can find effective ways of harnessing local opportunities that align with more immediate needs, in ways that overly generic national programmes often fail to do.

What are the implications of space for policy formation?

Why should a country, and any new political leadership, concern itself with matters of spatial differentiation in shaping national economic development policy? Firstly, we should recognise that a variety of factors generally combine to generate forms of spatial inequality across nation-states. These could be the result of explicit policies seeking to generate a bias of development in favour of one region[1] at the cost of another, or of geographic factors relating to topography or climate. Such divergent development paths are often, but not always, closely aligned with the character of urbanisation and related agglomeration effects. In recognising these processes, a case is often made that national policy frameworks need to be informed by the understanding that various programmes might have very different effects in different sub-national spaces. Some degree of awareness of such complexities is necessary, not only to optimise policy, but also to mitigate some of its unintended effects.

However, a second set of issues also comes into play when considering the imperative for a measure of spatial differentiation to inform national policy. These are primarily related to the emergence of regions, and more especially major urban conurbations, as the most critical nodes in any nation-state's engagement with global economic processes. Such spaces either thrive or struggle depending on the degree to which particular spatially bound factors (e.g. natural assets and proximity to other markets of significance) can be matched with more ephemeral factors in unique mixes to enable productivity increases, such as forms of innovation or other critical capabilities, to be developed. According to Ohmae (1995), traditional nation-states have become 'irrelevant' units in a global economy, and economically functional regions are often more significant. Storper (1997) claims that regional communities and firms are the building blocks of the resurgent regional economies that are driving globalisation processes today. Others point out that processes of knowledge sharing and networking, key to new economic processes, are connected to dynamics arising from proximity but they require something more than simply taking advantage of basic agglomeration effects. Helmsing (2001: 285) goes as far as to claim that 'the only justifiable form of industrial [trade] policy is in fact regional industrial development policy'.

This growing recognition of space in new forms of economic development and industrial policy is not something that has just exercised the minds of academic researchers. The key concepts have also been increasingly absorbed into policy frameworks the world over. Over a period of fifteen to twenty years the European Union has sought to harness the potential of local dynamics as a critical element of more diversified and resilient national economies. Individual countries within the European Union have further developed such frameworks. For example, programmes in France and the United Kingdom have emerged to support clusters and networks of innovation, thus enabling local stakeholders to harness unique local capabilities. Across the Atlantic in Canada it is striking how important the enhancement of localised opportunity is within both national and provincial economic development frameworks – not just as an afterthought, but rather as a key pillar. Furthermore, countries such as China, Brazil and India have also embraced notions of space and differentiation as a key element of policy despite histories of highly centralised policy frameworks. At the extreme this is represented by cities in China built around the identity of particular products such as toys or garment accessories. More often it has meant a higher degree of openness to the idea that locally crafted initiatives might have a comparative advantage over excessively centralised initiatives in responding effectively to global economic challenges.

Space and policy formation in South Africa

How then have South Africa's economic development programmes responded to these space-related issues in the past decade and a half? Certainly the early post-1994 policy frameworks tended to treat any notion of regional differentiation and sensitivity to space with deep suspicion.[2]

At a macro level the Growth, Employment and Redistribution (Gear) strategy made a case for accelerated trade liberalisation and enhanced export competitiveness as being key to the country's growth prospects. However, Gear limited itself to traditional macroeconomic policy instruments and did little to explore the ramification of such national choices on different sub-national areas, let alone propose policy responses.[3] With the benefit of hindsight, it can be said that Gear (and the processes that emerged from it) had profound regional impacts. Some of these were the result of the curtailment of social expenditure planned under the RDP. There was also the substantial loss of employment that particular areas suffered because of the decision to accelerate tariff reduction in clothing and textile sectors.

Out of a concern that Gear was not having the desired effects in generating growth, the Department of Trade and Industry (DTI) identified a number of 'infrastructure bottlenecks' that constrained exports (as well as incoming foreign direct investment). These bottlenecks were considered to be the result of more than a decade of reduced public investment, particularly in transport infrastructure. Consequently Spatial Development Initiatives (SDIs) were launched, with an initial focus on dominant export hubs and corridors (Johannesburg International Airport, Richards Bay, East London); these were subsequently expanded to incorporate areas that had prospects of significant tourism investment (Wild Coast, Lake St Lucia and Northern Cape). Specialist teams were put together to develop a case for major public investment so as to yield significant new private investment with an export orientation. While these teams tended to work closely with local role-players, the latter's prospects for securing public investment were linked to their ability to meet national goals; anything less than this was dismissed as parochial. This perspective was reinforced by a focus in the SDI process on large conglomerates and transnational corporations and the sidelining of enterprises serving local markets in the emerging programmes, such as the Industrial Development Zones (IDZs).

During the mid-to-late 1990s the provinces began to emerge as players in the field of economic development. The first Provincial Growth and Development Strategies emerged at this time and capacity started being built at the provincial level to support various regional growth and development initiatives. However, despite the existence of a national forum in the form of gatherings of provincial MECs and the national minister, the DTI did little in the way of developing systemic working relationships with provinces. More often than not, tensions emerged between national processes such as the formation of Trade and Investment South Africa (TISA) and the parallel formation of provincial-level investment and trade development agencies. At the time, the Minister of Trade and Industry regularly complained about how embarrassed his officials were when crossing paths in international airports and hotel lobbies with an assortment of provincial marketing bodies. Such tensions were often aggravated by competing perspectives of what regions had to offer: for TISA the Western Cape was a tourism hub but for Wesgro – the Western Cape Investment and Trade Promotion Agency – the province had a vibrant emerging manufacturing base with strong technological underpinnings.

This period also saw some of the country's major cities starting to assert themselves, not only in developing their own economic programmes, but also in trying to secure greater responsiveness by the DTI to the local needs of firms. This resulted in tensions with provinces that sought to be the exclusive voice in bringing regional issues to the national level and also placed greater pressure on the DTI.

Despite the emerging role of provinces, their impacts in direct and indirect terms on national policies and programmes, as well as that of the various larger cities, tended to be quite limited. Perhaps the one exception was that related to the DTI's attempt to initiate national cluster processes in some selected industry sectors. Some provinces and cities picked up the remnants of these less-than-successful endeavours and used the programmes, designed to support them, to initiate a wide range of inter-firm networking processes with a strong sub-national identity. Their success – e.g. that of the regional automotive industry clusters – suggested to the DTI that there was some scope to respond to new forms of industrial policy that might be more effective than homogenised national initiatives, or at least could add value alongside such national programmes.

The publication in 2002 of the Micro-economic Reform Strategy (MRS) and the Integrated Manufacturing Strategy (IMS) was closely observed by those in favour of greater attention to sub-national dynamics and processes in building lasting forms of competitiveness. However, the two documents – like their predecessor policies – remained largely focused on crafting policies in new fields with little or no consideration given to instruments that might connect more closely with sub-national agendas. These strategy frameworks did appropriately identify the importance of a host of issues such as skills, innovation and empowerment processes. But even in these fields there was not much suggestion that anything other than national departments might be able to formulate and orchestrate effective action in response to the challenges. The policy documents also remained largely silent on how localised forms of competitiveness could be nurtured to build new and more diversified foundations for the nation's economy.

The IMS led to the creation of a range of Customised Sector Programmes (CSPs), which were seen as tools to convert broader goals into programmes relevant to the specific dynamics of different sectors. Though the CSPs that have emerged in the past few years have in some cases identified important dimensions of the geography of production and competitiveness, their translation into action programmes has been less clear as the DTI has grappled with severe capacity constraints and competing agendas such as those related to empowerment. Where there has been some notable success, at least some of it appears to be closely related to the ability of local stakeholders to pick up on key strands of the CSPs and mobilise around them. Here a prime example has been the tool-making initiative that had its roots in initiatives within heavy industries in the Ekurhuleni Metro. In this case the national was by no means irrelevant, but it was local processes that allowed for a coherent set of actions to be crafted with a close alignment with the industries' specific needs.

During 2007, the DTI launched a new phase of industrial policy with the publication of the National Industrial Policy Framework (NIPF) and the related Industrial Policy Action Plan (IPAP). These documents tended to advance many of the key aspects of the IMS but identified four sectors of the economy that would receive priority attention for their potential to drive the growth and employment objectives of the government's Accelerated and Shared Growth Initiative of South Africa (Asgisa). The NIPF makes a claim for a more active industrial policy framework at a national level but once again reduces the spatial question to essentially two issues: infrastructure to support investment and exports; and the need to secure development outside the traditional growth poles of the economy.

The NIPF sets out a vision with the following focus areas: diversification away from traditional commodity and non-tradable services; a move towards knowledge-intensive industrialisation; the promotion of labour-absorbing productive activities; the promotion of greater levels of empowerment of marginalised groups and marginalised regions; and contributions to the development of the continent. There is little here for sub-national spaces to meaningfully hook into, beyond the (rarely mentioned) issue of areas denuded of economic activity.

With the minor exception of localised facilities in the craft and tourism sectors, IPAP does little more than the NIPF in setting out a coherent picture of how effective industrial policy interventions can be crafted in distinct and rooted ways at the sub-national level. In fact, to a large degree, the term 'local' in IPAP refers almost exclusively to the South African production of goods or services within a global context rather than any particular sub-national processes that might enable such opportunity to be exploited in one location rather than another.

The DTI has also, of late, proposed the implementation of a Regional Industrial Development Strategy (RIDS) with a distinct sub-national focus. The RIDS policy is an attempt to respond to calls for supporting forms of industrial development in impoverished areas of the country. It is expected that, in the first instance, the RIDS programme will allow for some measure of upgrading of infrastructure and institutional support for a number of the declining industrial estates created under the apartheid government's decentralisation strategy and a handful of medium-scale towns characterised by some level of industrial production. As the DTI has begun taking a much greater interest in the issue of local economic development, it has also started to explore more innovative forms of localised strategy response to economic challenges. However, this is very much a set of activities confined to the DTI's commitment to improving distributive impacts rather than driving the economic competitiveness of leading regions.

It is notable that this approach is somewhat in contrast to the Presidency's 2006 National Spatial Development Perspective (NSDP), which suggests that the country needs to recognise that meeting the bulk of citizens' developmental needs would require giving substantial attention to those urban centres with demonstrated economic potential. The proposal is that the unique and often quite different economic platforms of these urban centres must be placed higher up the national agenda where key national choices are being made. As these centres are already host to more than two-thirds of national economic activity and to more than 50% of the population, their economic prospects must be of particular concern in national policy frameworks. However, in real terms, the NSDP has not moved beyond being one of a number of 'perspectives' – for instance, in Asgisa there is little in the way of an explicit reinforcement of the intentions of the NSDP.

In the overall picture there is a remarkable absence of engagement with matters of space. In the first instance, the intelligence that underpins much of the policy is devoid of adequate spatial considerations. Furthermore, the way strategic national policy platforms are conceived more often than not completely ignores a considerable shift in global economic development and industrial policy practice, which has embraced the local as a central pillar in imagining new approaches to more meaningful policy interventions.

Reflecting on the implications

This overview of primarily DTI-related frameworks and programmes has shown only some occasional dipping into agendas which include a notion of regions as generating particular forms of competitive advantage. However, the overwhelming evidence is that these policies generally pigeon-hole spatial issues into (a) a need for supporting infrastructure in particular locales; and (b) a requirement to support a spatially more distributive spread of economic activity in which poor regions occupy a large place. There is almost no explicit recognition of the experience of many other countries that the framing of national competitiveness agendas must, at the minimum, seek to build differentiated regional or local capabilities through collaborative programmes responsive to unique local circumstances.

If this is the case, then to what degree might this be a problem for South Africa, and in what specific ways? In the first instance it is plain for many observers of the DTI that it has increasingly struggled to be relevant to the constituency of firms other than through its quasi-regulatory functions in the fields of company registration, trade administration and empowerment enforcement. Successes in the field of industrial policy have been few and far between, and developmental services to business have been generally patchy and have struggled to sustain themselves. A number of surveys have shown that firms see the DTI as at best distant and at worst irrelevant. Some of the DTI's own restructuring advisors have, for a number of years, suggested that a redefinition of the role of the DTI, in partnership with localised government and business associations, could enable it to be much closer to its constituency in terms of services and also help it generate a network of intelligence sources for the framing of national agendas that are rooted in diverse local processes. In these terms the failure by the DTI to respond to these new aspects of industrial policy has left the country with a less effective institutional base for industrial policy than might have been the case had a different approach been adopted. This is by no means to say that the conditions exist for some immediate form of decentralising of the DTI as an institution and in terms of its policy and programme development processes, but it does point to a serious gap that needs ongoing attention.

However, it is not only in terms of institutional design that South Africa could be losing out. The substance of policy and programmes has been overly concerned with a contrived sense of national agendas that are expected to be integrated, in delivery, through remote national bureaucratic manoeuvres. The assumption has been that nationally framed initiatives, hatched with a handful of industry lobby groups and self-appointed lead firms, can substantially alter competitive dynamics in what are often relatively fragmented and regionally heterogeneous clusters. International and local experience suggests that while such national processes are often necessary, they are more often than not insufficient to build the types of sustained networks and relationships between a variety of role-players required to support processes of competition that firms can tap into directly. For those with experience of such sub-national processes they report a combination of suspicion and disinterest by DTI officials, who often appear to be more accustomed to their Pretoria boardrooms than the meeting rooms of chambers of commerce or production-team meeting facilities of manufacturing enterprises.

South Africa's competitiveness challenge has its foundations in many factors. A substantial number of these relate directly to macroeconomic and global processes. Many also connect very clearly with particular national challenges unique to South Africa because of its distorted development path. These conditions suggest that a country such as South Africa needs to have a bold industrial policy framework that seeks to deal systematically with a wide range of constraints and to exploit a mix of opportunities that might exist. However, to enable the often very positive intentions underlying such frameworks to reach the bulk of enterprises in the country, they need to be informed by substantially deeper forms of localised intelligence. Furthermore, they require localised networks to make them real and accessible to producers not only in geographically isolated districts but also in complex urban centres which remain largely untouched by the economic agendas of the DTI and the government as a whole.

Jacob Zuma's direct experiences with industrial policy

Jacob Zuma first held government office as KwaZulu-Natal's MEC for Economic Affairs and Tourism in the immediate post-1994 period. During this time in office he was exposed first-hand to the frustrations of a region desperately seeking opportunities to engage with national industrial policy. He was also inundated by the emerging claims of a variety of locations in the province for greater degrees of sensitivity to their specific circumstances in the first Provincial Growth and Development process. This was perhaps most starkly represented by the rapid loss of garment firm employment in KwaZulu-Natal in the early to mid-1990s (over 30 000 jobs were lost). National programmes spoke only to the imperative of reducing tariff protection in support of a more competitive garment sector and little attention was given to how this might have differentiated impacts in specific regions with a substantial presence of garment firms. As firms began to shut down in the absence of any effective restructuring support, there was little interest from the DTI when its attention was drawn to the impacts of such policy shifts. Local and provincial government had not yet developed the confidence and the policy tools to test possible responses. Despite the pleas of unions and industry, firms in different locations within the province found themselves facing a massive growth of highly competitive imports and little in the way of capacity to hold on to diminishing market share.

In response Zuma supported the creation of an entity called the Regional Economic Forum, which brought together business, union and government stakeholders with the intention of charting a common path to respond to regional economic challenges. In the absence of any other tangible points of influence, the body sought to facilitate dialogue between local stakeholders with the intention of using this 'bottom-up' strategy to guide provincial government in its policy responses. Probably the most successful initiative in this framework was that related to the regional automotive sector, which had been identified as offering the country little strategic value as national policy favoured working with German automotive assemblers in relation to forms of direct support. The Regional Economic Forum brought direct regional support to a localised initiative and committed resources that enabled activities to be customised towards the real needs of local firms rather than the aggregated and generic programmes offered through the DTI. Although the latter were important in providing a measure of national endorsement, it is local resources and intelligence that assist the process of building a cluster network to connect with the specific interest of local firms.

Subsequent to this experience, Zuma has been exposed to other facets of national policy through his role at the centre of national government. To what degree this direct experience has had a lasting influence on him remains a matter of speculation. It is highly likely that many of his political colleagues and the established bureaucrats entrenched in inertia-filled national departments will suggest to him that what is required is a greater degree of centralised action from the national platform to drive programmes in the face of weak and directionless regional and local entities. In these circles the concept of the 'developmental state' holds sway, in which key priorities are driven through ambitious scaled-up interventions by government from the centre. After all, these advisors will point out that the enormous global and domestic challenges faced by the country can be most effectively met by a coherent and strong response from the national state.

Such a drive to enhance centralised forms of industrial policy would in all likelihood only serve to exacerbate the shortcomings of the national frameworks that have been in place to date. Not only our own experience but also that of many other countries suggests very strongly that it is unlikely that national policy-makers are sufficiently attuned to the diversity of local experiences and needs in a policy environment which has as its focus an aggregated set of national concerns. Furthermore, the kinds of networked communities of implementation required for the effective marshalling of agents of change have to be engineered in locations in which such actors are rooted – however tenuously – in order to exploit the opportunities that will present themselves in the future.

Notes

1. The term 'region' is used here in relation to sub-national spaces and not as a term describing a group of nation-states within a particular geographic region.
2. This was influenced, in part, by disputes over debates about federal solutions that had been supported by some parties at the pre-democracy negotiating table.
3. Gear did make some reference to a greater focus on regional development with respect to industrial policy in the introduction to the document but the only specific programme mention was an extension of the Regional Industrial Development Programme (RIDP) grant scheme for small and medium businesses. The RIDP had its root in a subsidy scheme to support businesses in apartheid-era decentralised industrial parks adjacent to bantustans but became available to any qualifying business regardless of location under the amended scheme.

References

Helmsing, A. 2001. Externalities, Learning and Governance: New Perspectives on Local Economic Development. *Development and Change*, 32 (2)

Ohmae, H. 1995. *The End of the Nation State*. Free Press, New York

Storper, M. 1997. *The Regional World: Territorial Development in a Global Economy*. Guilford Press, New York

8

Labour policy and job creation: too many holy cows?

Carel van Aardt

Much has been written about the South African labour market. The general conclusions are that sufficient jobs are not being created, that unemployment rates are very high, that people involved in the informal sector of the economy are generally compelled to do so as a result of being unemployed, and that the majority of poor people are virtually unemployable. However, few changes in economic and labour market policy have been effected to address these problems directly. Although the Growth, Employment and Redistribution strategy (Gear) and the Accelerated and Shared Growth Initiative for South Africa (Asgisa) both have a strong focus on job creation, the assumption made in these policy documents is that higher economic growth will ultimately translate into higher levels of job creation. Therefore, to create jobs a higher economic growth trajectory must be achieved. This essay will show why this assumption is to a large extent flawed.

The major reason why a dramatic increase in job creation will not be achieved is that most of the policy changes that need to be effected would require the removal of the holy cows of current thinking and practice, including stringent labour protection, labour market segmentation that is not merit-based and educational policies that are not directed at the labour market. It is a central thesis of this essay that the removal of these labour market rigidities and the revamping of the education system to become more labour-market-focused are both necessary to kick-start job creation. This approach is at odds with current labour policy and practice in South Africa. According to Ramady (2008) it is fairly clear what the pillars of economic wisdom are based on and what economically successful countries have done to become successful, viz. embracing the free market economy, science and technology, pragmatism, meritocracy, a culture of peace, the rule of law and a science-based education. South Africa's success in ensuring economic, employment and income growth will depend on its ability to design, introduce and implement policies in line with these 'pillars'.

This essay will show that there is a dire need for such policies to address constraints on higher levels of employment. The Harvard Group (2008) found that in comparable countries in Latin America, Eastern Europe and East Asia the proportion of the economically active population in employment was 50% higher than in South Africa. In a 2007 World Bank report (Clarke et al., 2007) focusing on the investment climate in South Africa, economic, employment and income growth in South Africa over the period 1994–2003 was compared with that of other emerging countries. Although South Africa did not do too badly growth-wise during this period, it lagged far behind other similar emerging countries with respect to economic, employment and income growth.

To answer the question of how more jobs can be created, this essay will focus on the following issues:
- the current size of the South African population that is available to work;
- the differential growth patterns of selected occupational categories;
- the educational attainment profiles of the employed and unemployed;
- employment dynamics in the formal and informal sectors;
- linkages between employment, income, poverty and income distribution; and
- linkages between job creation and GDP growth.

The essay will conclude with a discussion of some policy recommendations to strengthen the ability of the South African economy to create jobs.

Trends in the South African working population

It is clear from Figure 1 that the South African population, people of working age (POWA)[1] and the economically active population (EAP)[2] grew rapidly during the period 1990–2008, necessitating the creation of numerous jobs. As Table 1 shows, during the period 1990–9 growth rates for annual population, POWA and EAP were generally higher than those for employment, with the consequence that a growing number of economically active people were not able to obtain employment. This situation changed from 2000 onwards when employment growth rates increased and

Figure 1: The size of the South African population, POWA and EAP, 1990–2008

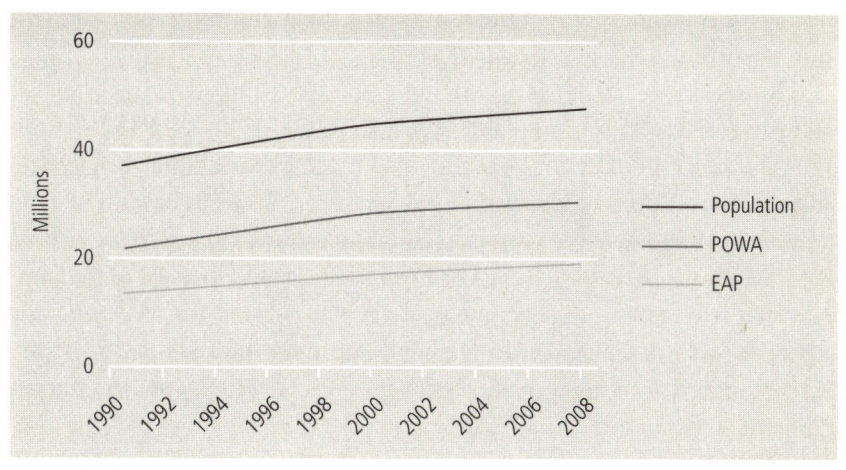

Source: BMR estimates

Table 1: Population, POWA, EAP and employment growth rates, 1990–2008

	Population growth (%)	POWA growth (%)	EAP growth (%)	Employment growth (%)
1990	2.23	2.88	2.18	−1.30
1991	2.18	2.83	2.14	−0.82
1992	2.12	2.77	2.11	−0.52
1993	2.08	2.73	2.16	−0.33
1994	2.03	2.68	2.27	0.28
1995	2.00	2.65	2.39	0.44
1996	1.89	2.54	2.46	1.61
1997	1.74	2.37	2.44	1.62
1998	1.69	2.21	2.35	1.46
1999	1.60	2.09	2.21	1.17
2000	1.48	1.90	2.01	3.12
2001	1.31	1.68	1.83	5.51
2002	1.13	1.43	1.58	5.22
2003	0.92	1.14	1.38	1.13
2004	0.78	0.97	1.18	5.62
2005	0.64	0.81	1.02	1.95
2006	0.52	0.69	0.88	4.06
2007	0.42	0.60	0.78	3.39
2008	0.38	0.54	0.71	2.36

Source: BMR estimates

were generally higher than those for population, POWA and EAP. However, these were not sufficient to ensure that unemployment rates dropped significantly.

The jobs created were, however, not equally distributed throughout the occupational spectrum (see Table 2). During the period 1997–2008 the highest average per annum growth rates were experienced in the higher-skilled occupations (i.e. administrative, managerial, professional and technical occupations) while the average per annum growth rates in lower-skilled occupations (i.e. artisanal, clerical, sales, production and mining) were fairly low. This is indicative of a labour market with an increasing demand for highly skilled workers and a decreasing demand for lower-skilled workers.

Although there was substantial growth in employment over the period 1996–2004, compared to international trends unemployment in South Africa was strangely high, given the number of jobs created over 1997–2008 (see Table 2) and the availability of informal sector employment (including self-employment) as a socio-economic safety net for the unemployed (Kingdon and Knight, 2004, 2006). Various reasons have been given for why more unemployed people did not take up informal sector employment, including the following:
- many unemployed people prefer not to work and can afford to remain out of work instead of joining the informal sector;
- many unemployed people receive social grants, which makes it unattractive for them to become involved in the informal sector; and
- about 56% of unemployed people reside in households whose incomes are higher than R2500 per month and are therefore discouraged from taking up very low-paid work in the informal sector.

From Table 2 and Figure 2 it appears that during the period 1997–2008 many jobs were created in the skilled categories. For example, in the professional and technical category alone more than half a million jobs were created. Such high growth rates gave rise to a large increase in the number of employed and a concurrent drop in the number of unemployed. The drop in unemployment should not be ascribed solely to job creation but also to the departure of skilled emigrants from South Africa, which opened up employment opportunities for unemployed skilled people. There has also been a structural change in employment in South Africa among highly skilled workers: increasing numbers of such people have moved from employment to self-employment (Barker, 2003; SA Government, 2008;

Table 2: Growth of selected occupational categories, 1997–2008

Occupational category	1997	2008	Average growth p.a. (%)
Administrative and managerial	370 007	687 044	5.79
Artisanal and related	1 032 927	1 083 155	0.43
Clerical and sales	2 915 161	2 437 955	−1.61
Production and mining	1 728 057	1 934 197	1.03
Professional and technical	1 285 313	1 807 504	3.15
Service	1 501 695	2 279 322	3.87
Transport and communication	458 053	779 749	4.96

Source: SAARF (2008)

Figure 2: The number of employed and unemployed, 1990–2008

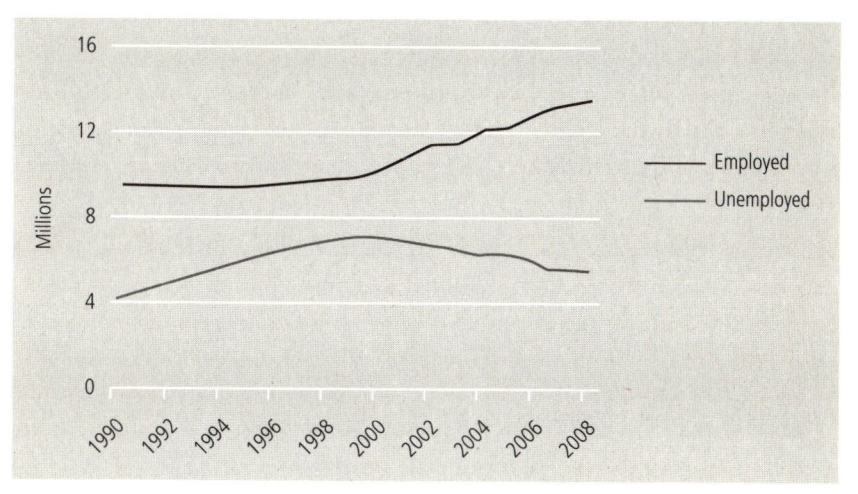

Source: BMR estimates

SAARF, 2008). This dynamic impacts positively on total employment in four important ways:

- posts are vacated that can be filled by the highly skilled unemployed;
- in becoming entrepreneurs, people grow the pool of self-employed;
- the self-employed eventually create jobs for others when their businesses grow; and
- the demand of the self-employed for intermediary goods and services creates strong multiplier effects, stimulating employment growth in supplier institutions.

Table 3: Employment status by educational level, 2008

	Unemployed (%)	Working full-time (%)	Working part-time (%)	Total
No education	54	32	14	100
Some primary education	53	29	18	100
Primary education complete	51	27	22	100
Some high school education	51	34	16	100
Matric	41	47	13	100
Post-matric certificate	11	82	7	100
Technikon diploma/degree	10	81	9	100
University degree	7	86	7	100
Total	**42**	**44**	**14**	**100**

Source: AMPS 2008

Formal- and informal-sector employment and incomes

Although an increasing number of jobs were created during the period 2000–8, which were mostly filled by skilled incumbents, such new employment opportunities were not created equally across the different economic sectors. If the findings in Figure 2 are read in conjunction with those of Table 2, it appears that there were high levels of employment growth in managerial, administrative, professional, technical and service occupations (highly skilled occupations) in the utilities, construction, trade, finance and services sectors while the lowest levels of job creation occurred at the arti-

Table 4: Employment growth by sector, 2000–8

	2000	2001	2002	2003
Agriculture	1 285 675	1 301 516	1 312 563	1 209 388
Mining	521 379	544 764	567 044	593 565
Manufacturing	1 575 626	1 597 439	1 613 423	1 607 924
Utilities	76 007	81 326	86 688	84 795
Construction	521 964	571 861	624 156	663 521
Trade	2 046 026	2 180 535	2 315 088	2 299 003
Transport	564 272	573 317	580 302	568 126
Finance	947 095	1 023 301	1 101 452	1 116 114
Services	1 681 364	1 859 583	2 048 904	2 207 849
Private households	955 698	1 001 910	1 046 379	1 073 716
Total	**10 175 106**	**10 735 553**	**11 296 000**	**11 424 000**

Sources: Statistics South Africa (2008), BMR estimates

sanal, clerical, sales and production levels (lower-skilled occupations) in the agricultural, mining, manufacturing and transport sectors. Ironically, the latter are the sectors where one would expect – from comparable trends in other emerging economies with similar sectoral contributions to GDP to those of South Africa – large numbers of artisans, clerks and production workers to be employed every year (Clarke et al., 2007; World Bank, 2007).

A further feature of employment in South Africa (as shown in Figure 3) is that two distinct phases in employment creation can be distinguished during the past two decades. In the period 1990–2001 job creation occurred primarily in the informal sector (the formal sector showed a decline in employment numbers for a large part of this period). This was followed in the period 2002–8 by higher levels of job creation in the formal sector and a decrease in job creation rates in the informal sector of the economy. The higher job creation rates in the formal sector could be ascribed to a large extent to higher GDP growth rates than those experienced during 1990–2001.

Although there was strong growth in job creation in both the formal and informal sector during 2002–8 (see Figure 3), this – as well as fairly high GDP growth rates – did not have the expected strong positive effects in reducing poverty and giving rise to a more equal disribution of income. Rather (as appears from Figure 4) the percentage of the population living below the minimum living level (MLL) – an indicator of poverty – did

2004	2005	2006	2007	2008	Average annual growth
1 287 915	893 481	876 815	946 925	871 260	–4.75
590 657	452 570	448 578	504 748	474 007	–1.18
1 582 699	1 777 423	1 765 406	1 785 391	1 798 707	1.67
94 636	107 048	77 083	96 987	98 399	3.28
714 662	863 804	1 133 757	1 199 299	1 366 479	12.78
2 508 388	2 854 264	2 908 799	3 069 162	3 234 029	5.89
572 165	593 534	707 661	580 878	572 856	0.19
1 225 912	1 286 698	1 310 405	1 302 543	1 326 870	4.30
2 390 910	2 351 880	2 363 868	2 512 270	2 546 903	5.33
1 097 556	1 120 296	1 207 628	1 235 799	1 256 998	3.48
12 065 500	12 301 000	12 800 000	13 234 000	13 546 510	3.64

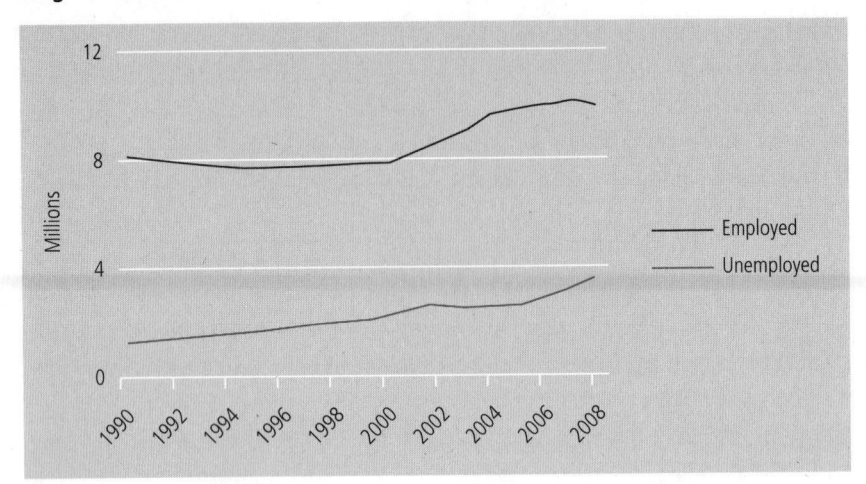

Figure 3: The number of formal- and informal-sector employed, 1990–2008

Source: BMR estimates

not decrease markedly over the same period while income inequality (as measured by the Gini coefficient) increased instead of decreased. The question can be asked: Why does a higher employment rate not give rise to a lower poverty rate and a more equal income distribution? One possible explanation is that informal-sector employment does not necessarily take a person out of poverty, given the very low incomes earned there. This postulate is explored in Figure 5 where the number of informal-sector workers was combined with that of the unemployed, and the relation between the number of unemployed and informal-sector workers and the percentage of people living in poverty is explored.

As Figure 5 reveals, unemployment, in conjunction with informal-sector employment, was a strong predictor of poverty especially during 1990–2003. In other words, the higher the number of people unemployed or working in the informal sector of the economy, the higher the poverty rate. Since 2002 strong growth in formal-sector employment (see Figure 3) has caused this to weaken. However, it remains true that the informal sector is an impoverished sector in South Africa. In this regard Burger and Yu (2006) show that during 2000–5, on average 21% of the employed had work in the informal sector of the economy but only earned about 6% of total earnings. Thus, while the per capita earning of non-agricultural workers in the formal sector in June 2008 was R9612, that of informal-sector workers was R1345 (Statistics South Africa, 2008; BMR estimate).

Figure 4: The EAP employed, people living in poverty and the Gini coefficient, 1990–2008

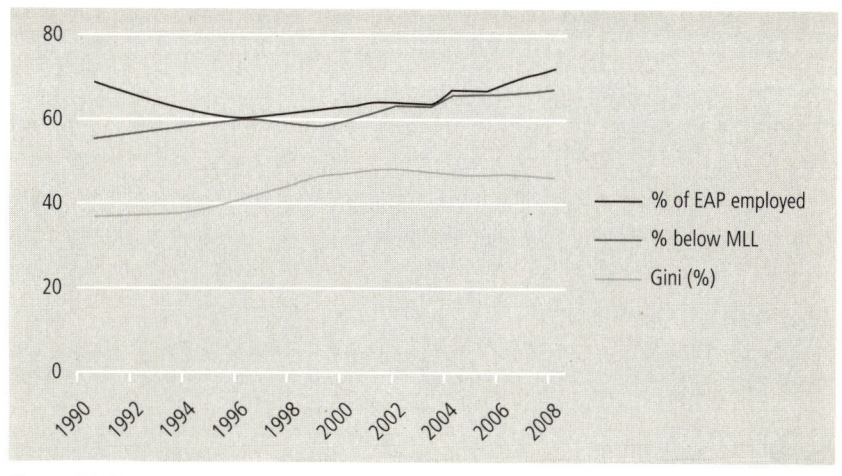

Source: BMR estimates

Figure 5: The EAP unemployed and employed in the informal sector, people living in poverty and the Gini coefficient, 1990–2008

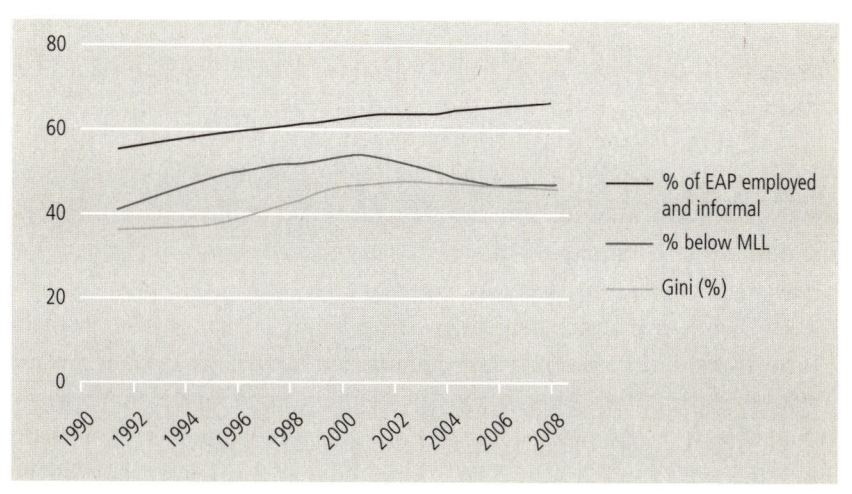

Source: BMR estimates

According to Barker (2003), the reasons for the low incomes in the informal sector are its focus on retailing and personal services, its lack of craft skills and resulting inability to add substantial value through production activities. Barker adds that the average wage in the informal sector is close to the monthly subsistence value.

The trend observed in Figure 5 becomes clearer when the total number of unemployed and informal-sector employed is compared with the total number of poor people in South Africa. As Figure 6 shows, there is a correlation between the number of poor people on the one hand and the number of unemployed and informal-sector employed on the other, but this correlation is weakening over time, especially since 2002 (see Figure 5). One should note that although employees in the informal sector are generally poor, they would have been even poorer if they had not been informally employed. If we view the number of poor, unemployed and informal-sector employed in real figures (instead of percentages) in Figure 6, the real extent of poverty, unemployment and informal-sector survival in South Africa becomes evident.

GDP, employment, income and expenditure linkages

Given the relation between formal-sector employment and incomes, and in view of the much higher per capita income earned in the formal sector as against the informal sector, one can ask whether formal-sector employment is a predictor of average household income. Having now established that workers in the informal sector receive on average very low incomes, we can infer that formal-sector employment is the driver of income growth in South Africa and, by implication, of poverty reduction. In the long term formal-sector employment growth will also give rise to a more equal income distribution in South Africa, while over the short term the informal sector acts as a social safety net, providing an opportunity for the poor to derive income.

In Figure 7 we can see that there is a positive relationship beween formal-sector employment and household income per capita growth in South Africa. To ensure poverty reduction and household income growth in South Africa, employment growth in the formal sector needs to be strengthened. To do this, there needs to be skills development, GDP growth and a flexible labour policy dispensation. Table 5 and Figure 8 show the strong effect of GDP growth has on employment, which in turn has a strong impact on household disposable income, and thus on household income expenditure. This in turn will have a positive impact on GDP, if we keep in mind the Keynesian aggregate demand equation, and thus complete the virtuous circle. The level at which GDP growth translates into employment will be determined by the level at which a flexible labour regime, labour-intensive production and high skills levels among the labour force are present in South Africa.

■ **Figure 6:** The unemployed, the informally employed and the poor, 2000–8

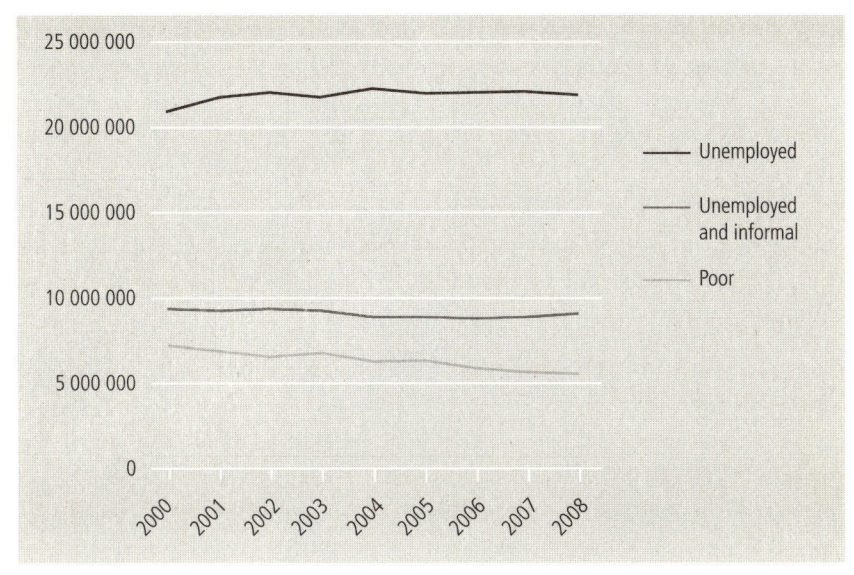

— Unemployed
— Unemployed and informal
— Poor

Source: BMR estimates

■ **Figure 7:** GDP per capita, household disposable income per capita and formal-sector employment, 1990–2008

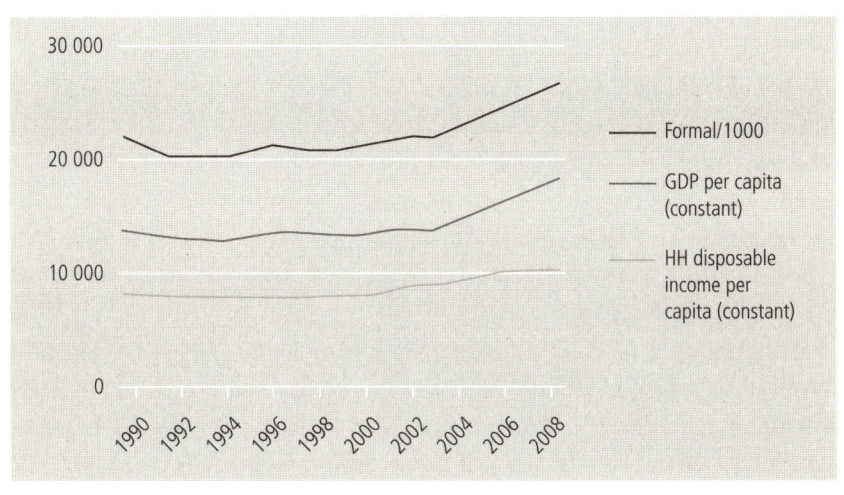

— Formal/1000
— GDP per capita (constant)
— HH disposable income per capita (constant)

Source: BMR estimates

Table 5: GDP growth, employment growth, household income and household consumption expenditure growth, 2000–8

	GDP growth	Employment growth	Household disposable income growth	Final household consumption expenditure growth
1990	−0.30	−1.30	0.40	2.30
1991	−1.00	−0.82	0.40	2.30
1992	−2.10	−0.52	−1.50	1.90
1993	1.20	−0.33	1.00	1.20
1994	3.20	0.28	2.00	0.80
1995	3.10	0.44	4.80	−6.00
1996	4.30	1.61	4.50	3.80
1997	2.60	1.62	3.00	2.10
1998	0.50	1.46	0.60	−2.20
1999	2.40	1.17	1.50	0.40
2000	4.20	3.12	3.90	2.90
2001	2.70	5.51	3.20	3.10
2002	3.70	5.22	3.10	4.60
2003	3.10	1.13	3.50	6.30
2004	4.90	5.62	6.30	6.20
2005	5.00	1.95	6.60	4.80
2006	5.40	4.06	7.60	5.20
2007	5.10	3.39	6.90	5.00
2008	3.10	2.36	4.19	3.04

Sources: BMR estimates; SARB, 2008

According to Barker (2003), the employment coefficient is an excellent measure of the level at which changes in GDP growth rates give rise to changes in employment growth.

An employment coefficient of 1 or higher is indicative of a situation where an increase in economic growth rates will result in a strong increase in employment growth. If the employment coefficient is low, the implication is that GDP growth does not fully translate into employment growth, and could signify jobless growth when the employment coefficient is near 0. The employment coefficient is dynamic over time and will increase if production becomes more labour-intensive and will decrease if production becomes more capital-intensive.

Figure 8: Employment growth, GDP growth, household income and household consumption expenditure, 2000–8

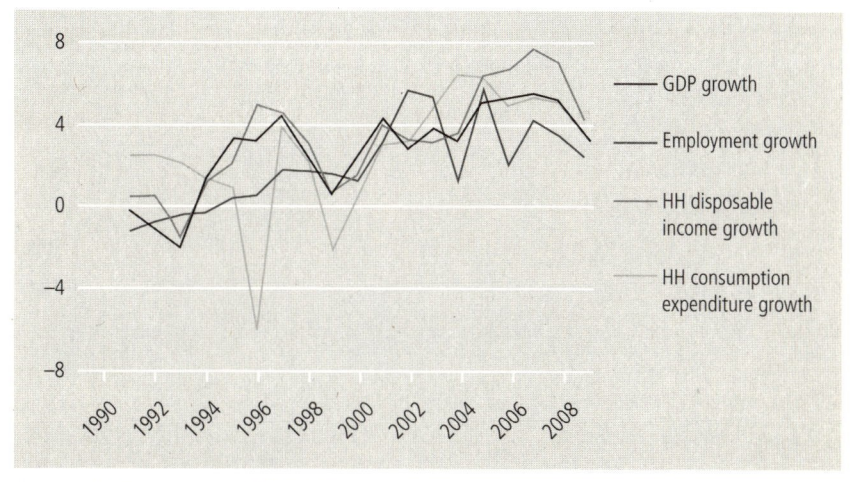

Sources: BMR estimates; SARB, 2008

Figure 9: Employment coefficients, 1990–2008

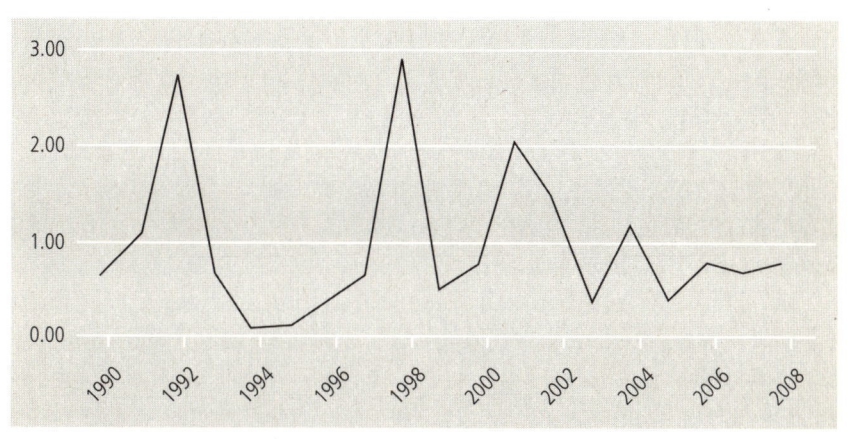

Source: BMR estimates; SARB, 2008

It is evident from Figure 9 that employment coefficients for 6 of the 19 years shown in Figure 8 were below 0.5. This is indicative of a fairly inelastic relation between economic and employment growth during these years. For a further 7 years the employment coefficients were between 0.5 and 1, indicative of an elastic but fairly weak relation between economic and employment growth.

If one analyses employment coefficients over a period longer than 1990–2008, it appears that they have been declining over the past few decades. The average employment coefficients for the period 1961–1993 – preceding the data provided in Figure 9 – were as follows:
- 1961–1972: 0.49
- 1973–1978: 0.76
- 1979–1984: 0.45
- 1985–1993: -0.33

The key question is: Can anything be done in terms of policy to change this trend? Can the government devise policies that will lead to an increase in the employment coefficient extending into the future?

Some recommendations for labour market policy

The relation between wage rates and employment in the South African context is graphically depicted in Figure 10. In this figure the y-axis represents wage rates and the x-axis represents the labour force. The area L to L^1 represents the total labour force while the line L to P^1 represents the segment of the labour force employed in the primary employment sector, which is nearly exclusively formal. The area P^1 to S represents the segment of the labour market employed in the secondary employment sector, which is nearly exclusively informal. The area S to L^2 represents the unemployed. The area P^1 to P^2 represents that segment of the labour force which is currently employed in the secondary employment sector but which can be absorbed in the primary sector should existing labour market rigidities be removed.

The Harvard Group has calculated that the line P^1P^2 represents about 6 million people when comparing the proportion of the economically active population who are employed with that of other emerging economies where less labour market rigidity is experienced. If an extra 6 million people had been part of the primary employment sector, the secondary employment sector (and pool of unemployed, S to L^2) would have been substantially smaller. That is, if the total size of the primary employment sector had been the current 9.9 million plus an extra 6 million, the total number of economically active people operating in the secondary employment sector would have been about 1.8 million, leaving about 1.5 million people unemployed (7.8% of the economically active as against the current 28%).

According to Figure 11, employment could be boosted further by

Figure 10: Wage rates and labour supply dynamics in South Africa

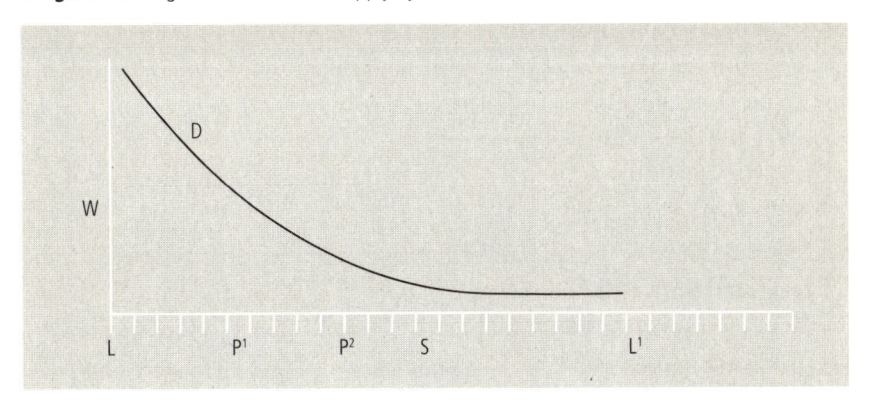

Figure 11: Wage rates and labour supply dynamics in a scenario of higher skills levels

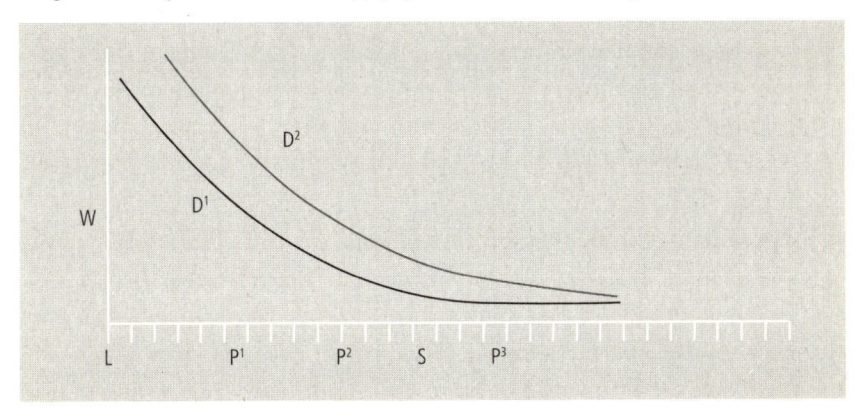

ensuring a more highly skilled workforce and making employers more willing to employ more workers at higher wage rates. By this means the current demand curve for labour (D^1 in Figure 11) could be shifted to demand curve D^2. By ensuring both a more flexible labour dispensation and a more highly skilled workforce, the area of possible employment outcomes in Figure 11 shifts from the area D^1 to P^1, where it is at present, to D^2 to P^2. In employment terms the implication would be that in addition to 9.9 million people being employed in the primary employment sector (as at present), a further 7.5 million people could be added, bringing total primary sector employment to 17.4 million. If a further estimated 920 000 economically active people were involved in the secondary employment sector, total employment would be 18.32 million compared to the current 13.5 million, bringing the total number of unemployed to 600 000 (3.2%

of the economically active), as compared to the current 5.4 million (28.5% of the economically active).

A variety of policy proposals have been made by various labour market experts and institutions to optimise formal employment opportunities. Such proposals include the following:

- Making the creation of 'decent' work opportunities the primary focus of economic policies.
- Investing in priority skills and education to ensure that people have the necessary skills to be employable.
- Directly absorbing the unemployed through labour-intensive production methods and procurement policies, a significant expansion of public works programmes and an expanded national youth service.
- Instituting a wage subsidy allowance for 18-year-olds to facilitate the school–work transition and, by doing so, allow the youth to demonstrate their abilities. During the probation period in which the allowance is used, employers might dismiss them without any justification. According to the Harvard Group, this will provide young workers with a kick-start into employment, and will encourage more experimentation by employers and a more efficient matching of workers to jobs.
- Improving labour market information systems and ensuring that information about available jobs reaches all economically active people.
- Encouraging high-skilled immigration to ensure that a bigger skills pool becomes available and a higher economic growth path is maintained.
- Curtailing social grants and minimising minimum wage regulations to encourage the unemployed to become involved in the informal sector and lower-paid segment of the primary employment sector.
- Curtailing labour legislation that increases the indirect costs of labour. This includes especially provisions of the Basic Conditions of Employment Act, which reduces the hours of work and increases overtime premiums; the Labour Relations Act, which makes it very difficult for employers to shed non-performing workers; and other labour legislation (i.e. minimum wages legislation), which makes it difficult for employers to increase productivity.

The need for change in labour policies has been brought home by the findings of the 2008/9 Global Competitiveness Report (Porter and Schwab, 2008). South Africa does not compare well with other countries with regard to labour market practice:

- South Africa is 119th out of 134 countries with regard to cooperation

between labour and business;
- South Africa is 123rd out of 134 countries with regard to flexibility in respect of wage determination;
- South Africa is 81st out of 134 countries with regard to the rigidity of employment;
- South Africa is 129th out of 134 countries with regard to hiring and firing practices; and
- South Africa is 81st out of 134 countries with regard to pay and productivity.

Whereas policy recommendations require policy changes and legislative amendments, the findings from the 2008/9 Global Competitiveness Report require changes in mindset and practice. First and foremost are changes to labour–business relationships in South Africa to facilitate joint solutions to labour market challenges. In other emerging economies like China, Thailand, Vietnam, Malaysia and Taiwan, labour and business were successful in tackling labour market challenges together to the benefit of both. The labour market policy ideas that emanated from the 2007 ANC Polokwane Conference are not helpful in strengthening labour–business relationships and in ensuring higher levels of job creation in South Africa.

Furthermore, various rigidities in the labour market remain a serious impediment to job creation in South Africa. According to the World Bank report (Clarke et al., 2007), the major rigidities or inflexibilities are labour regulations discouraging employers from employing more people, regulatory policies making it difficult to structure employment contracts flexibly, and labour inspections that turn the state into a watchdog. As an example of wage inflexibilities in South Africa, the World Bank provides the following comparative analysis of median monthly compensation for South Africa and China:

- Unskilled workers: $70 in China, $230 in South Africa;
- Skilled workers: $70 in China, $500 in South Africa;
- Professional workers: $140 in China, $800 in South Africa;
- Managers: $140 in China, $1 850 in South Africa.

Lastly, while productivity is continually optimised in other emerging economies through training, South Africa is doing less well with worker training. According to the World Bank (Clarke et al., 2007), in South Africa about 45% of skilled workers are receiving firm-based training compared to 77% in Brazil, 69% in China and 80% in Poland.

Conclusion

This essay has reviewed the key trends in the South African labour market over the period 1990–2008. The review indicates that it is growth in formal-sector employment that is necessary for economic (GDP) growth to translate into a reduction in poverty levels. The informal sector, while providing a safety net of sorts for formally unemployed people, has not been, and will not be, the engine of income growth for this country.

Research by the Harvard Group suggests that there is potential for formal employment to increase by approximately 50%. However, for this to happen, labour policies need to be changed to make people more attractive to formal employees. Protecting the rights of existing workers will put limits on the entry of potential workers to the formal workplace. Their ability to rise out of poverty is being constrained by the policies designed to protect them when they become employed. This situation needs to change.

Notes
1 People of working age (POWA) are those between the ages of 15 and 64 years.
2 The economically active population (EAP) consists of people of working age (POWA) who present themselves for employment.

References
ANC. 2007. *ANC 52nd National Conference 2007: Resolutions.* ANC, Johannesburg
Barker, F.S. 2003. *The South African Labour Market.* Van Schaik, Pretoria
Burger, R. and D.Yu. 2006. Wage Trends in Post-apartheid South Africa: Constructing an Earnings Series from Household Survey Data. *Labour Market Frontiers,* October 2006, 1–8
Clarke, R.G., J. Habyarimana, M. Ingram, D. Kaplan and V. Ramachandran. 2007. *An Assessment of the Investment Climate in South Africa.* The World Bank, Washington
Harvard Group. 2008. *Final Recommendations of the International Panel on Growth* (www.treasury.gov.za)
Kingdon, G. and J. Knight. 2004. Unemployment in South Africa: The Nature of the Beast. *World Development,* 32 (3), March 2004
Kingdon, G. and J. Knight. 2006. The Measurement of Unemployment When Unemployment Is High. *Labour Economics,* 13 (3), June 2006, 291–315
Oosthuizen, M. and H. Bhorat. 2005. *The Post-Apartheid South African Labour Market.* DPRU, University of Cape Town, Cape Town
Porter, M.E. and K. Schwab. 2008. *The Global Competitiveness Report 2008–2009.* World Economic Forum, Geneva
Ramady, M.A. 2008. Economics, Peace and Laughter Revisited: or Learning from the Asian 21st Century. Unpublished paper

SAARF. 2008. *2008 All Media and Product Survey.* SAARF, Johannesburg
SA Government. 2008. *SA Government 15 Year Review.* The Presidency, Pretoria
SA Reserve Bank. 2008. Reserve Bank online database (www.resbank.co.za)
Statistics South Africa. 2008. *Quarterly Employment Statistics,* June 2008. Statistics South Africa, Pretoria
World Bank. 2007. *World Development Indicators.* The World Bank, Washington

9

Health policy and growth

Oludele A. Akinboade, Thabisa Tokwe and Mandisa Mokwena

> Studies compiled from the twelfth century onward show that the poor, quite simply, are sicker than the non-poor and that this is true in both rich and poor countries.
> – Farmer, 1999

Our health is 'everything'. Whether you are a toddler, a child, a teenager or an adult, good health enables you to perform the daily functions of life. Health is also critical for the overall success of the South African economy. The objective of achieving a 6% rate of economic growth, and halving unemployment and poverty by 2014, as set out in the Accelerated and Shared Growth Initiative for South Africa (Asgisa) policy document, will remain a dream unless South Africans get public health right. Many of the successful economies have consciously invested in achieving and maintaining levels of health as a prerequisite for their growth.

Health plays the key role in determining human capital. Better health improves the efficiency and the productivity of the labour force, and ultimately contributes to economic growth and human welfare. To attain better, more skilful, efficient and productive human capital resources, many governments subsidise healthcare facilities for their people. In this regard, the public sector pays some part (or all) of the cost of utilising such services.

This essay sets out to describe and explain the relationship between health and economic growth in South Africa. The next section provides an overview of the South African healthcare system, the challenges facing the new government in this area and the responses to date. The section thereafter discusses previous contributions that have examined the link between health and economic performance. An analysis of the trends of public healthcare spending by provinces in South Africa is then presented. In the next section we look at the empirical relationship between public healthcare spend and economic growth in South Africa over the period 1982–2006. We carry out causality tests to find out whether health expenditure stimulates growth or vice versa, and conclude by giving policy recommendations.

Overview of the healthcare sector in South Africa

The democratic government elected in 1994 inherited a highly fragmented and bureaucratic system that had provided health services in a discriminatory manner (Ntsaluba and Pillay, 1998). Services for whites were better than those for blacks, while those in the rural areas were significantly worse off in terms of access to services then their urban counterparts. With 14 different health departments, the system was characterised by fragmentation and duplication. There was no real attempt to deliver primary health care to the majority of people, and the health sector was largely focused on hospitals. Those living in rural areas had to travel long distances for medical care.

Even prior to its electoral victory in 1994, the ANC had prepared, through a widely consultative process, its National Health Plan. This was one of the first comprehensive sectoral plans for post-apartheid South Africa that firmly entrenched the principles of social justice and equity. In terms of its vision, 'The health of all South Africans will be secured and improved mainly through the achievement of equitable social and economic development such as the level of employment, the standards of education, and the provision of housing, clean water, sanitation and electricity' (ANC, 1994a). The key goals of the plan were incorporated into the Reconstruction and Development Programme (RDP), which was adopted by the new government as its guiding policy document. The RDP described a package of social and economic policies that were aimed at redressing the massive inequities within all spheres of South African life. Many of the broader social sector policies (e.g. improved access to water and sanitation) were specifically motivated in terms of their likely positive impact on health status. In addition, the health sector was given a relatively high priority in the overall RDP, as it was argued that there could be more rapid 'delivery' in meeting RDP targets through health service improvements relative to other sectors (ANC, 1994b). Thus, health equity goals were seen as an integral part of the overall political commitment to tackling poverty and redressing inequity.

On the basis of the National Health Plan and the RDP, the government drafted the White Paper for the Transformation of the Health System in South Africa (DoH, 1997a), which mapped out the proposed direction and programme of action for the transformation of the health sector. Equity and social justice were central themes of the White Paper. The White Paper was used as a basis for the drafting of the National Health Act No. 61 of 2003. The object of the Act is 'to regulate national health and to provide uniformity in respect of health services across the nation' by establishing a national health system which encompasses public and private providers of health services; and provides in an equitable manner the population of the Republic with the best possible health services that available resources can afford.

Since 1994 the health sector has undergone rapid change to make it more equitable and accessible to the needy. More than 1300 clinics have been built or upgraded. Free health care has been made available to children under the age of six, and to pregnant or breastfeeding mothers. The policy of universal access to primary health care, introduced in 1994, forms the basis of healthcare delivery programmes. The number of people using these facilities has increased significantly across provinces. In addition to that, a new administrative structure is being put in place which will see primary healthcare clinics fall under the auspices of district authorities while hospitals remain under the control of provincial authorities. A district-based health system is being developed to ensure local-level control of public health services, and to standardise and coordinate basic health services around the country to ensure that health care is affordable and accessible.

In spite of these achievements, the challenges and opportunities facing the South African healthcare system are considerable. There is a greater need for more efficiency and more equity. A mix of public and private health services has already emerged and seems likely to continue. The public sector will almost certainly provide care for most of the population and should emphasise primary care because it tends to be more cost-effective than focusing on secondary and tertiary services. The private sector can serve as an alternative for those willing and able to pay for what will probably be higher-cost care. It can also serve as a testing environment for new technologies. Improved efficiency can provide some additional resources to meet expanded services for appropriate care. Research is needed to identify which services each South African can expect as an entitlement, and ultimately South Africans must decide how much, if any, of their other resources should be shifted to health services.

Amongst the challenges faced by public health workers are poor salaries, high workloads, poor work environments and few opportunities for advancement. These have been push factors in the migration of health workers from South Africa. There is a resulting chronic shortage of health professionals, which impacts directly on the quality of care. The issue of remuneration has also driven health professionals to other disciplines and to the private sector. Furthermore, the reintegration of South Africa into the global economy has created opportunities for South African professionals to pursue opportunities elsewhere in the world. It is this migration of skills that has resulted in a visible shortage of managerial and planning skills in public health.

Health care in South Africa is a paramount issue for citizens and government alike. Nearly 50% of provincial budgets go toward health-care spending. Add to that increased costs, antiquated infrastructure and an ageing population, and many see a healthcare crisis looming.

Investment in health is not only a desirable but also an essential priority for most societies. However, South Africa's health systems face tough and complex challenges, in part derived from new pressures, such as ageing populations, growing prevalence of chronic illnesses, and intensive use of expensive yet vital health technologies. Moreover, the government must deal with the higher expectations of citizens and resolve persistent inequities in access and in health conditions among different groups. The main concern is how to ensure the financial sustainability of health systems, while making a positive contribution to macroeconomic performance. As a result, health has moved to the top of the policy agenda in all the South African provinces. Much of the work undertaken in South Africa's health projects has aimed at providing policy-makers with the evidence they need to champion greater value for money in the health sector, while ensuring universal access and equity and raising quality of care. The government has learnt a lot, though there is more to discover.

Health and the economy

Health is one of the most important assets a human being has. It permits us to develop our capacities fully. Life-cycle models have explained how one's health status can determine future income, wealth and consumption (Lilliard and Weiss, 1997; Smith, 1998, 1999). These models demonstrate that the economic value of health is huge and health gains have the economic consequence of widespread economic growth and escape from the ill-health traps of poverty (WHO, 1999).

Health performance and economic performance are interlinked. Over time, as countries get richer, they tend to spend more on healt;h care. Therefore, wealthier countries have healthier populations for a start. On the other hand, ill health is a major cause of poverty, and poverty, mainly through infant malnourishment and mortality, adversely affects life expectancy. Researchers found that about 22–30% of the growth rate is attributable to health capital. Moreover, improvements in health conditions equivalent to one more year of life expectancy are associated with higher GDP growth of up to 4 percentage points per year (Bloom and Canning, 2003; Bloom, Canning and Sevilla, 2004; Gyimah-Brempong and Wilson, 2004).

The effects of health on economic development are clear in the sense that countries with weak health and education conditions find it harder to achieve sustained growth. Lower life expectancy discourages adult training and damages productivity. Similarly, the emergence of deadly communicable diseases has become an obstacle for the development of sectors like the tourism industry, on which so many countries rely. If health financing is inequitable, it can expose whole populations to huge cost burdens that block development and simply perpetuate the disease–poverty trap. At the same time, health systems need financing and investment to improve their performance, yet this need cannot in turn impose an unfair burden on national spending or competitiveness. In other words, if policy-makers want to raise investment in health spending, they may need to find cuts elsewhere in the economic system.

African health systems face huge funding challenges. Compared to a global average of 5.4% of GDP, current government spending averages 2.5% of GDP and falls far short of that needed even to provide basic care. While spending on health care in high-income countries exceeded US$2000 per person per year, in Africa it averaged between US$13 and US$21 in 2001 (Commission for Africa, 2004). The Commission on Macroeconomics and Health (2001) recommended that spending for health care in sub-Saharan Africa should rise to US$34 per person per year by 2007, and to US$38 by 2015, which represents roughly 12% of GNP. This is the minimum amount needed to deliver basic treatment and care for the major communicable diseases (HIV/AIDS, TB and malaria), and early childhood and maternal illnesses. Similarly, some argue for a massive scaling up of public health and other social sector expenditure.

There are a number of key questions for policy and health sector strategy. How far has public expenditure been effective in bringing about the progress in health status experienced in developing countries over the past few decades? And what programmes have been particularly effective (Roberts, 2003)? To answer the first of these questions, research has sought econometric estimates of the strength and significance of the factors most likely to influence health status based on a generally agreed list of factors determining health outcomes. At the micro level, the proximate determinants of the health status of members of a household are usually taken to be:

- personal and socio-cultural (household income, asset holding and access to insurance, income and asset distribution, other personal characteristics of household members including lifestyle, sexual practices, and knowledge of good nutrition, diet, hygiene and health maintenance practice, and genetic pre-disposition to illness);
- geographical and environmental (location whether urban or rural, access to clean water and sanitation, prevalence of communicable diseases and of environmental health hazards); and
- health services (relevance, quality, availability, price and accessibility of public and private preventive and curative health services).

A growing literature in recent years has tried to examine the link between health expenditure and health outcomes especially as it affects mortality of under-fives and infants. Early studies (summarised by Musgrove, 1996) found no evidence that total spending on health has any impact on child mortality. According to empirical evidence presented by Filmer and Pritchett (1997), public spending on health is not the dominant driver of child mortality outcomes. Income, income inequality, female education, and 'cultural factors' such as the degree of ethnolinguistic fractionalisation explain practically all of the variation in child mortality across countries. Based on these findings, policies that encourage economic growth, reduce poverty and income inequality, and increase female education would do more for attaining child mortality reductions than increasing public spending on health. Filmer and Pritchett (1999) found that government health expenditures account for less than one-seventh of 1% variation in under-five mortality across countries, although the result was not statistically significant. They conclude that 95% of the variation in under-five mortality can be explained by factors such as a country's per capita income, female educational attainment, and choice of region. A number of other studies have linked changes in mortality rates to such factors as resource use at hospital, managed care, educational status of parents, females and children, and technological change (Cutler, 1995; Kessler and McClellan, 2000; McClellan and Noguchi, 1998; Mazunder 2007; Glied and Lieras-Muney, 2003). Burnside and Dollar (1998) found no significant relationship between health expenditure spending and change in infant mortality in low-income countries.

Expenditure on health care in South Africa

The collapse of apartheid led to a major shift in resource allocation in South Africa's public health sector. The heavily skewed expenditure pattern that favoured facilities in white neighbourhoods relative to non-whites, and tertiary care over primary care, was abandoned. Funding for the large and internationally recognised medical centres was cut dramatically, as was that of other well-financed hospitals. Greater resources were made available for primary care in existing and new clinics in both rural and urban non-white areas. Increasingly, the 15–20% of the population (largely white) with private health insurance has sought hospital care from private hospitals. The private sector, which accounts for 60–70% of health spending, has grown rapidly as those with private insurance have fled the public services (Health Systems Trust and World Bank, 1995).

Within South Africa, it is important to consider resource differences between the public and private sectors relative to the populations that they serve. The private sector accounts for over 60% of healthcare expenditure, yet it serves a minority of the population. There are certain concerns about the financing of the private sector, particularly in relation to medical schemes, which account for the largest share of private-sector spending. Medical scheme contributions continue to increase faster than inflation and are increasingly unaffordable for many South Africans. At the same time, schemes continually limit the healthcare benefits they provide, and the elderly, chronically ill and others are consequently 'dumped' on public hospitals when medical scheme benefits run out.

There have been a number of notable interventions at a national level with the aim of improving access to health services, which have yielded positive results in all provinces. It is well known that South Africa spends a considerable amount of money on health services compared to other middle-income countries. Yet the average health status of South Africans is relatively poor. There are two key issues that help to explain this poor relationship between healthcare expenditure and health status. Firstly, there

Table 1: Provincial health spending patterns in R billions, 1995–2007

PRO	1995	1996	1997	1998	1999	2000
EC	2.206	3.066	3.031	3.048	3.496	3.790
FS	1.183	1.470	1.659	1.692	1.654	1.777
GP	3.092	4.643	5.299	5.478	5.805	5.942
KZN	3.285	4.234	4.806	4.900	5.110	5.772
NP/L	1.424	1.999	1.954	2.081	2.221	2.524
MP	541	817	1.047	1.058	1.147	1.117
NC	277	330	376	302	433	466
NW	933	1.276	1.375	1.342	1.384	1.561
WC	2.346	2.780	2.937	3.032	3.125	3.468
Total	16.097	20.615	22.484	23.023	24.375	26.417

Source: National Treasury

are a number of factors (other than health care) that influence health status, such as income, education, and access to water and sanitation. A high level of spending on health services will not by itself result in good health. Secondly, people may not be using the healthcare resources they currently have, most effectively.

Most of the funding for health services in the public sector comes from general tax revenue. A very small amount of money comes from user fees at public hospitals. Though overall government expenditure has declined since the first democratic elections in 1994, as a big share of tax revenue is being used for debt repayments, the government has been careful to protect social service budgets. While there has been considerable variation in the success of the different provinces in securing a reasonable share of provincial budgets for health care, overall allocations to the health sector have increased as a percentage of the total budget. Table 1 shows the pattern of health spending in the country's provinces from 1995 to 2007.

According to Table 1, the national budget for the public health sector has grown almost three times from R16 billion during 1994/5 to almost R57 billion in 2006/7. In 2007, the total public sector health budget was R59.2 billion, which constituted 3.05% of GDP and 11.08% of government expenses. Although the state contributes about 40% of all expenditure on health, the public health sector is under pressure to deliver services to about 80% of the population. Despite this, most resources are concentrated in the private health sector, which sees to the health needs of the remaining 20% of the population.

2001	2002	2003	2004	2005	2006	2007
3.992	4.493	5.242	5.173	6.122	6.693	7.658
1.953	2.194	2.563	2.797	3.099	3.250	3.470
6.838	7.685	6.190	8.597	9.973	10.404	11.011
7.033	7.535	8.343	8.950	10.517	11.737	12.796
2.664	3.166	3.724	4.196	4.790	5.448	6.912
1.457	1.689	2.007	2.263	2.654	2.912	3.194
517	609	833	832	1.098	1.291	1.401
1.699	2.012	2.263	2.595	2.957	3.428	3.778
3.731	3.984	4.597	5.172	5.707	6.323	6.774
29.884	33.367	35.762	40.575	46.917	51.486	56.994

How these public resources are allocated, and the standard of health care delivered, varies from province to province. With fewer resources and more poor people, cash-strapped provinces such as the Eastern Cape face greater health challenges than wealthier provinces such as Gauteng and the Western Cape. In 2006, spending between provinces became more equitable, with under-resourced provinces like Mpumalanga and Limpopo acquiring more funding. There was also a notable growth in the funding of district health services, including HIV, primary health care and emergency medical services, and in the upgrading of health infrastructure.

The relation between government spending on health care and economic growth

In a separate exercise we briefly reviewed the empirical relationship between annual government spending on health care and economic growth (as measured by the rate of growth of GDP) in South Africa over the period 1983–2006. As illustrated in Figure 1, we found a very strong positive correlation between the growth in the level of healthcare spending and the rate of growth of GDP.

The approach we adopted allowed us to separate out the short- and long-run (equilibrium) relationships between the two variables. Looking at this more closely, we found strong, positive, statistically significant relationships between the rate of growth of GDP and the levels of health spend over the four years. We also found a significant long-run relationship between the two.

The strong positive correlation and relationship suggest the existence

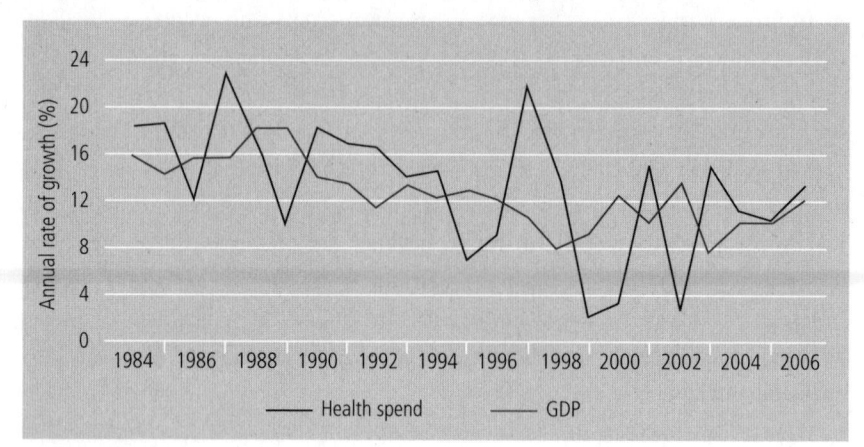

Figure 1: Annual growth rates of nominal health spending and GDP, 1984–2006

of a casual link between the two variables. However, when we tested for causality between the two variables we found that the rate of economic growth 'causes' the level of healthcare spending, rather than vice versa, as was initially expected. To unlock this puzzle our analysis needs to be extended to include other potential drivers of growth such as investment, human capital formation and technological developments.

Conclusion and recommendations

The results of our econometric tests indicate a high degree of correlation and a significant relationship between health spending and economic growth. Some may argue that an even higher percentage of the government budget should be directed towards health care. However, this is unlikely to happen.

There was a substantial reallocation of budgets from protection services (including defence, and police and prisons) shortly after the 1994 elections. As there is limited potential for reallocating more resources in this way, additional resources for health services would probably be secured at the expense of other social services (such as education and social welfare payments). Given that improved education (particularly for women), access to potable water and sanitation, and other socio-economic conditions contribute substantially to health improvements, it would be unwise to jeopardise these services by over-emphasising health service resource requirements. Thus, it is unlikely that additional tax revenue will be available in the near future for public-sector health services.

Before seeking additional sources of healthcare funding, it is important to improve equity and efficiency in the use of existing resources. In particular, there is a need to shift budgets gradually towards currently under-resourced areas and in favour of primary-care services. This means that hospital budgets, particularly for the large urban-based tertiary hospitals, would decrease gradually. In order that referral hospital services are not jeopardised, dramatic improvements in hospital efficiency are required: efforts must be made to offer a similar quality and quantity of hospital services with fewer resources. In particular, attention should be paid to losses of drugs and other consumables (either through theft or because of expiry of drugs through poor stock management) and inappropriate staff numbers and skills mix.

This redistribution of financial resources needs to be accompanied by proactive efforts to develop adequate management capacity (e.g. appropriately skilled managers and functioning information systems) in these areas and facilities, to ensure that budgets are translated into service delivery improvements. As staff account for the greatest share of healthcare spending, it is also important to develop adequate staff relocation mechanisms, including incentives for staff to work in rural and peri-urban areas and in primary-care facilities.

A key mechanism available to draw additional funds into public-sector health services is through user fees at hospitals. On the one hand, it is not advisable to increase fee levels for those who do not have any form of health insurance, as few public hospital users can pay substantial amounts of money in times of illness. However, some public hospital patients are covered either by medical schemes or other forms of insurance such as workmen's compensation. At present, substantial fee revenue is lost due to poor billing systems. Sometimes, accounts are issued so late that medical schemes refuse to pay them. Improved issuing of accounts and collection of fee revenue could increase the resources available for public health services, if provincial treasuries agree to these funds being kept within the health sector (rather than being placed in general provincial funds). Another possible funding source currently under discussion is social health insurance (SHI), whose introduction would extend health insurance coverage to a larger number of South Africans. While SHI may address a number of healthcare financing problems, it requires careful consideration before it can be taken forward.

In summary, to meet some of the key challenges facing healthcare fi-

nancing in South Africa, the government needs to:
- implement the new Medical Schemes Act effectively;
- strengthen provincial-level negotiations for a fair allocation to healthcare budgets (particularly in provinces where health budgets per person are below the national average), without jeopardising allocations to other social services;
- improve equity and efficiency in the use of existing resources;
- strengthen billing systems for hospital user fees; and
- explore in detail the possible advantages and disadvantages of introducing social health insurance.

The task of ensuring that resources are distributed equitably between provinces in South Africa is one of the most critical in improving the health status of people across the country. However, although this is an essential project for the country as a whole, it must be remembered that improving health is not simply about changing the allocation of healthcare resources. Levels of health are influenced by many other factors and, inevitably, poverty means ill health. Thus the alleviation of poverty and improvement of living conditions are also crucial in this respect. The pursuit of annual economic growth of about 6% by the government is not misplaced.

References

ANC. 1994a. *A National Health Plan for South Africa*. ANC, Johannesburg

ANC. 1994b. *The Reconstruction and Development Programme: A Policy Framework*. ANC, Johannesburg

Bhargava, A., D.T. Jamison, T.J. Lau and C.J.L. Murray. 2001. Modeling the Effects of Health on Economic Growth. *Journal of Health Economics*, 20: 423–440

Bloom, D. and D. Canning. 2003. The Health and Poverty of Nations: From Theory to Practice. *Journal of Human Development*, 4 (1), 47–71

Bloom, D.E., D. Canning and J. Sevilla. 2004. The Effect of Health on Economic Growth: A Production Function Approach. *World Development*, 32 (1), 1–13

Burnside, C. and D. Dollar. 1998. Aid, the Incentive Regime, and Poverty Reduction. Macroeconomics and Growth Group, World Bank, Washington

Commission for Africa. 2004. *Our Common Interest*. CFA

Commission on Macroeconomics and Health. 2001. *Macroeconomics and Health: Investing in Health for Economic Development*. WHO, Geneva

Cutler, D.M. 1995. The Incidence of Adverse Medical Outcomes under Prospective Payment. *Econometrical*, 63 (1), 29–50

Department of Health. 1997a. *White Paper for the Transformation of the Health System in South Africa*. Government Printer, Pretoria

Farmer, P. 1999. *Infections and Inequalities: The Modern Plagues*. University of California Press, Berkeley

Filmer, D. and L. Pritchett. 1997. Child Mortality and Public Spending on Health: How Much Does Money Matter? World Bank Policy Research Working Paper no. 1864, Washington

Filmer, D. and L. Pritchett. 1999. The Impact of Public Spending on Health: Does Money Matter? *Social Science and Medicine*, 49 (10), 1309–1323

Glied, S. and A. Lieras-Muney. 2003. Health Inequality, Education and Medical Innovation, NBER Working Paper no. 9738

Gyimah-Brempong, K. and M. Wilson. 2004. Health Human Capital and Economic Growth in Sub-Saharan African and OECD Countries. *Quarterly Review of Economics and Finance*, 44 (2), 296–320

Health Systems Trust and World Bank. 1995. Health Expenditure and Finance in South Africa. Health Systems Trust, Durban

Jacobs, P. and J. Rapaport. 2002. *The Economics of Health and Medical Care*. Aspen Publishers, Gaithersburg

Kessler, D. and M. McClellan. 2000. Is Hospital Competition Socially Wasteful? *Quarterly Journal of Economics*, 115, 577–615

Lilliard, Lee A. and Y. Weiss. 1997. Uncertain Health and Survival: Effects on End-of-Life Consumption. *Journal of Business and Economic Statistics*, 15, 254–268

Mazunder, B. 2007. How Did Schooling Laws Improve Long-term Health and Lower Mortality. Federal Reserve Bank of Chicago, Working Paper Series, WP-06-03

McClellan, M. and H. Noguchi. 1998. Technological Change in Heart-Disease Treatment: Does High Tech Mean Low Value. *American Economic Review Paper and Proceedings*, 88, 90–96

Musgrove, P. 1996. Public and Private Roles in Health. Technical Report 339, World Bank, Washington

Ntsaluba, A. and Y. Pillay. 1998. Reconstructing and Developing the Health System: The First 1000 Days. *South African Medical Journal*, 88 (1), 33–35

Roberts, R. 2003. Poverty Reduction Outcomes in Education and Health Public Expenditure and Aid. Working Paper 210, Centre for Aid and Public Expenditure, ODI, London

Smith, J.P. 1998. Socioeconomic Status and Health. *American Economic Review*, 88, 192–196

Smith, J.P. 1999. Healthy Bodies and Thick Wallets: The Dual Relation between Health and Socioeconomic Status. *Journal of Economic Perspectives*, 13, 145–166

WHO. 1999. WHO on Health and Economic Productivity. *Population and Development Review*, 25 (2), 396–401

10
Politics and human-oriented development

Adam Habib

The first year of South Africa's second decade of democracy witnessed the opening of a political drama whose outcome may define the future character of the society.* This piece of theatre, about who was to succeed President Mbeki in the African National Congress (ANC), involved a formidable political cast, comprising not only the ex-President of the Republic and Jacob Zuma, now president of the ruling party, but also almost every other significant figure in South Africa's ruling political hierarchy. Moreover, the script was organised around a political contest between different sets of heroes and villains, most notably Thabo Mbeki and Jacob Zuma. The distinguishing feature of this theatre was that its heroes and villains changed depending on who was telling the narrative.

In one version, South Africa's transition was presented in a positive light. It was a story of macroeconomic stability, sustainable growth, low inflation, high productivity, and demographic and racial transformation. South Africa was presented as the prime example of the modern African state, one taking its place responsibly in the world community of nations. The benefits of the democratic transition were seen to be broadly shared across the society. Where they were not, it was suggested that this had less

---

* I would like to record my appreciation to Bill Freund, David Everatt, Enver Motala, Garth le Pere, Geoffrey Modisha, Imraan Valodia, Lenny Markovitz, Michael MacDonald, Omano Edigheji, Steven Friedman, Raymond Suttner and Vishnu Padayachee for commenting on earlier drafts of this paper. This essay was first published in *Social Dynamics*, 2008, vol. 34, no. 1, pp. 46–61 (© Taylor and Francis).

to do with the policies pursued, and far more with the structural dynamics of South African society. The heroes in this story were Thabo Mbeki, Mosiuoa Lekota, Trevor Manuel, Tito Mboweni and the cadre of officials and technocrats that surrounded them. The villains were the populists located mainly in the Congress of South African Trade Unions (Cosatu), the South African Communist Party (SACP) and the ANC Youth League (ANCYL) who surrounded Jacob Zuma and misled what was in effect a rabble of largely young, uninformed, lumpen elements.

The second version presented South Africa's transition as having been derailed. Of course there was an acknowledgement of the positive features of this transition. Its peaceful character, the establishment of new democratic institutions, and the racial transformation of the state were recognised as advances on South Africa's apartheid past. But the story was also cast as one of missed opportunities, the enrichment of the elite few, the capture of the ANC by a new breed of politically connected businessmen, and the marginalisation of the interests of poor urban and rural communities. The heroes in this version were Jacob Zuma, Zwelinzima Vavi, Blade Nzimande and the groups of activists who were seen to have stood up courageously to the imperial presidency and the comprador bourgeoisie that surrounded it. The villains were former President Mbeki, his cabinet and the technocrats who operated so well in the unfeeling world of statistics and who were alienated from the lived realities of South Africa's poor and marginalised.

These competing explanations have survived even though Thabo Mbeki's political reign has now come to an end. His departure has provoked concern especially among South Africa's business community and its urbanised upper classes. In December 2007 he was unceremoniously defeated in the election for the ANC's presidency at Polokwane. Nine months later, the new leadership in the party forced his resignation as State President seven months prior to the end of his tenure. The resultant political instability, including the resignation of a number of cabinet ministers most closely identified with Mbeki, has raised concern. Is democracy imperilled? Will the prudent economic policy of the Mbeki years be jettisoned? How did Jacob Zuma win the presidency of the ANC and what can we expect in his political tenure?

These are important questions but let us begin addressing them by trying to understand what Polokwane was all about. Most people would recognise that Polokwane represented a rebellion by ANC delegates against Thabo Mbeki's rule. And it was motivated by two factors. First – and almost everyone seems to agree with it – Mbeki is said to have centralised power, not consulted enough, aggravated tensions in the party, and been aloof and divorced from the membership. Second – and many in the ANC leadership seem to reject it – delegates felt that the transition under Mbeki had benefited the rich disproportionately and worked to the disadvantage of the poor. Delegates were concerned about the inequalities that have defined the first 13 years of our transition, and the enrichment of the narrow politically connected elite that has become the hallmark of the black economic empowerment agenda.

How do we explain this? Most commentators explain the centralised management style or the exclusivist economic agenda as a product of Mbeki and his personality. Xolela Mangcu's recent book *To the Brink* (2008) and Mark Gevisser's biography of Mbeki, *The Dream Deferred* (2007), are two examples. For Gevisser, the centralised style of management is the product of a personality growing up in no man's land – in between the rural and urban, in between modernism and traditionalism, in between father and comrade, and in between the international and the national. This profoundly affected Mbeki, generated the aloof personality that we have come to know, and defined both his technocratic orientation and the centralised management style of his presidency.

But this explanation is not a comprehensive one. It does not recognise the issue of institutional constraints, that individuals, however powerful their personalities, are constrained by the positions they occupy and the pressures they are subjected to. In the celebrated words of Karl Marx, 'Men make their own history, but they do not make it just as they please; they do not make it under circumstances chosen by themselves, but under circumstances directly found, given and transmitted from the past.'

A more all-embracing explanation has to look at the systemic rationale for both macroeconomic policy choices and the centralisation of power under Mbeki. When the ANC came into power in 1994, it inherited a nearly bankrupt state, was confronted with an ambitious set of expectations from the previously disenfranchised, and faced an investment strike by the business community. To get investment and growth going, the ANC leadership felt that they had to make a series of economic concessions most of which were captured in the Growth, Employment and Redistribution strategy (Gear). As soon as they made this decision, they confronted another problem: how to get the programme passed, for they feared that their own comrades in the national legislature would defeat it? So they bypassed the very structures of democracy that they had inaugurated. They endorsed Gear in Cabinet and set about implementing it. This established a centralising dynamic in the South African political system. From there it was a short step to appointing premiers and mayors and marginalising Cosatu, the SACP and others who disagreed with Mbeki from the decision-making structures of the party and state.

Mainstream political and economic elites recognise the force of this story and suggest that there was no alternative. Cosatu and the SACP of course do not share this political conclusion, but they seem to think it necessary to construct an alternative political trajectory by getting their own band of heroes to ascend to high political office in the ANC and the state. This essay, however, posits an alternative solution for individuals and groups such as these that are interested in achieving a more explicitly human-oriented development agenda. Development should not be seen as a product of individuals in high office. Consequently, replacing the existing political elite is not a sufficient, or indeed a necessary, solution.

This essay does not look for a solution at the level of policies or personalities. Neither does it focus on social and institutional relationships. Instead, it investigates the broader structural political conditions, especially the configuration of power, under which human-oriented development occurs. Its conclusion is that a human-oriented development agenda requires effective competition for political power. It is not sufficient simply to have the right people at the top.

Democracy and development: some comparative reflections

A wealth of scholarship has been built up over the last decade on the South African transition. While this body of academic work has provided some understanding of the dynamics of the transition and its evolution, it does not adequately investigate the political conditions under which human-oriented development can occur. Instead it is focused either on legitimising or critiquing the present development trajectory and, where alternatives are advanced, these are largely constructed at the level of policy. This, together with the fact that the leadership battle within the ANC is organised mainly around personalities, indicates that there is an excessive focus on agency and very little reflection on how institutional and structural location aligns agential behaviour and choice with a human-oriented development trajectory. Moreover, there is currently very little realistic thinking on how institutional and structural constraints can be transformed. This is a pity since there are a number of historical cases across the world where economic and political elites were prompted to undertake a human-oriented development trajectory. Does it not make sense, then, to establish a research agenda on the politics of policy-making, with the express aim of trying to understand under what conditions elites can be made to behave in systemically beneficial ways?

There is of course a substantial body of literature that tackles this issue. And, despite their varied focuses, there is a surprising amount of unanimity among them on the political conditions that prompt elites to behave in human-oriented and systemically beneficial ways. Three distinct sets of literature are relevant in this regard. First is the literature that attempts to explain the rise of corporatism – a political system in which power is exercised through large organisations (businesses, trade unions, etc.) working in concert with each other, under the direction of the state – in diverse political contexts. Three schools of explanation have emerged: those of 'historical continuity', 'societal reflection' and 'crisis response'. The historical continuity school predictably explains the rise of corporatist institutions by suggesting that they are a product of the diffusion throughout society of norms, values and traditions that emphasise hierarchy and obedience to authority (Wiarda, 1981). The societal reflection school, by contrast, suggests they are a natural outcome of socially segmented societies (Rogowski and Wasserspring, summarised in Stepan, 1978). The crisis response school, which focuses on concrete political circumstances and the pressures generated by conflicts among various social groups in society, is perhaps the most persuasive in accounting for the rise of corporatism in the modern world (Panitch, 1986; Maier, 1984; Stepan, 1978; Schmitter, 1974). Not only does this school make a persuasive case for understanding the rise of corporatism in the authoritarian parts of Latin America, but it also accounts for corporatism's development in the very different conditions of Western European social democracies. In both contexts, the school explains the rise of corporatism through a focus on the vulnerability experienced by political elites as a result of the political mobilisation by social groups like workers and peasants, and the expansion of communism in the international and regional environments.

The second set of literature that provides an understanding of the conditions that prompt elites to behave in systemically beneficial ways is that on the development states of East and Southeast Asia. Again, this literature has different orientations. Some scholars have a policy bent and are mainly descriptive in approach, detailing the particular policies that generated positive socio-economic outcomes in these development states.[1] Others tend to have a more institutional focus, emphasising the embedded but relatively autonomous character of the state, which speaks to the structural linkages and social interactions between political and economic elites (Evans, 1995). But a description of policies, institutions and networks cannot explain why elite coalitions adopt national development agendas. Nor can they explain why international political elites would allow these development states to implement a series of policies that discriminate against foreign capital.

The third set of literature relevant to this concern is that focusing on the consolidation of democracy. Returning to the classic elements of democracy, this literature highlights the necessity of competitive political systems for making political elites accountable to their citizens. Robert Dahl made the case for democratic oppositions three decades ago in his pioneering study *Political Oppositions in Western Democracies*. More recently, Schedler (2001) argues that political uncertainty is the essence of democracy. He proceeds on the basis of this foundation to draw a distinction between what he terms institutional and substantive uncertainty. The former, which he views as involving the rules of the game, is bad for democracy, whereas the latter, which relates to the uncertainty of political elites about their chances of continuity in office, is really good for democracy. It is precisely this uncertainty, Schedler argues, that forces political elites to become responsive to the needs and wishes of citizens, and herein lie the prospects for a more equitably shared development trajectory.[2]

The three sets of literature, then, all suggest that a substantive uncertainty on the part of political elites is positive for a more human-oriented development trajectory. Of course this uncertainty has to be conditional if it is to have developmental effects. Firstly, it must occur within an overall context of commonality — a democratic constitution widely supported by the citizenry, for instance — if the uncertainty is not to produce instability and dictatorship. Secondly, the literature indicates that this beneficial substantive uncertainty is normally a product of two distinct political processes: social mobilisation and extra-institutional action, and elite contestation. Both political processes have the net effect of dispersing power in society. It is precisely this dispersal of power that enhances citizens' leverage over national political elites, and that of the latter over their international counterparts.

Since the end of the Cold War, elite contestation, at least for the foreseeable future, can only be realised at the national level. In this sense Amartya Sen is correct to argue that political freedom (read 'democracy') is necessary for economic growth and development. But the statement requires qualification because his insistence on the positive value of democracy to economic growth and development is founded, as was that of an earlier generation of philosophers, on its having an instrumental and constructive value: instrumental in the sense of 'enhancing the hearing the people get in expressing and supporting their claims'; and constructive in that it helps build a democratic culture of discussion, debate and exchange of ideas (Sen, 1999: 5). This presupposes, however, that such democracies always achieve their primary purpose: to diffuse power in society. As a result they enhance the leverage of citizens and thereby promote the accountability of state elites to their citizenry. But what if such diffusion of power does not take place and such accountability is not realised? After all, this is the essential conclusion of much of the later literature on the Third Wave of democratisation, lamenting the rise of the phenomenon of illiberal and delegative democracies, which, as Guillermo O'Donnell (1994, 1993) maintained, are political systems in which representative political structures are weakened sufficiently to enable power to be centralised in and delegated to a leader or leadership.

Elite contestation can therefore not be assumed but must rather be actively promoted in both new and established democracies. This is because such contestation is necessary, as is social mobilisation, for enhancing the leverage of citizens with their political elites, and thereby promoting the substantive uncertainty that is so necessary for prompting these actors to embark on a human-oriented development trajectory. This strategic lesson goes against the grain of much of the democratisation literature on the Third Wave of transitions, which tends to urge political caution and socio-economic pragmatism instead of robust political engagement (O'Donnell and Schmitter, 1986; Huntington, 1991).[3] But the lesson also goes against the strategic perspective of significant components of the liberation movement in South Africa who tend to emphasise unity within the Tripartite Alliance or the need to win the heart and soul of the ANC (Cosatu, 2006; SACP, 2006a, 2006b) and who, by implication, are given over to an excessive focus on the role of agency. The net effect is that an inordinate amount of time is spent on ensuring that the right candidates get into positions of influence in both the ruling party and the state. What this strategic perspective ignores is the need for a competitive political party system at this historical juncture that will make political elites accountable to their citizens, and thereby create the political condition for human-oriented development.

But how is this political condition to be created? What are the precise actions, behaviour, reforms and strategies that could generate the substantive uncertainty which has been identified as so essential?

Structural reforms for human-oriented development

Even if the need for a substantive uncertainty is recognised, how is it to be created in South Africa at this moment? Of course the character of the contemporary international system is unlikely to assist in this regard. Not only are the impulses to substantive uncertainty severely weakened as a result of the erosion of the bipolar world of the Cold War, but the economic and technological transformation of the last two decades, hitherto captured by the term 'globalisation', has also strengthened predictability through a concentration of power in favour of transnational capital and international financial agencies and to the disadvantage of national political elites and marginalised social groups (Marglin and Schor, 1992). Neither a revolution nor a national revolt, on the scale of that which occurred in South Africa in the 1980s or in Malaysia in 1969, is on the cards for the foreseeable future. After all, the ANC for now still commands overwhelming support in the country. The revolts that do spontaneously occur, although numerous, are sporadic, localised, and largely concerned with accessing rights and do not constitute an immediate political challenge to national elites (Ballard, Habib and Valodia, 2006). Substantive uncertainty has to be created within the framework of the current democratic political system, which is not only an advance on apartheid, but also the product of the endeavours of poor and working people.

There is a long tradition of thought in progressive and socialist circles on how to advance the interests of workers and the poor within democratic non-socialist contexts. The most recent scholarly exercise on South Africa in this regard was undertaken by John Saul who, following Boris Kagarlitsky, essentially made the case for what he termed structural reform, that is reforms that have a snowballing effect and facilitate the emergence of other reforms, all of which collectively constitute a project of self-transformation. In addition, such reforms are, in Saul's words, 'rooted in popular initiatives in such a way as to leave a residue of further empowerment – in terms of growing enlightenment/class consciousness, in terms of organizational capacity – for the vast mass of the population, who thus strengthen themselves for further struggles, further victories' (Saul, 1991: 6). But Saul floundered when he came to specifying the reforms defined as structural. Caught up in the euphoria of the transition, and the rhetoric of intellectuals, progressive academics and union leaders, he proceeded to give credence to a whole slew of policies, both economic and other, that could hardly be described as transformative (Desai and Habib, 1994).

Nevertheless, Saul's conceptual departure point, structural reform, can be usefully harnessed to an understanding of how to advance a human-oriented development trajectory. For reforms to warrant the title 'structural' they must enhance the leverage of working and marginalised communities, diffuse power in favour of these social groups in society, and promote the substantive uncertainty of political elites.[4] What actions, behaviours, policy reforms and strategies can advance this agenda? Of course these have to be determined in a contextually specific manner. They must emanate from a concrete analysis of a spatial context in a specific time. And for South Africa, in this historical period, five decisions, developments or reforms can be identified.

1. Reform of the electoral system

Electoral reform would go a long way to enhancing citizens' leverage over political elites. Presently, the proportional electoral system enables the representation of a maximum number of political parties. This positive feature, however, is counterbalanced by a negative, the empowerment of the party leadership over rank-and-file legislative representatives. Given that electoral votes are cast for the party rather than individual candidates, and that the parliamentary list is largely determined by the party leadership, the accountability dynamic of legislative representatives to their constituencies is severely weakened. Indeed, accountability is structured hierarchically to party leaders, which has the consequence of ensuring that individual legislative representatives are conditioned to act not with their conscience, but in line with party diktat.

These consequences have prompted a number of civic actors and political parties to call for an overhaul of the electoral system. Indeed, the Slabbert Commission appointed in May 2002 to investigate the issue recommended that the electoral system be changed to a Mixed Member Proportional System (MMP) with 75% of legislative representatives elected from 69 multi-member constituencies, while the remainder would come from the party list to ensure overall proportionality in accordance with the mandate of the Constitution.[5] This recommendation reflected, according to the majority on the Slabbert Commission, a popular view that while the national-list PR system was fair and representative, it did not enable individual legislators to be accountable to the voters (Mattes and Southall, 2004). The express purpose of the majority recommendation of the commission was to enhance the leverage of citizens over their representatives and contribute to a political system that generates a substantive uncertainty on the part of its political elites. It should be noted that this majority view was contested by a minority report, which found in favour of the status quo, a recommendation that was ultimately accepted by the ANC government.

2. *Establishment of a viable competitive political system*

At present, South Africa has all the institutional characteristics of a robust democratic political order. Yet its political system cannot be regarded as competitive. This is not only because the ANC is overwhelmingly dominant in terms of electoral support, but also because it has increased its margin of support in three consecutive national elections.[6] Even more important is the fact that the largest opposition parties are unable to serve as serious competitors to the ruling party because their support base is largely constructed among minority racial groups. As a result, not only does a viable political system not exist, but it also has no prospect of emerging from the collection of parties that are currently represented in the national legislature (Habib and Taylor, 2001).

The only way a competitive political system will be established is if the Tripartite Alliance was to fracture or the ANC itself was to split. Until recently both of these outcomes were not deemed to be realistic, at least in the short term. This was because most analysts before Polokwane, myself included, believed that an organisational break would only emerge with Cosatu and the SACP splitting from the ANC. Yet this was seriously opposed not only by the leadership of these organisations but also by some of the leading lights in the progressive academic establishment.

Two objections were often made when this idea of a break in the Alliance was ever raised. First, it was feared that leaving the Alliance would enable the upper classes, both black and white, to have free rein in determining the policy agenda of the ruling party (Marais, 2001). This, however, was to make the assumption that policy influence is only exerted through participation in internal forums. Yet as many studies demonstrate, policies can as easily be influenced by extra-institutional action or the external deployment of other forms of leverage by social actors within society. With regard to the latter, it is worth noting that capital was able to influence the ANC's policy after 1996 without much substantive presence within the party itself (Habib and Padayachee, 2000). Finally, as Cosatu and the SACP themselves would recognise, the alliance with the ruling party did not prevent for the first decade of South Africa's transition a slide to what they perceive as neo-liberalism.

Second, a possible break in the Tripartite Alliance was often dismissed on the grounds that the overwhelming majority of workers and shop stewards preferred the Alliance to continue. This preference was articulated not only by the leadership of Cosatu and the SACP, but by a group of scholars loosely associated with the Sociology of Work Programme (Swop) in the University of the Witwatersrand, who have demonstrated over three surveys in the last decade that more than two-thirds of Cosatu's rank and file are supportive of the Alliance (Buhlungu, 2006). A mere resort to survey data, however, cannot replace analysis. Demonstrating that a majority of workers are supportive of the Alliance does not address the issue of whether a break could strategically advance the agenda of the working and unemployed poor.[7] All it showed was that the subjective will for the Alliance did not yet exist. After all, it is worth noting that majorities have been known to support inappropriate or even incorrect strategic perspectives.[8]

In any case, instead of occurring as a result of a walkout by Cosatu and the SACP, the split within the ANC seems to have been initiated by people on the right of the political centre, by some of the defeated Mbeki-ites – Mosiuoa Lekota, Sam Shilowa and Mluleki George – who have decided that their political future lies in an independent parliamentary opposition. Yet the emergence of a viable parliamentary opposition cannot be taken for granted even if it arises from within the ruling party. There have been similar splits before and they have all petered out. But none has arisen from such deep and serious fissures within the ANC, and none has involved such a formidable collective of national political figures. Nevertheless, if this political initiative is to be significant and sustainable, then it will have to overcome four serious challenges.

- The establishment of a viable opposition party is going to require seriously deep financial pockets. Shilowa has indicated that this is not a problem, and South Africa's political rumour mill suggests that a number of BEE giants, Saki Macozoma, Mzi Khumalo and Khaya Ngqula in-

cluded, also support this initiative. Even if this is true, however, the question has to be asked if these BEE entrepreneurs will be in for the long haul, as would be necessary if this initiative is to be successful.
- The successful launch of this political alternative is going to require a national organisational infrastructure. To date, Lekota, Shilowa and others have tried to work off the ANC's institutional base, which explains why the leadership moved so quickly to isolate them. But now that they are on their own, the success of the initiative depends on how many of the ANC branches and provinces will throw in their lot with them. At present it does seem as if they will have some footprint in the Eastern, Northern and Western Cape. In addition, they will need at least a significant presence in the Free State, Gauteng, Limpopo, Mpumalanga, North West, and a small existence in KwaZulu-Natal if they are to be perceived as serious national actors.
- The political initiative would need to be supported by a wider array of national figures. Lekota and Shilowa are formidable political actors in their own right. But the initiative would get a great boost if Mbeki were to give it his public blessing, which he now has decided not to do. In fact, he has publicly come out against the initiative. Given this, a wider array of figures in the Mbeki camp need to be seen supporting this initiative not only to contradict the view of it as an attempt by disgruntled political leaders to hang on to power, but also if it is to carry the necessary liberation pedigree and have legitimacy among older members of South Africa's black population.
- Finally, the political alternative has to go beyond personalities and root itself in a distinct policy agenda. To date, the breakaway has been presented as a separation compelled by personality differences or unhappiness with the leadership of the ANC for not sharing the spoils of office equitably. Obviously this promotes the view of its origin in a rupture among political elites to advance their own interests and lays the initiative open to the charge that it is being driven by ambitious politicians who cannot come to terms with the outcome of internal party processes. If it is to go beyond this, the political alternative has to root itself in a policy programme and a track record distinct from that claimed by the Zuma leadership within the ANC.

Perhaps the greatest prospect for the initiative lies in the hands of the current leadership of the ANC. This might seem an odd conclusion to arrive at but it is worth noting that the political challenge only became a reality because the existing ANC leadership underestimated the consequences of driving Mbeki from office. If a triumphalist attitude continues to prevail within the post-Polokwane leadership of the ANC, and if sufficient bridges are not built between the two camps within the organisation, then the political alternative is likely to grow if only because 'dissidents' have no other option. It does seem as if leaders like Kgalema Motlanthe and even Jacob Zuma are aware of the threat, but there is also a strong strand within the leadership that responds to challenge and contestation with disciplinary hearings and expulsions. Obviously a balance has to be struck between maintaining internal political plurality and disciplining individuals for using the structures of the organisation against itself. But if an appropriate balance is not achieved, as seems to be the case currently, then the leadership may be creating the conditions for a serious challenge at the polls.

Such a challenge will also be hastened by the political behaviour of the current leadership of the ANC. These same political actors who played such a useful role just a year ago by introducing political plurality and thereby a substantive uncertainty have now begun to make decisions and behave in ways that introduce institutional uncertainty into the political system. They have attacked the National Prosecuting Authority, the courts and even individual judges. As a result they have begun to delegitimise the institutions of justice and other state structures. Some of their inflammatory statements about resorting to killing if the courts do not find in their favour not only entrench a culture of violence, but also undermine the rule of law. Also, the new political elite's decision to continue treating state positions as the spoils of war blurs the divide between party and state and undermines the very foundation of democracy.

While some of these decisions and behaviours may serve their short-term political and personal goals, others will come to haunt ANC leaders in the future when they occupy political office. It needs to be borne in mind that economic development, service delivery and poverty alleviation are dependent on a state with legitimacy and capacity. Behaviour that undermines the legitimacy and capacity of state institutions will compromise the new political elite's own long-term goals. Moreover, it may even alienate potential voters from the ANC. While previously the leadership could afford to remain complacent, this will no longer be the case if Lekota and Shilowa get their political alternative off the ground. Perhaps the greatest contribution that these two will bequeath South Africa is that, by creating a viable political alternative, one rooted in all of South Africa's population, they will make it difficult for political elites to take the country's citizenry for granted. And therein lies the potential for strengthening democratic accountability in South Africa.

3. The erosion of the corporatist institutions and processes that evolved in the 1990s

This is probably treasonous to argue given the ideological orthodoxy that has developed in favour of corporatism in both the academy and the public sector. But it is worth bearing in mind that corporatism facilitated social democracy in Western Europe in particular because of the Keynesian macroeconomic environment, itself a product of a particular configuration of power in the global order (Maier, 1984: 49; Panitch, 1986). Its presence in a more neo-liberal economic climate is therefore unlikely to lead to the same outcome. Indeed, as Przeworski (1991) maintained, corporatist institutions can become mechanisms of co-optation in the present era, enforcing a predictability that distracts political elites from accountability to their citizens.

The alternative, of course, need not involve a pristine non-engagement or a wish for revolutionary rupture as corporatist advocates often caricature it. Indeed, it may simply involve the establishment of a pluralist labour system, similar to that existing in the United States, where participation and negotiations are not institutionalised and governed by formal political rules or by a broader public discourse that stresses the necessity of partnerships among conflicting social forces. Rather, the negotiations that do occur are simply the outcome of the everyday interplay and contested engagements of social actors in the economic and market arena. It would be useful to note of course that this pluralist labour system has precedents in South Africa; it existed in the 1980s, and its reintroduction can only compel the organised expressions of workers and the poor to focus on a politics of power in which collective organisation forms its essential component.[9]

4. The emergence of a robust civil society

Related but distinct from this is the emergence of an independent, robust, plural civil society. Already there has been much progress made in this regard. In two separate reflections on the issue, I have argued that not only has civil society been fundamentally transformed in the post-1994 era, but that sections of it are also having a dramatic systemic impact by contributing to a substantive uncertainty that makes elites more responsive, at least partially, to the concerns of poor and marginalised citizens. The first of these reflections, entitled 'State–Civil Society Relations in Post-Apartheid South Africa', essentially demonstrated that political democratisation and economic liberalisation have essentially transformed an ostensibly homogeneous, black, progressive, anti-apartheid civil society into one composed of at least three distinct blocs – NGOs, survivalist agencies and social movements – all with very distinct relationships with the state. It concluded that the 'diverse roles and functions undertaken by [these] different elements of civil society, then, collectively create the adversarial and collaborative relationships, the push and pull effects, which sometimes assist and other times compel the state to meet its obligations and responsibilities to its citizenry' (Habib, 2005). The second contribution, co-edited with Richard Ballard and Imraan Valodia, focused on post-apartheid social movements, maintaining that they 'contribute to the restoration of political plurality in the political system', facilitate 'the accountability of state elites to our citizenry', and 'contribute to the emergence of a political climate that prompted government's recent shift to a more state interventionist and expansive economic policy with a more welfarist orientation' (Ballard, Habib and Valodia, 2006). These developments have the effect of what Jeremy Cronin recently termed enabling a popular agency, necessary for the dispersal of power, which at least makes possible the emergence of a more human-oriented development trajectory.[10]

5. A strategic foreign policy

Finally, a strategic foreign policy can be instrumental in establishing the political space and enhancing the capacity of national stakeholders, including its political elites, to pursue a human-oriented development. The literature review undertaken above of the political conditions under which elites become responsive to their citizens clearly indicates that a contested international environment defined by rivalry among global elites and great powers is positive for human-oriented development. Moreover, it suggests that resource endowments, such as mineral wealth, strategic location and even population size, can become a useful leverage for national political elites in their engagements with their foreign and global counterparts.[11] The application of these lessons to the South African case involves two elements. First, it requires South Africa to undertake the role of leadership in the continent or, in the words of the international relations literature, to play the role of benevolent hegemon which prioritises not only stability, democracy and economic development, but also the development of regional and continental common markets. These increases in market size can greatly enhance the leverage of national and continental politicians in their relations with other actors in the global economy, and can be particularly favourable for attracting foreign investment. Second, it requires South Africa to prioritise multilateral institutions and endeavours and strategic alliances both within the South and between Northern and Southern countries in order to contain the unilateralism of the United States and that of big economic powers when they act in concert, as often happens in global trade negotiations.[12]

Some of these roles are already being undertaken by South Africa. It has increasingly begun to play the role of regional and continental hegemon, even if done unevenly and sometimes reluctantly (Habib and Nthakeng, 2006).[13] South Africa has also played a role in multilateral institution-building both at the continental and international levels. Moreover, it has begun to prioritise strategic alliances, as in the case of the India–Brazil–South Africa partnership and the Group of 20, both of which were crucial in preventing, particularly in the trade negotiations in Cancún, an unfair trade deal being imposed on the countries of the South.[14]

Yet despite these successes, there are significant weaknesses in some of South Africa's foreign policy engagements. First, it has to prioritise South–North strategic alliances, in addition to the South–South ones, if power is to be significantly dispersed in the global setting and development opportunities for the South are to be maximised. Second, some of South Africa's politicians have to learn to transcend their market fundamentalism so apparent in some of the documentation of Nepad (Bond, 2004), their refusal to regulate South African investment on the continent (Habib and Nthakeng, 2006), and the almost timid reforms undertaken in respect of the IMF and World Bank. It is useful to note that the current success story of China is not simply one of its resort to the market, but also its pragmatism in manipulating the market, through a fixed currency for instance, to suit its own ends (Breslin, 2006). Third, South Africa's foreign policy practitioners and trade negotiators need to become bolder in their engagements. This would involve a greater willingness to involve South Africa in the politics of brinkmanship, as occurred in Cancún, and in engaging global civil society, which could be far better engaged than at present to advance a human-oriented development agenda. Finally, none of this would be possible without more significant capacity being built in respect of both technical skills within state institutions, and the internalisation of these strategic perspectives among state personnel far beyond the narrow band that currently occupies the presidential and foreign policy apparatus (Alden and Le Pere, 2004).

In any case, the five developments or reforms suggested above are not meant to be an exhaustive list. Many more may be conceived as relevant. To earn the title of 'structural', however, all must be directed to dispersing power so as to make elites substantively uncertain of their futures, a necessary political precondition for establishing a shift to a more human-oriented development trajectory.

Conclusion

It is worth noting that the strategies and policies recommended here suggest that not only is human-oriented development the product of a political process, but it requires an intricate mix of representative and participatory democratic elements. The first two strategic and policy reforms are intended to strengthen the representative character of the political system so as to promote a contestation between political elites. The second two speak to strengthening the participatory character of the political system, to facilitate what Friedman (2005) has so often termed 'providing voice to the poor'. This mix of representative and participatory democratic elements is meant to create the substantive uncertainty which is the political foundation for the accountability between elites and their citizens so necessary for realising a human-oriented development agenda. The political programme then challenges the perspectives of those who view participatory and representative democracy as distinct political systems. The view advanced here argues that it is the intricate mix of participatory and representative elements that enhances the accountability of political elites to their citizens.

The role of substantive uncertainty in facilitating a more ideologically diverse public discourse and a reconsideration of policy is also evident in the succession crisis within the ANC. A number of public commentators have indicated that one of the positive consequences of the contest between Mbeki and Zuma has been the opening up of the policy discourse in particular on AIDS, the macroeconomy, and Zimbabwe (Friedman, 2006). Yet, as I argued in a panel debate with Aubrey Matshiqi and Steven Friedman at the Institute of Security Studies (ISS), this openness is vulnerable and unlikely to be sustainable so long as it is premised on a contest between two leaders in the ruling party. For it to be truly sustainable, the uncertainty must be institutionalised within the political system as a whole.[15] And now, for the first time, South Africa has a real possibility that such an institutionalisation could occur through the establishment of Lekota's and Shilowa's political initiative, which could compete with the ANC for the allegiance of the country's entire electorate. But this has not yet happened.

In any case, this contradiction will never be resolved by clever technocrats in rational conversation. It will be fundamentally determined by the configuration of power and how it evolves over the next few years. This, then, is one of the principal lessons to be learnt from some of the comparative development experiences across the world. South Africa has had some policy shifts in recent years that have benefited poor and marginalised communities. But if their interests are to be addressed more fully, this cannot be done through rational conversation between policy technocrats. It will only happen when power is dispersed and reconfigured in the social setting, political elites are made substantively uncertain of their futures, accountability is thereby re-established between them and citizens, and policy as a result becomes responsive to the interests of the poor and marginalised.

Notes

1 The structural adjustment literature of the World Bank, especially in the 1980s, was typical of this.
2 There are some scholars who are critical of this perspective. Raymond Suttner, for instance, in response to some of the democratisation literature on dominant parties, accuses 'experts' who stressed the necessity of elite contestation as being 'dogmatic ... deeply conservative ... [and supporting] a specific version of democracy, that of formal, representative democracy without substantial social and economic transformation or significant popular involvement'. The problem with this view of course is that it sets up a false divide between representative and participatory forms of democracy.
3 For some of these scholars like O'Donnell, it was the then recent memory of authoritarian rule which prompted them to recommend political caution, lest the transition be disrupted. This caution, however, led to a set of political dynamics that facilitated the rise of illiberal or delegative democracies. See Habib and Padayachee, 2000.
4 It is worth noting that this perspective is similar to that articulated by the SACP. In part two of its controversial discussion document released by its Central Committee in May 2006, entitled 'Class Struggles and the Post-1994 State in South Africa', the SACP argues that 'if it is to have any prospect of addressing the dire legacy of colonial dispossession and apartheid oppression, a national democratic strategy has to be revolutionary, that is to say, it must systemically transform class, racial, and gendered power...'. This is not new. For instance, the

slogan adopted by the SACP at its 1995 strategy conference, 'Socialism is the Future: Build it Now', reflects similar sentiments.
5   Cosatu is in favour of the general recommendation, although it suggests that the proportion between constituency and party list be 65% and 35% respectively.
6   Its support is just shy of 70%, up from 66.36% and 62.65% in 1999 and 1964 respectively. Although critics sometimes qualify this point by noting that voter turnout in national elections has declined to 76%, down from 88% in 1999, this should not detract from the fact that the party has increasingly consolidated its electoral support in the country.
7   This is the peculiar logic that has become common in this debate. See a number of the chapters in Buhlungu, 2006.
8   Ultimately, Jeremy Cronin, deputy general secretary of the SACP and chairperson of the Transport portfolio in the national legislature, is probably correct to recognise that were the Alliance to break, it would not do so neatly, but would probably fracture almost all of the constituent units. But then political and social advance is often a messy affair, and it is precisely the acrimony and broken relationships that give rise to the substantive uncertainty of elites, which is so necessary for a policy agenda responsive to the interests of working and poor communities. Is this likely to happen? Almost certainly, not in the short term. As indicated earlier, the political will among both the leaders and their supporters just does not exist currently for such a radical course of action. It may, however, in the future. The problem is whether Cosatu and the SACP will at that point be sufficiently viable so as to constitute an alternative political pole of attraction.
9   Cosatu has itself begun to reflect on the organisational lessons of its practice of the 1980s, although it is careful to acknowledge that this experience must not be romanticised.
10 He suggested this at a seminar, hosted by the Centre for Conflict Resolution (CCR) of the University of Cape Town on 18 October 2006, where he served as a discussant in a presentation I made on our co-edited book on social movements, *Voices of Protest*.
11 Note, for instance, how China has used population and therefore market size as a leverage to attract foreign investment.
12 Note, for instance, the coincidence of interests on agricultural subsidies that prevailed for so long between the US and Europe in the World Trade negotiations.
13 There are of course scholars who dislike the term 'hegemon', preferring instead to describe South Africa as a pivotal state.
14 The negotiations ended in stalemate and generated enormous criticism of both the US and Europe and increased pressure on them from domestic stakeholders to reconsider their positions.
15 Panel discussion on the theme 'The Presidential Succession and the Tripartite Alliance', hosted by the Institute for Security Studies (ISS), Pretoria, 14 September 2006.

References

Alden, C. and G. le Pere. 2004. South Africa's Post-Apartheid Foreign Policy: From Reconciliation to Ambiguity. *Review of African Political Economy*, 31 (100), 283–297

Ballard, R., A. Habib and I. Valodia (eds.). 2006. *Voices of Protest: Social Movements in Post-Apartheid South Africa*. UKZN Press, Pietermaritzburg

Bond, P. 2004. *Talk Left, Walk Right: South Africa's Frustrated Global Reforms*. UKZN Press, Pietermaritzburg

Breslin, S. 2006. Interpreting Chinese Power in the Global Political Economy. Paper presented to the Conference on Regional Powers in Asia, Africa, Latin America and the Middle East, hosted by the German Institute of Global and Area Studies (GIGA), 11–12 December 2006

Buhlungu, S. 2006. *Trade Unions and Politics: Cosatu Workers after 10 Years of Democracy*. HSRC Press, Cape Town

Cosatu. 2003. Resolutions of the Cosatu 8th National Congress, Electoral System, Part 5

Cosatu. 2006. Cosatu Political Discussion Document: Possibilities for Fundamental Change. Paper prepared for the 9th National Congress, 18–21 September 2006

Dahl, R.A. 1966. *Political Oppositions in Western Democracies*. Yale University Press, New Haven

Desai, A. and A. Habib. 1994. Social Movements in Transitional Societies: A Case Study of the Congress of South African Trade Unions. *South African Sociological Review*, 6 (2), 68–88

Evans, P. 1995. *Embedded Autonomy: States and Industrial Transformation*. Princeton University Press, Princeton

Friedman, S. 2005. South Africa. In J.S. Tulchin and G. Bland (eds.), *Getting Globalization Right: The Dilemmas of Inequality*. Lynne Rienner, Boulder, Co.

Friedman, S. 2006. Spring of Hope, Winter of Worry for South African Democracy. *Business Day*, 6 September 2006

Habib, A. 2005. State–Civil Society Relations in Post-Apartheid South Africa. *Social Research*, 72 (3), 671–692

Habib, A. and S. Nthakeng. 2006. Constraining the Unconstrained: Civil Society and South Africa's Hegemonic Obligations in Africa. In Walter Carlsnaes and Philip Nel (eds.), *In Full Flight: South African Foreign Policy after Apartheid*. Institute for Global Dialogue, Midrand

Habib, A. and R. Taylor. 2001. Political Alliances and Parliamentary Opposition in South Africa. *Democratization*, 8 (1), 207-226

Habib, A. and V. Padayachee. 2000. Economic Policy and Power Relations in South Africa's Transition to Democracy. *World Development*, 28 (2), 245–263

Huntington, S. 1991. *The Third Wave: Democratization in the Late Twentieth Century*. University of Oklahoma Press, Oklahoma

Maier, C. 1984. Preconditions for Corporatism. In J. Goldthorpe (ed.), *Order and Conflict in Contemporary Capitalism*. Clarendon Press, Oxford

Marais, H. 2001. *South Africa: Limits to Change: The Political Economy of Transition.* Zed Books, London

Marglin, S. and J. Schor. 1992. *Golden Age of Capitalism: Reinterpreting the Post-War Experience.* Oxford University Press, Oxford

Mattes, R. and R. Southall. 2004. Popular Attitudes towards the South African Electoral System. *Democratisation,* 11 (1), 51–76

O'Donnell, G. 1993. On the State, Democratization and Some Conceptual Problems: A Latin American View with Glances at Some Post-Communist Countries. *World Development,* 21 (8), 1355–1369

O'Donnell, G. 1994. Delegative Democracy. *Journal of Democracy,* 5, 55–69

O'Donnell, G. and P. Schmitter. 1986. *Transitions from Authoritarian Rule: Tentative Conclusions about Uncertain Democracies,* vol. 4. Johns Hopkins University Press, Baltimore

Panitch, L. 1986. *Working Class Politics in Crisis: Essays on Labor and the State.* Verso, London

PCAS. 1986. The Presidency, Towards a Ten Year Review: Synthesis Report on Implementation of Government Programmes, October 1986

Przeworski, A. 1991. *Democracy and the Market.* Cambridge University Press, Cambridge

SACP. 2006a. Class, National and Gender Struggle in South Africa: The Historical Relationship between the ANC and the SACP, Part 1. *Bua Komanisi,* Special Edition, May 2006, 3–16

SACP. 2006b. Class Struggles and the Post-1994 State in South Africa, Part 2. *Bua Komanisi,* Special Edition, May 2006, 16–31

Saul, J. 1991. South Africa: Between 'Barbarism' and 'Structural' Reform'. *New Left Review,* 188

Schedler, A. 2001. Taking Uncertainty Seriously: The Blurred Boundaries of Democratic Transition and Consolidation. *Democratisation,* 8 (4), 1–22

Schmitter, P. 1974. Still the Century of Corporatism. *Review of Politics,* 36 (1), 85–131.

Sen, Amartya. 1999. Democracy as a Universal Value. *Journal of Democracy,* 10 (3)

Stepan, A. 1978. *The State and Society: Peru in Comparative Perspective.* Princeton University Press, Princeton

Wiarda, H. 1981. *Corporatism and National Development in Latin America.* Westview Press, Boulder, Co.

11

The role of the state

Raymond Parsons

> A middle course is best,
> Not poor not proud;
> But this, by no clear rule defined,
> Eludes the unstable, undiscerning mind,
> Whose aim will surely miss.
> – *Euripides,* The Oresteia

> State intervention is like the little girl who had a little curl right in the middle of her forehead: when she was good, she was very, very good; and when she was bad, she was absolutely horrid.'
> – *David Landes*

What constitutes good government has vexed political philosophers, and more lately economists, for centuries. The American republican John Adams believed that of all the arts the only one not to have improved since ancient Athens was that of politics. Citizens and their leaders so often blunder into folly, knowing it as folly and yet somehow unable to escape it. Perhaps this suggests that we should abandon Plato's question 'Who shall rule us?' and focus instead on Karl Popper's question 'How can we stop our rulers from ruining us?' Certainly in recent decades there has been ample literature, empirical evidence and 'growth diagnostics' available to help us in answering some questions around good governance and the creation of prosperity.

Yet the biggest puzzle in economic development remains why sustained economic growth is so hard to achieve. Indeed, in the early 1970s the late Professor Harry Johnson once remarked that 'growth economics merely describes what happens when economic growth occurs; it does not explain *why* economic growth occurs' (Allen, 2000: 15). This is also reflected in the fact that only a handful of the world's two hundred economies have discovered how to do it for the majority of their citizens, and a single successful formula remains elusive.

More recently, commenting on an evaluation of the latest World Bank World Development Report (WDR), a leading economic publication says:

> Despite the bank's best efforts, economic growth remains a mystery: no one really knows why some countries sustain it over decades and others do not. Bill Easterly of New York University criticises the WDR for not helping poor countries decide what to do when things are so uncertain. That may seem harsh, given that the reports have contributed more than their fair share to the world's stock of knowledge. Thanks to them, economists now know much more about what does not work. But it is not so clear they understand any better what does. (*The Economist*, 24 January 2009: 62)

And in country after country where there *has* been significant growth, policy-makers continue to worry about distributional outcomes. Across a range of economies, including South Africa, higher growth rates have reduced poverty but have been accompanied by rising inequality. The media and others rightly refer to 'those left behind' and to 'bringing more people into the mainstream of the economy'. We know that South Africa's unemployment and inequality levels are among the highest in the world. What can or should be done to address these concerns without endangering growth performance? How do we resolve this conundrum? What, if any, are the trade-offs? These have been relevant questions for high-growth countries – as well as for South Africa seeking to *accelerate* its growth rate in the years ahead.

What of the role of the state? It is safe to say that politics over the past century has been heavily shaped by controversies over the appropriate size and strength of the state. States have a wide variety of functions, for good or ill. And the state in South Africa? In an emerging market like South Africa the relationship has to be carefully defined, based on the country's stage of growth, as well as the capacity of the state to deliver. In addition, it must be emphasised that South Africa's public policy choices are *not* between economic growth and social equity, but should be based on a recognition that economic growth facilitates social equity and vice versa. There *is* a virtuous circle possible of economic growth and social equity on a sustainable basis.

That said, and given that the development strategies articulated by the South African government of the democratic era since 1994 have been oriented to improving the lot of the historically disadvantaged majority black population, the most disappointing aspect of post-apartheid economic performance is the emergence and persistence of extreme levels of unemployment, particularly for less-skilled younger blacks, together with the continuation of widespread poverty and the widening of inequalities. The failure to bring unemployment down decisively is probably the greatest source of popular discontent about the government's economic policies, despite numerous other successes, and it naturally leads to pressure to try more radical and activist solutions which risk being wasteful and counterproductive.

'Everything of importance has been said before, by someone who did not discover it.' Philosopher A.N. Whitehead's dictum is probably true of growth policy for South Africa. Many would argue that by now we should *know* much more about what needs to be done. From the RDP (1994), Gear (1996), the Jobs Summit (1998), the Growth and Development Summit (2003), Asgisa (2005), the analysis of the Harvard Group as well as the HSRC, OECD and the Growth Reports (2007/8) – everything that needs to be done in South Africa has been pronounced upon again and again. Leaving aside exogenous factors, our growth has been held back not by our lack of imagination but by our unwillingness – or inability – to follow through with much of what we have decided needs to be done, and by a refusal to accept responsibility when there is a failure of delivery. It is now time to 'walk the talk' more convincingly.

The Asgisa approach is broadly appropriate

Both the Harvard Group (Hausmann, 2008) and the OECD Report (2008) support the approach by Asgisa of identifying 'binding constraints' that inhibit higher rates of sustained economic growth in South Africa. They agree that the key constraints have been appropriately identified. The Harvard Group puts forward 21 specific recommendations for addressing these constraints. The OECD Report is more indirect and focuses on much broader aspects of economic policy. Three areas of economic policy which need attention are identified: education, competition policy, and deregulation and labour markets.

The Report then concentrates on justifying why these three areas need attention and what benefits could flow, rather than on identifying the specific policy instruments necessary for their attainment. The Growth Report (CGD, 2008) is more nuanced in its approach. Its analysis of the 13 high-growth economies globally indicates that policy lessons are not always consistent. What worked in one country in a particular time often failed elsewhere at a different time. Policy flexibility and experimentation, it concludes, are key lessons to be drawn from global experience.

While accepting the goals identified by Asgisa, the OECD Report warns that the policy instruments suggested (including the Harvard Group's 21 specific recommendations) are often too weak to address the identified constraints. For example, Asgisa focuses on some aspects of employee training but offers little to improve basic education – whereas the OECD believes the greatest return actually lies in this area. Some policy prescriptions, the OECD notes, are contradictory; e.g. while Asgisa emphasises the need for increasing competition, industrial policy runs the risk of preserving the apartheid-era pattern of protected national champions insulated from foreign competition and enjoying high mark-ups. If the overall thrust of these various studies and programmes is broadly accepted by policy-makers in South Africa, the prospect is opened of improving the existing system without any drastic upheaval.

Most importantly, the OECD Report warns that there is a contradiction between the weaknesses of state capacity to support economic development identified in Asgisa and the emphasis on state programmes and policies to address the same constraints. It notes also the 'striking' lack of policies to improve the functioning of the labour market despite very high levels of unemployment. Asgisa, in the OECD's view, correctly identifies a shortage of skilled labour as a problem but fails to address the problem of how to deal with the far larger number of people who are jobless.

It remains a central choice facing all societies to decide on the role of the state. Economic success requires getting the balance right between government and the market in country-specific circumstances. South Africa has a 'mixed economy', in which both the private and public sectors have their respective roles to play. Economic prosperity is not guaranteed by what is called 'the market' but would be impossible without it. If markets are to work well, the stable and favourable socio-economic environment they need must include a wide range of services which have to be provided largely by the state, including a regulatory framework where appropriate.

The OECD points out that the state remains an important player in the economy, not only through regulation and the provision of goods and services, but also with its ownership of substantial productive assets. According to official data, about 43% of the country's capital stock was in the hands of the state and municipal authorities at the end of 2006 – concentrated mainly in capital-intensive sectors such as mining, defence industries, the power sector and utilities.

State control in South Africa has nonetheless in recent years advanced considerably in the form of an unprecedented volume of new legislation from both Parliament and other levels of government. While parliamentary officials sometimes boast of the number of new laws passed by Parliament annually, the emphasis should really be on quality rather than quantity. And the compliance costs on business, especially small business, in constantly having to adapt to changing legal requirements have become extremely onerous. 'A closely linked but different issue', adds the OECD, 'relates to the instability of the regulatory framework: high regulatory uncertainty may indeed prove as problematic as the regulatory burden, in particular if combined with weak administrative capacities' (CGD, 2008: 65–6). Surveys have also shown that in South Africa almost one-fifth of businesspeople consider policy uncertainty as a major or severe constraint on investment and growth.

Is this really a successful 'mix'? A large part of the answer depends on the flexibility of the private enterprise system in South Africa, a matter about which we can entertain a fair degree of confidence, especially with the steady emergence of new black entrepreneurs. But much of it depends on the wisdom of official policy, and especially on how far the state will facilitate or hinder the functioning of private enterprise, a matter about which recent experience gives much less ground for confidence. What are the challenges here?

Role of the state

When we refer to the role of the state and its performance, it is important to understand what exactly is meant by these concepts. The World Bank (1997: 20) has defined the state, in its broader sense, as 'a set of institutions that possess the means of legitimate coercion, exercised over a defined territory and its population, referred to as a society'. The state executes policy-making through the medium of an organised government. When the government is less well organised, government failure occurs, which Dollery (2003: 90) defines as 'the inability of public agencies to achieve their intended aims'.

Referring to the research done by Michael O'Dowd in 1978, Dollery specifies three so-called types of government failure, namely inherent impossibilities (where government attempts to do the impossible, such as enforcing apartheid); political failures (where what is attempted is possible in theory but owing to political constraints is impossible in practice), and bureaucratic failure (in cases where government has the intention of implementing a policy, but the administrative capacity to implement it in accordance with its stated policies is fundamentally lacking). While there may be examples of the first type of failure (e.g. implementation of inappropriate labour policies while trying to reduce unemployment), it is bureaucratic failure that has proved to be the Achilles heel of public sector efficiency and delivery in South Africa.

This also raises the pertinent question whether from the standpoint of economic efficiency it is more important to enlarge state scope or increase state strength. International evidence suggests that state *strength* is more important than *scope* in determining long-term economic growth rates. And from the perspective of economic history, given the nature of large, lumpy social overhead capital, there was a time when the stage of South Africa's economic development (say, from the 1920s) dictated that the state had to play an extremely important role in the process of building social overhead capital. But how true is this still in 2009? Should there now be a shift in emphasis in the state's role? The present juncture in South Africa's political and business cycle seems a good moment to address this question and seek answers that will better serve the cause of delivery and economic performance in this country.

In this regard it is useful to distinguish between the constraints on future growth presented by 'bottlenecks' and by 'ceilings'. A 'bottleneck' is a short-term phenomenon and can usually be quickly overcome provided the economy is flexible. A high elasticity of supply makes it easier to accommodate unbalanced growth. The pressures created by lack of balance in economic growth may render factors of production, and particularly entrepreneurial decisions, more responsive to economic incentives. Examples might include a shortage of cement or insufficient commercial or industrial property development in a particular region.

A 'ceiling', on the other hand, is usually the result of factors outside the control of the average decision-maker, such as when cost or capacity is controlled by a monopoly or the state, or supply has simply ceased to be readily available at *any* price (e.g. electricity, bulk railway transport or skilled labour). In such cases, economic activity deprived of its complement is bound to be abortive. The 2008 global liquidity crisis, unusually, may have had the characteristics of a 'ceiling', where for several economies lending and borrowing simply seized up. Both ceilings and bottlenecks can arise simply from a failure to plan ahead, but a 'ceiling' is more difficult to address when it is reached.

The 2008 Eskom power outages were a clear example of a 'ceiling' being reached. There is a solution – the construction of more power plants – but this will take a number of years during which our generation margin will remain worryingly tight. Another ceiling to our future growth is the lack of hard skills, especially technical skills. 'Ceilings' or 'binding constraints' are by definition not always easily addressed and the simple fact that they have been recognised in Asgisa and the Joint Initiative for the Promotion of Skills Acquisition (Jipsa) does not mean they have magically gone away.

The OECD Report warns that there is a contradiction between the weaknesses of government identified by Asgisa and the excessive reliance of Asgisa on the state to solve the identified constraints on growth. This does not mean that government is powerless. Both the OECD Report and the Harvard Group desire a proactive role for government in increasing domestic competition and in alleviating poverty. But government's role or ability to 'pick winners' in industrial policy is downplayed by both reports. What matters more for competitiveness is *not* minimal government but competition-enhancing efficient government.

The Growth Report confirms that there is no single recipe for success. But successful countries do share certain characteristics. *Effective* government – not big government or small government – is one of these factors. Successful countries are not those whose governments came up with more brilliant plans than others, but rather those who, as Deng Xiaoping described his approach, 'crossed the river by feeling for the stones'. 'High growth', concludes the Growth Report, 'requires committed, credible, and capable governments ... The high-growth economies typically built their prosperity on sturdy political foundations. Their policy-makers understood that growth does not just happen. It must be consciously chosen as an overarching goal by a country's leadership' (CGD, 2008: 21).

But what politician would *not* choose high growth? In practice many do not, argues the Growth Report, not because they do not want high growth, but because its achievement is difficult. 'In the fast-growing economies', the authors say, 'policymakers understood that successful development entails a decades-long commitment, and a fundamental bargain between the present and the future. Even at very high growth rates of 7–10% it takes decades for a country to make the leap from low to relatively high incomes. During this long period of transition, citizens must forgo consumption today in return for higher standards of living tomorrow. This bargain will be accepted only if the country's policymakers communicate a credible vision of the future and a strategy for getting there. They must be trusted as stewards of the economy and their promises of future rewards must be believed' (CGD, 2008: 26).

In assessing the challenges facing modern governments in the 21st century, former British Prime Minister Tony Blair put it as follows:

> Globalisation is profoundly changing the nature of our society. It forces businesses and people to step up a gear simply to keep abreast with the pace of change: commercial transactions are completed without delay; communications happen instantly; goods can be moved rapidly across huge distances.
>
> Government is not immune to these changes. For it to continue to maintain its legitimacy, it needs to change its outlook radically. The technological innovations driving global change have not just opened up new opportunities for delivering services, but increased people's expectations of what they want from those who serve them.
>
> To meet these challenges the State must provide the same level of customer service as the public have come to expect in every other aspect of their lives. To achieve this, the role of the State is not to control, but to enable. Making modern public services the cornerstone of the enabling state – where the State provides strategic direction not micro-management – requires a transformation of how we deliver our services. (Barber, 2007: 332)

It is therefore necessary that current and future policy-makers in South Africa again ask themselves three key questions:
- What should the state *do*?

- What should the state *not do*?
- How should the state *ensure* that what needs to be done, is done?

Ideally, the answers to these questions should lie in a pragmatic approach. We should not allow the necessity of implementation to become a casualty of ideological fault-lines. Leaving aside the normal anti-cyclical roles of monetary and fiscal policies, we need to unpack the different dimensions of 'stateness' to understand how they relate to economic development. The OECD analysis has highlighted the degree of state ownership and intervention as a major barrier to entry in South Africa. Too many are keener on the grand rhetoric of redefining the state's role than on the practicalities of designing effective and affordable delivery. The mere fact of asking questions opens a range of new possibilities. The demarcation between the public and private sectors must be driven by new practical tools to promote delivery. Most importantly, once it has been decided what government should do itself and ensure is done by others, mechanisms must be put in place to ensure that delivery actually occurs. There is no point in arguing that the state should do something and then not doing it. This is to accept failure upfront.

The delivery challenge

The 2009 ANC election manifesto has argued that the state will be centre-stage in future economic policy. Many economists and businesspeople will agree — but not because they desire or even foresee the state in a massively heroic role in a future 'developmental state' as many others may do. Rather, the success or failure of the state to deliver its core responsibilities will be the key determinant of whether or not we grow at sustainably higher rates of growth in the future. A critical issue therefore facing an emerging market like South Africa is adequate state capacity and finance to implement programmes and projects successfully — and the functions for which the state alone (rightly or wrongly) is solely responsible.

Just as the 'Washington Consensus' in the 1990s failed to assign sufficient importance to the dangers of market liberalisation in the absence of effective institutions, so the advocates of yet further state intervention in South Africa greatly underestimate the high degree of state capacity needed to implement it successfully. The poor track record of state-driven structures like Eskom, the Land Bank and SAA is salutary, and looming crises in health services and water supply management now also seem likely. Crime levels also leave much to be desired. A recent Institute of Security

Studies report (2008) asserts that the state has failed to protect its citizens against crime. As institutional capacity and experience cannot be acquired overnight, we are setting ourselves (and the intended beneficiaries) up for considerable further disappointment and recrimination.

All the evidence suggests that citizens are impatient for change and are sceptical about the collective capacity to deliver. Over the past two years there have been an estimated 2000 civic protests, some violent, about the lack of delivery. Much of the tense dispute about provincial boundaries stems from some municipalities wanting to be in what are perceived to be better service-delivery jurisdictions. It is now more than ever the quality of execution that decides whether funded developmental and other policies bite – and make a difference on the ground. Indeed, looming financial constraints and delivery problems are converging to create formidable challenges here. The issue of affordability will now increasingly occupy centre-stage in the delivery scenario.

And when there is just simply non-delivery there must be accountability and action. Blame is a key component of progress. We need to ask ourselves why it is that, of all government functions, the department that stands head and shoulders above all others in terms of delivery is SARS. Why is it that we are excellent at collecting taxes, which presumably most people do not really want to pay, but are often poor at educating children, who are eager to learn? There are, of course, many excellent schools and many dedicated teachers. But equally there are many schools where nobody passes at all and certainly where nobody passes in the critically needed disciplines of mathematics and science. Is it because at SARS an incentive scheme was put in place to measure and reward delivery, yet there is no distinction between a teacher whose pupils pass and one whose pupils fail?

The argument for introducing market-like pressures (so-called 'quasi-markets') under the right conditions into the public sector is clear – people like choice and efficiency, and a degree of competition drives productivity improvements in other sectors of the economy, so why not in the public sector? Furthermore, as dedicated as bureaucrats and professionals may be, they can never have the degree of concern for users that users have for themselves. The potential benefit for the state of putting the user more in the driver's seat goes beyond improved performance, and also includes the possibility that the 'system' constantly strengthens itself and therefore does not need to be driven ('flogged' as Tony Blair once said), as it does under a command-and-control option.

Successful development is therefore more than a vision and a strategy – ideas have to be converted into policies and projects. If the creation of institutions like the public service's new national leadership and management academy in Pretoria is to be successful, a strong delivery culture needs to be developed or embedded in our public sector – and we need to get beyond crisis management. We need an approach in which the quality and impact of public sector delivery is given overriding priority. In short, meeting the delivery challenge is inextricably linked to the socio-economic goals of any new government in South Africa. Seen as a whole, it would be more realistic – and strike more resonance with the population at large – if we in future speak more about the need for a *delivery state*.

What the 2009 election thus creates is a window of opportunity provided by widespread public interest in the question of governance and public administration. As citizens' expectations of public services have risen, so their confidence in the capacity to deliver has fallen. Levels of cynicism are high but at least our political leaders have recognised the challenge. There is broad political agreement across the major political parties about the need to ensure successful public service delivery and to provide a new set of measures to enable government departments and local government to strengthen their capacity to deliver significantly. The ANC's 2009 election manifesto is committed to a review of the structure of government. The stage South Africa happens to be at in its electoral cycle means that right now the opportunities – and the practical inclination – are there to improve the government machine. What can be done?

In a key study of his efforts to improve public service delivery in the UK made at the request of Tony Blair, Michael Barber (2007: 369) lists the ten lessons learnt and how to make early progress irreversible. At a British cabinet meeting in July 2003 he outlined the following:

- A week may be a long time in politics but five years is unbelievably short.
- Sustained focus on a small number of priorities is essential.
- Flogging a system can no longer achieve goals; reform is the key.
- Nothing is inevitable: 'rising tides' can be turned.
- The numbers are important but not enough; citizens have to see and feel the difference and expectations need to be managed.
- The quality of leadership at every level is decisive.
- Good system design and management underpin progress.
- Getting the second step changed is difficult and requires precision in

tackling variations and promoting best practice.
- Extraordinary discipline and persistence are required to defeat the cynics.
- Grinding our increments is a noble cause ... but where progress is slow, it's even more important for people to understand the strategy.

When asked what his greatest challenge had been as Prime Minister, Harold Macmillan once famously replied, 'Events, dear boy, events.' Although governments are usually driven by events and crises, it is the steady routine of sustained implementation that delivers results. Barber (2007: 333) says that 'stubborn persistence and attention to detail are vastly underestimated in the literature on government and indeed political history'. Good government, as the influential economic journalist Walter Bagehot once noted, is dull government.

South Africa's parliamentary Joint Budget Committee (JBC) recently highlighted the need for more coordinated and integrated planning in the three spheres of government to bring about closer alignment. In evaluating the latest Medium Term Budgetary Policy Statement, the Committee said that 'to ensure coordinated planning, government should consider setting cross-cutting performance indicators for the respective government departments' (*Business Day*, 17.11.2008). It also criticised those departments – such as Water Affairs – where there was evidence of underspending. It seems from successive Auditor-General reports that often we find a situation of 'too much money chasing too little capacity' in the public sector.

In summary, what appears to be needed from the public sector is to build confidence in its strategic thinking, in dealing with poor performance, managing change effectively, learning from mistakes and working across government departments. This tells us that raising the rate of growth in South Africa and achieving a fairer society have much to do with strengthening state capacity where it matters, or otherwise devising new and innovative mechanisms to ensure effective delivery. Policies do matter, but so do the institutions and mechanisms through which they are approved and implemented.

Problem of coordination

The vexed problem of coordination – or a lack of it – in state action is something which both the public and private sectors have also come to recognise as a serious challenge. Among the recent striking examples of poor coordination and interdepartmental conflict have been the electricity crisis (the Department of Mineral and Energy Affairs, the Department of Public Enterprises and Eskom); industrial policy (the Department of Trade and Industry, and the Treasury); the new social security proposals (the Department of Social Welfare and the Treasury); and the implementation of the environmental impact legislation (the departments of Environmental Affairs and Water Affairs), to mention a few. The 2008 ANC–Cosatu–SACP Economic Summit (2008: 2) therefore proposed a planning commission in the Presidency to 'align the work of all departments of government and organs of state to the development agenda'.

This may or may not be a workable institutional response to the challenge of coordination – but for better implementation of policies and projects we will need to look elsewhere. A planning commission is a focus, not a substitute, for decision-making. It furnishes no more than a systematic way of trying to coordinate decisions and improve on coordinated or uncoordinated decisions. Although uncoordinated decisions may be bad or costly, so also may coordinated decisions. There is no magic about a planning commission that transforms the quality of decisions beyond the virtue that coordination lends.

Does this mean that nothing can be done? Even with a planning commission, are there other ways to promote coordination in policy and action in an imperfect world? What we are looking at here are a number of mechanisms or institutions which, if properly utilised, could enhance the performance of the state (in some instances simultaneously) in respect of

- coordination
- capacity-building
- capacity evaluation
- value for money
- consultation
- consensus-building

to mention a few advantages. We need to overcome a strange and frequent paradox: the lack of coherence and coordination in policy-making in South Africa in the midst of a plethora of 'advisory' processes and structures.

These options include:

- *Greater use of consultative documents*
In 1997 a White Paper on energy presciently predicted, among other things, that South Africa would reach an electricity 'bottleneck' within a decade. And so it happened. In the past few years the authorities have made

less and less use of 'green' papers (for discussion purposes) or 'white' papers (intended policy direction) as instruments of consultation and coordination for official policy. It is difficult to recall when last the ground was carefully prepared for far-reaching new legislation or policy through these mechanisms, which seem to have been abandoned for planning purposes. Unfortunately, there have been some bad experiences in the past with White Papers as tools of policy-making.

There have also been long-standing complaints about draft legislation being presented to the social dialogue process at Nedlac for immediate attention, with little or no background or motivation. This does not make for good policy-making or a particularly coordinated one. Yet, on reflection, it is clear that a government anxious to canvass widespread support for its legislation and policies would be well advised to make effective use of these instruments for that purpose. Summits and workshops are not adequate substitutes for this process.

The advantages of 'green' and 'white' government papers nonetheless include the following:

- They act as an early warning system to both government as a whole and the private sector about official intentions in a specific area of policy, say health or transport. Where there is real analysis, they create an opportunity to offer a coherent, well-argued and evidenced case for whatever the government is proposing. It is then possible to begin to identify any unintended consequences that may flow from such proposed actions in a structured way. By reducing sudden legislative or policy 'shocks', they are likely to have a favourable impact on business and investor confidence.

- They communicate official intentions and offer a simple and straightforward way of letting everyone know what is intended, but before the policies are cast in concrete. The government can thus 'test the waters' and tap into the wisdom of other constituencies. The documents also force attention on any obstacles to the fulfilment of new policies, and so help to secure early amendments for overcoming them. It means better drafted legislation for Parliament, which enacts so much legislation every year. This process needs to be made more effective to prevent legislation reaching the parliamentary agenda that has to be referred back or substantially redrawn within a very short time.

- They become instruments of coordination, as policy proposals usually start from a world that is already moving, not one that has to be set in motion. There is an institutional history and background. They compel the participants in the process, whether from government or the private sector, to examine the extent to which these documents cover earlier ground on the policy concerned. They also provide an evaluation of the success or failure of earlier decisions in a particular area of policy, as well as in related policies. Here they could also be integrated with the regulatory impact assessment process mentioned below.

In short, therefore, effective use of well-structured 'green' or 'white' papers provides a declaration of intended policies as well as a method of communication and consultation on draft policies – and ultimately generates a coordinated focus for official decision-making by their very preparation.

- *Regulatory impact assessment (RIA)*

What permeates virtually all reports on South Africa's performance is the need to lighten the regulatory burden on small and emerging businesses. South Africa needs a more competitive-friendly regulatory framework – especially for small business, where the greatest potential for job creation exists. Government can still do much by streamlining laws and regulations to reduce the transaction costs of doing business in South Africa and by microeconomic reforms to raise global competitiveness. South Africa is still far from having this kind of regulatory culture, which should extend to parliamentary processes.

The full introduction of an RIA mechanism in South Africa should therefore be expedited. The central RIA Unit, established in February 2007 under the political leadership of the Deputy President, needs to gain momentum. It is evidence of the 'vicious circle' to which state capacity is subject that the introduction of RIA (a partial solution) has been slow because of a lack of capacity within the state machinery! We need over time to make for easier regulation where it matters and create a framework of 'smart tape' rather than 'red tape' in South Africa. RIA must be introduced early in the official decision-making process, not least because one of the key questions in the initial analysis should be whether regulation is the best tool to deal with a problem.

Another advantage of RIA could be to coordinate the work of different regulators. The compilation of an RIA will encourage a government department to evaluate the variety of regulations in a particular sector and to consider afresh how such regulation could be coordinated, even if that regulation is not under direct control of the department. Indeed, the OECD Report also points out that the poor scoring on regulatory processes in South Africa reflects in part the failure to allow more room for market solutions, as well as some coordination problems among different state agencies (CGD, 2008: 64).

- *Public–private sector partnerships (PPPs)*

Increased use of PPPs is another useful mechanism for coordinated activity and active implementation. Only about 3–5% of infrastructural expenditure by central government is presently allocated to PPPs in terms of Asgisa and the National Treasury. By world standards this is low. A more positive attitude towards the use of PPPs is necessary and any remaining obstacles should be addressed. We need to experiment with all kinds of new partnerships between the state and private enterprise. A target closer to, say, 20% of infrastructural spending would mobilise private financing (both internal and external) into public assets on a much bigger scale. Apart from its other advantages, this could be helpful in a period in which global financial developments will make public financing considerably more difficult.

Emerging economies like South Africa are clearly not immune to the negative global forces as the pool of international liquidity has lately dried up and as the world economy slows. Given the country's very low domestic savings rate, South Africa has been borrowing savings from the rest of the world to help fund the economy's rising rate of investment. But in the absence of any substantial rise in domestic savings rates, the country will have to try to borrow funds in tight foreign markets to fund the massive investment programmes for companies like Transnet and Eskom, in addition to the private sector's investment plans of about R1.5 trillion over the next five years. What it does basically mean is that the amount of capital available is less and also more expensive.

Given these constraints on the availability of global capital, the room for South Africa to manoeuvre in terms of access to foreign borrowings and in terms of macroeconomic policy choices has narrowed. There is not only less room for error but also a need to become more competitive if South Africa is to be a preferred investment destination for foreign investment. Yet we find that the roll-out of PPPs is seriously hampered by a lack of capacity and skills in government departments and provincial authorities.

It is also helpful to distinguish between 'high-powered' investment and 'ordinary' investment. Transportation, Eskom and the like are 'high-powered', in the sense that they can have a meaningful effect on cost reduction and on the productivity of all sectors that depend on the basic infrastructure. State-owned enterprises alone are estimated to control about 20% of capital stock in South Africa, whereas much factory investment, while satisfying consumers, does not necessarily add to the productivity of industry *in general*. Public resource development can open up private investment opportunities, but we do not need to be locked into the mode that *only* the government can successfully run parastatals. There is scope for better business models and South Africa should be prepared to explore them. Mobilising strategic minority interests could be one of them.

We may, in passing, also note the recent comments of David Lewis, chairperson of the Competition Tribunal, on the weak performance of state-owned enterprises (SOEs) as a constraint on economic growth. He went on to say:

> In South Africa, the approach adopted by government to these state-owned enterprises is critical from the perspective of the credibility of competition policy, and more important from the perspective of the country's economic fortunes … I have absolutely no doubt that the returns – whether from a growth or redistribution perspective – from developing an effective regulatory framework for our telecommunications, energy and transport markets, are significantly greater than the return that will be earned from any of the range of industrial strategies that are endlessly peddled in rounds of policy documents, which all sound the same as policy documents you heard of five years ago, ten years ago, or even fifteen years ago. (*Engineering News*, 27.10.2008)

Importantly, the OECD's recommendations include the public sector in its competition focus. It emphasises what it calls 'network' industries – telecoms, transport and electricity – where it also sees current state monopolies as problematic. This brings us back to the earlier reference to state *strength*, rather than state *scope*, as being more important to the long-term economic growth rate.

- *Making the role of Nedlac more effective*
Nedlac was established in 1995 to promote social dialogue and consensus-seeking in public policy choices in South Africa. It is one of only two similar structures (government, business, labour and community) in the world which are negotiation-driven in respect of key legislation and policy. Most of the institutions of its kind internationally are mechanisms that play consultative and advisory roles only. Nonetheless, over the years Nedlac has also become a channel for consultation and coordination, even though its primary purpose is negotiation with the social partners. Bringing important draft legislation and policy to Nedlac – and sharing information between the social partners and government – inevitably facilitates coordination. Even where consensus is not reached, a process of consultation has taken place.

If Nedlac did not exist in South Africa, it would therefore be necessary to invent it. Yet after 14 years of existence it is generally accepted that Nedlac needs to be more effective. A recent International Labour Organisation report commissioned by Nedlac has made various recommendations for strengthening and improving the efficacy of Nedlac. This needs to be supplemented by examining the extent to which the Nedlac process can play an even more aggressive role in promoting coordination in socio-economic policy simply by having the key stakeholders under one roof. Nedlac must be an active driver of social dialogue, not just its passive custodian, especially at a time when there is such an emphasis on the need for better coordination and delivery.

- *Enhancing the role of local government*
By now the perceived failure of 'democratic centralism' to deliver public satisfaction in the conduct of public services has led a few students of the state machinery to question its basic premise. Might the trouble be not a lack of sufficient command-and-control at the centre, but too much of it? Is this partly the cause of the perceived lack of coordination in outcomes? Any mistakes tend to be big ones. Progress in tackling problems is often slower than might be hoped for, or than circumstances warrant, simply because mobilising and coordinating action in Pretoria is a time-consuming business. All this might have been an acceptable price to pay for sound administration and competent management. Unfortunately the evidence suggests that government and management do not mix well if unduly centralised.

Global experience suggests that the best public sector structure is one that is able to shift flexibly from one level of centralisation to another in response to changing pressures and conditions. Of course, this is a formidable area of economics and public administration. The challenge is to find the optimum degree of decentralisation between national, provincial and local governments. There are a host of complex technological and other factors bearing on the appropriate degree of decentralisation in the public sector. Furthermore, issues of delegated authority are often approached not merely from a functional but also from a normative standpoint. Today, decentralisation is more often associated with high levels of popular participation and control, and hence with positive values like democracy, and is desired as an end in itself.

But for as long as we choose as a country to be generally reliant on the public sector (whether national or local) for much of our transport, power, water and other infrastructural requirements, it is critical that the necessary investment to expand our capacity *efficiently* in these areas should take place. The public sector also has large social delivery obligations, especially at the local level where 60% of social delivery in South Africa takes place. The fact remains that in nearly half of our rural towns over 50% of households are indigent. A lack of capacity in the poorest municipalities means a failure to spend limited capital funds.

In South Africa about half of the 282 local authorities are reportedly dysfunctional or almost dysfunctional, so there is no alternative but to build capacity urgently at that level, if necessary with the assistance of the private sector. Yet the public sector is nonetheless going to be increasingly squeezed in the period ahead between financial stresses on the one hand and citizens' expectations on the other. Local government will be no exception. 'The economic slowdown will hit municipalities hard', says one analyst, 'since it is more difficult for them than for national government to run counter-cyclical policies when revenues fall' (*Business Day*, 10.12.2008).

One important sphere in which social dialogue, partnership and capacity-building should therefore be strengthened is the tier of local government. After all, it remains the level of government closest to the people. The new mantra is 'to think like a mayor'. An immediate challenge is to see whether the social dialogue 'culture' can be replicated to a greater extent at municipal level in ways that will lead to enhanced capacity and better delivery. In general, enhanced delivery will require better alignment of functions between national, provincial and local government. This, in turn, will underpin our collaborative and coordination efforts at national level.

We should therefore be looking to several existing instruments and institutions to see whether they can be more effective in policy coordination and implementation, irrespective of what is eventually decided about a possible planning commission located in the Presidency. An improved framework will bring much-needed discipline to policy-making by ensuring that, more than ever, hard evidence is taken into account in preparing policy proposals, and this will make long-term success more likely.

A 'collectivism index'?

For those who remain concerned about the dangers of excessive state intervention, or 'collectivism', it may be helpful for a reputable 'think-tank' to construct a 'collectivism index' (Skidelsky, 1995: 24–6) to provide an empirical basis for the future monitoring of state involvement in the South African economy. Ignorance of the facts of the situation can be a major barrier to the making of wise policy in future. Policy should derive from a process of experiment and observation, not from dogma.

This index could be distilled out of elements such as:
- The proportion of output the state spends and the ratio of public to private investment. The public spending to GDP ratio is a vital measure of 'collectivism', because the larger the share of national income spent by the state, the greater its ability to shape what is produced.
- The share of output produced by the state, such as in the fields of transportation, energy and communications, where the state has direct control of production.
- The degree of intervention with cross-border flows of goods, capital and labour, which would measure the degree of self-sufficiency existing.
- The progressiveness of the tax system and the extent to which it is an instrument of redistribution.
- The degree of regulation and the regulatory burden, such as through the expansion in the market of regulatory agencies.

Pending the creation of such an index, what we need to establish is whether on *prima facie* grounds South Africa has reached a stage at which diminishing returns have set in for the efficacy of the state – as evidenced in chronic delivery problems, excessive bureaucracy, and especially corruption and 'rent-seeking'. The status quo is becoming increasingly untenable. 'Democratic centralism' has been honestly intended to drive the nation's agenda forward but in fact it has often held everything up. It has had serious unintended consequences, often outweighing the intended ones. Economists cannot see inefficiency without asking whether there could be a better way.

The trend in any 'collectivism index' will to some extent be decided by the success or otherwise of the business community, and especially new black entrepreneurs, in influencing what they see as the appropriate dividing line between the public and private sectors in the South African economy. If business wants a larger share of the action for itself – and wants to reduce the burden of regulation on it – it will need to do the following.

- As a point of departure, accept that the debate is to some degree an intellectual one – a battle of ideas – and that at the highest level the advocates of enlarging or protecting the private sector must generate new ideas as to how this can best be achieved in South African circumstances. It is not enough to simply fall back on the pure ideology of markets but it is necessary to mobilise empirical evidence of how markets can work successfully, and in what circumstances, to achieve key socio-economic goals. If a system can be demonstrated to deliver where others have failed, ideology will be less important to the general public. This is a challenge to the private sector.
- Avoid creating the impression that narrow vested interests dominate the national economic agenda by pushing their own business interests to the exclusion of broader considerations of public policy. Abuse of market power undermines the competitive system. The OECD Report referred to earlier, as well as Asgisa, puts particular emphasis on the need to enhance competition levels in South Africa. The public mood and the attitude of the competition authorities have hardened into one of zero tolerance for flagrantly anti-competitive behaviour. When markets go bad they have to be made to work better. To that extent the competition authorities are rightly going to pursue a more proactive policy to promote competition in future.
- Take up the cudgels vigorously, especially through organised business, on behalf of broad business interests and the development of a strong entrepreneurial culture, especially for small business. Successful businesses are engines of growth. Advocacy and lobbying on behalf of the market economy and overall business interests need to be backed with empirical research and persuasive arguments. Here business needs to talk with a united voice as far as possible.

The exact division of labour between the state and the private sector in a country like South Africa is therefore not something that falls like manna from heaven – but is the result of the interplay of political, economic and social forces, which business itself has a critical role in shaping. Business, after all, is a key agent of change. Is there an 'ideal' relationship between government and business? Ultimately, the ideal relationship in practice between the state and the private sector is probably one of 'creative tension': let neither be suspicious of the other, let there be maximum cooperation – but let both be watchful.

Conclusion

The extensive nature of the issues around the role of the state in South Africa underlines the uncomfortable reality that there is no 'silver bullet' for good governance, notwithstanding the siren calls of the media and the manifestos of politicians. We do not need to reinvent government but we do need to make the machinery we have work properly. We need administrative machinery that works to deliver public services much more efficiently. Indeed, radical government reorganisation usually involves a large amount of time, energy and political capital to achieve, with little prospect of graceful withdrawal.

That said, what then are the ultimate boundaries between the state and the private sector? Truly effective and competitive markets occupy a delicate middle ground between the absence of rules and the existence of suffocating rules. Laws do not usually create prosperity. Ideally we in South Africa, like elsewhere, want a transparent, level playing field where everyone has a fair chance of participating and those who provide the best value for money prevail. The debate around the degree of state intervention thus needs to chart a narrow path between the Scylla of excessive government intervention – scattering sand in the gearing wheels of the economy – and the Charybdis of too little government to facilitate economic growth and equity.

While the absence of rules makes the playing field uneven, too many rules of the wrong kind – which often seems the case in South Africa – could inhibit the economy to the point at which the country remains in a 'low-growth' trap of 3–4%. If South Africa still aspires to a 6% growth rate by 2014, it will be essential to get the balance 'right'. Both internal and external factors converge on the importance of what needs to be decided about the respective roles of the public and private sectors in future.

Another powerful reinforcing financial imperative is now also embedded here. The changed global economic situation and the current low growth phase in the South African economy highlight one overriding reality – the increasing *constraint of finance*. Either over-ambitious socio-economic programmes must be cut back, or new sources of finance found in higher taxes or increased state indebtedness. Or else South Africa must find its way back dynamically to the Asgisa 6% growth path so as to be able to tackle the challenges of unemployment and poverty successfully. There will be no soft options, only tough decisions, awaiting a new government in 2009.

There therefore remains a clear and urgent choice for South Africa. Either strengthen the public sector delivery, keeping government affordable and the tax burden reasonable, or face a continued failure to ensure delivery, leading to rising costs, reductions in services and greater financing challenges. In other words, either economic growth with all its benefits, or the yoke of low growth and its creeping socio-economic costs, and welfare dependency. We want to turn many more South Africans into a nation of victors over adversity and deprivation, rather than victims trapped on welfare.

On what note should we conclude? We must ultimately remain wary of deifying either markets or the state, or attributing vast powers of omniscience and omnipotence to them. Both are capable of 'failure', although under normal circumstances government 'failures' are usually on a larger scale, tend to be highly politicised and are much harder to remedy. Given South Africa's experience to date with 'statism', the onus is on those who wish to extend it to prove their case and to demonstrate where additional state involvement will produce superior outcomes.

Yet these political and economic systems will not, by themselves, create a 'good society' and good lives for most of us. They will produce what is good, desirable and valuable only if we *decide* what is good, desirable and valuable, whether as voters, consumers, workers or businesspeople. The way people think about economics, business, competition and related values shapes the quality of the strategic choices they make. A democracy thrives or develops by the ability of its people to choose and act wisely.

References

Allen, W.A. 2000. *Financial Markets and National Economies.* Royal Institute of International Affairs, London

Barber, Michael. 2007. *Instruction to Deliver: Tony Blair, Public Services and the Challenge of Achieving Targets.* Methuen, London

CGD. 2008. *The Growth Report: Strategies for Sustained Growth and Inclusive Development.* The Commission on Growth and Development, May 2008

Declaration of the Alliance Economic Summit, Johannesburg, 19 October 2008

Dollery, B. 2003. The Decline of the South African Economy: Review Note. *South African Journal of Economics,* 71 (1)

Hausmann, R. 2008. *Final Recommendation of the International Panel on Asgisa.* Working Paper no.161, May 2008

Landes, D. 1998. *The Wealth and Poverty of Nations.* Abacus, London

OECD. 2008. *South Africa: Economic Assessment 2008.* OECD Economic Surveys, July 2008

Skidelsky, R. 1992. *John Maynard Keynes: The Economist as Saviour 1920–1937.* Macmillan, London

Skidelsky, R. 1995. *The World after Communism.* Macmillan, London

World Bank. 1997. *World Development Report 1997. The State in a Changing World.* Oxford University Press, New York

12

Recapitulation and coda: 70 key findings and recommendations

1. **Overture: theme and variations** *by Raymond Parsons*
   - International evidence suggests that sustained growth and development are essential to address unemployment and poverty successfully. However, economic growth is a complex process that is difficult to achieve. It should be inclusive but this is not guaranteed.
   - Until recently South Africa's challenge was mainly to navigate a domestic economic downswing; now the negative global economic outlook is at least as important in shaping policy responses for stability, growth and development. The changed global economic environment will inevitably shape South Africa's future public policy choices.
   - Changes in the business cycle are also coinciding with major domestic political shifts, which have important implications for South Africa's economic direction after the 2009 elections. Markets and business will need reassurance about future economic policy.
   - The political assumption is that the ANC–Cosatu–SACP Alliance will win the 2009 elections and that ANC president Jacob Zuma will become President of South Africa.
   - The Accelerated and Shared Growth Initiative for South Africa (Asgisa) remains a relevant framework for assessing opportunities and risks if South Africa is to prosper and be globally competitive in the years ahead. South Africa must build on its achievements to date, learn from its mistakes, and explore the new opportunities that emerge.
   - There *is* a 'virtuous circle' of high growth, democratic governance and social development possible in South Africa. The transition to

a high-skill, high-productivity and rising wage economy is both economically necessary and politically desirable. The forces of globalisation abroad, and the dynamics of transformation within, must meet in a faster 'catch-up' growth for South Africa, of the kind experienced by several other emerging economies.
- In the final analysis, *shared* economic prosperity remains the only secure guarantee of a democratic order in South Africa.

2. **South Africa's economic performance since 1994: can we do better?** *by Charlotte du Toit and Johann van Tonder*
   - South Africa's higher economic growth rate of 5% during the period 2004–2007 can be regarded as a 'blessing in disguise', as it revealed policy and implementation constraints limiting the economy's capacity to produce goods, absorb labour and reduce poverty. South Africa can still do better.
   - The majority of the 'wealth creators' arising from this growth have been in the formal sector through increased asset and income growth. The gap between poor and rich has widened and South Africa's poverty rate has decreased only marginally despite the past four years of higher economic growth. Higher employment rates have been mainly driven by job creation in the informal sector.
   - Obstacles to higher employment emanate from both the supply and demand sides of the economy, and the formal sector is unable to absorb more labour. A range of institutional factors not only prevents job creation but also contributes to job vacancies not being filled. These need to be urgently addressed in a holistic manner.
   - The current account deficit of the balance of payments has become persistent in nature. The contribution of exports to foreign receipts is dwindling. The existence of exchange control may have protected South Africa from the global credit crisis, but it has also contributed to distortions in the exchange rate and interest rates. South Africa has had to rely heavily on short-term portfolio capital to finance its current account deficit.
   - Recent high interest rates have had a negative impact on private fixed investment growth. South Africa has been unable so far to attract sufficient new foreign direct investment (FDI).
   - The tertiary or services sector appears to be the new engine of growth in South Africa.

3. **Economic policy: some lessons from Southeast Asia**
   by Lefentse Nokaneng and Chris Harmse
   - There needs to be a shift from labour-intensive agricultural peasant production to small- and medium-scale manufacturing.
   - Export-oriented industrialisation is more essential to growth than import-substitution.
   - The inflow of FDI and the accompanying upgrading of industrial infrastructure transformed manufacturing production in East Asian economies. A naturally beneficial cycle between investment and manufactured exports has been at the heart of industrial policy in the East Asian economies.
   - The relationship between increased demand and supply underpins the success of East Asian economic growth. Increased demand for intermediate imports has been matched by expanded exports and domestic capacity creation. Current account deficits have been rapidly converted into surpluses.
   - An outstanding feature of East Asian economic development has been that increased efficiency in production has led to welfare gains in the shape of higher per capita income, increased employment and a more equitable distribution of incomes.
   - Moving towards favourable agricultural policies and land reform and away from subsistence farming helps to provide food security.
   - Resource allocation through markets was encouraged amongst the East Asian countries. Efficient labour markets improved job creation and made for a better allocation of labour. Joint ventures with foreign firms helped to amplify the economic success.
   - Although on the surface the policy frameworks of South Africa and several East Asian economies may appear similar, implementation of policy has been less successful in this country.

4. **Inflation targeting: a pillar of post-Polokwane prosperity**
   by Stan du Plessis
   - Inflation targeting has attracted considerable controversy in South Africa since its adoption in February 2000. The monetary policy debate is now faced with a potentially significant shift in the social and political support for low and stable inflation as the appropriate goal for monetary policy. In its own terms inflation targeting has nonetheless been a success in South Africa.

- The evidence presented supports the interpretation of South Africa's inflation target as a highly flexible monetary policy regime. Widening the mandate of the South African Reserve Bank (SARB) to include output with inflation would have little practical impact on the way monetary policy is being currently implemented.
- Monetary policy under inflation targeting in South Africa has not destabilised the economy. Instead, the evidence suggests that it has contributed to significant stabilisation of the economy.
- A numerical inflation target – which allows the public to monitor the SARB's commitment – provides a constraint on the discretion of the Bank and a disincentive for it to renege on its commitment to low and stable inflation.
- It is equally important for the SARB to develop a track record for honesty and credibility in monetary policy; this requires a prolonged and extensive communication strategy to anchor inflationary expectations.
- Critics of inflation targeting in the ANC–Cosatu–SACP Alliance and elsewhere have gained prominence but have ignored the extensive empirical support for the beneficial impact of inflation targeting on both developed and developing countries.
- If the political space for the SARB to use monetary policy independently and flexibly to keep inflation low and stable is compromised, South Africa may be served with a bill of high inflation and no gain in growth – a bill for which the relatively poor will pay in diminished welfare more than the relatively rich.

5. **Fiscal policy beyond 2008: prospects, risks and opportunities**
   by Iraj Abedian and Tania Ajam
   - A combination of rapid economic contraction and the imminent change of political leadership in South Africa in 2009 has opened an interesting new vista for South Africa's fiscal policy prospects. Key macroeconomic policies underpinning fiscal structures are under review. Assuming that the ruling ANC Alliance will win the 2009 election, their recent pronouncements about possible macroeconomic policy change have caused concern locally and internationally.
   - Given the emergence of a serious global recession, what is highly probable is a fall in the country's fiscal revenues over the next few

years. Meanwhile, the ANC Alliance has mooted the adoption of fairly ambitious fiscal commitments going forward. Much of the proposed fiscal programme is welfarist and some of it developmental. The welfarist, populist elements of the mooted policies are known to create medium- to long-term fiscal liabilities that are hard to escape from.
- Developmental fiscal commitments require a well-known set of technical prerequisites that are lacking in the South African public sector at present. Not enough is currently said about the weaknesses and fault-lines within fiscal management institutional structures.
- It is vital to take account of the key risks facing the country's fiscal management over the next few years. These risks vary from global to local, from institutional to managerial. Yet their collective threat to the country's fiscal integrity is real and needs consistent political management. Failure in this regard is more than likely to reverse the remarkable fiscal achievements made over the past ten years. This is particularly significant given the global financial and economic circumstances that are likely to prevail over the next decade.
- Some key fiscal opportunities exist that provide constructive options for public sector intervention over the next period. Herein lies the scope for the next generation of fiscal reform and modernisation. Admittedly, some of these reforms are complex, require time and call for consistent leadership of the political economy arena.
- We must not create a populist, welfarist fiscal framework that is detrimental to the sustainable upliftment of the poor and inimical to economic performance.

6. **Trade, industrial and competition policy** *by Riaan de Lange and Reyno Seymore*
    - The approach to trade, industrial and competition policies should be on an integrated basis, as they are ultimately interdependent concepts and policies.
    - Although the National Industrial Policy Framework identified four 'lead sectors' and is intended to be the definitive industrial policy, many questions still exist that generate uncertainty. The policy needs to be better aligned with South Africa's existing 'revealed comparative advantage'.
    - Regarding South Africa's tariff policy there is need for a 'back-to-

basics' approach. The Tariff Book requires simplification and should be reviewed in its entirety.
- The role of the Competition Commission has become even more important. Pro-competition policies must continue to be implemented. Competition policy should take account not only of the practice of import parity pricing, but also that of export parity pricing.
- The principle of contestability should also apply to the public sector and parastatals.

7. **Industrial policy and national competitiveness: the spatial dimension** *by Glen Robbins*
   - Any new government must seek to understand and embrace the possibilities that would come with incorporating a spatial dimension to industrial policy, so as to move away from the state intervention dilemma and to broaden public policy choices in this sphere.
   - International and local experience suggests that – although a national industrial policy is necessary – it is inadequate to build the types of sustained networks and relationships between a variety of role-players required to support processes of competitiveness into which firms can directly tap. South Africa needs a bold industrial policy that seeks to address in systematic ways a wide range of constraints and exploit the mix of opportunities that exist.
   - ANC president Jacob Zuma has had direct experience of industrial policy, in his former capacity as KwaZulu-Natal's MEC for Economic Affairs and Tourism. In tackling the loss of competitiveness experienced by the garment industry in particular, Zuma supported the creation of the Regional Economic Forum, which brought together business, labour and government to chart a common path by way of responding to regional economic challenges and crafting policies to meet regional-specific needs.
   - Future industrial policy needs to a far greater extent to accommodate the diversity of local experiences – and the mobilisation of local agents of change – if national policies are to be successful.

8. **Labour policy and job creation: too many 'holy cows'?** *by Carel van Aardt*
   - We need to recognise that it is the private sector that must create the bulk of jobs in the long run.

- The creation of 'decent work' opportunities should become the primary focus of relevant policies.
- There should be investment in priority skills and education to ensure that people have the necessary skills to be employable. Education remains a high priority.
- South Africa needs to absorb the unemployed through labour-intensive production methods and procurement policies, a significant expansion of public works programmes and an expanded national youth service.
- A wage subsidy allowance should be instituted for 18-year-olds to facilitate the school–work transition and, by doing so, allow the youth to demonstrate their abilities. This will provide young workers with a kick-start into employment. It will also encourage more experimentation by employers and a more efficient matching of workers to jobs.
- Labour market information systems should be improved and steps taken to ensure that information about available jobs reaches all economically active people.
- High-skilled immigration should be encouraged so that a bigger skills pool becomes available to help sustain a higher economic growth path.
- Labour legislation that unduly increases the indirect costs of labour should be reviewed.
- One important change is better labour–business relationships to facilitate joint solutions to labour market challenges. In emerging economies comparable to South Africa – such as China, Thailand, Vietnam, Malaysia and Taiwan – labour and business have been more successful in jointly tackling labour market challenges.

9. **Health policy and growth** *by Oludele A. Akinboade, Thabisa Tokwe and Mandisa Mokwena*
   - Health is critical to the overall success of the South African economy. The Asgisa goals of 6% growth and halving unemployment and poverty by 2014 will remain a dream unless South Africa gets its public health 'right', as health plays a key role in determining human capital.
   - South Africa has essentially two separate and distinct health systems – a large public sector and a smaller but fast-growing private sector.

The public sector is stretched and under-resourced in places, while the mushrooming private sector, run largely on commercial lines, caters to middle- and high-income earners, who tend to be members of medical schemes and, to a lesser extent, of health insurers.
- South Africa needs to implement the new Medical Schemes Act effectively.
- There is need for improved equity and efficiency in the use of existing resources allocated to health.
- The task of ensuring that resources are distributed equitably between provinces in South Africa is one of the most critical in improving the health status of people across the country. However, although this is an essential part of making access to health services more equitable, it must be remembered that improving health is not simply about changing the allocation of healthcare resources.
- Health is influenced by many other factors and inevitably poverty means ill health. The alleviation of poverty and improvement of living conditions are thus also crucial in making the health status of South Africans more equitable.

10. Politics and human-oriented development *by Adam Habib*
- Effective competition for political power is required for a human-oriented development agenda. It is not simply sufficient to have 'the right people at the top'.
- Five conditions are necessary as a way of holding South African political elites more accountable to the electorate:
  – reform of the current electoral regime
  – development of a viable, competitive political system
  – erosion of corporatist institutions and processes that evolved in the 1990s
  – emergence of a robust civil society
  – the development of a strategic foreign policy.
- The only way a competitive political system will be established in South Africa is if the ANC–Cosatu–SACP Alliance is to fracture, or if the ANC faces a breakaway, as has now happened with the formation of Cope. Nevertheless, if the Cope political initiative is to be a significant and sustainable one, it needs to address some serious challenges.
- The greatest prospect for the Cope initiative lies in the hands of the

current leadership of the ANC. If a 'triumphalist attitude' continues to prevail within the current ANC leadership, and if sufficient bridges are not built between the two camps, the political alternative is likely to grow if only because the 'dissidents' have no other option.
- If Cope creates a viable political alternative – one rooted in all of South Africa's population – political elites will no longer be able to take the country's citizenry for granted. And herein lies the potential for the strengthening of democratic accountability in South Africa, as well as human-oriented development.

11. The role of the state: where to draw the line?
by Raymond Parsons

- In an emerging market like South Africa, the role of the state has to be carefully defined, based on the country's stage of development as well as the capacity of the state to deliver. If markets are to work well, the stable and favourable environment they need must include a wide range of services and a sensible regulatory framework that only the state can provide.
- The 2008 OECD Report highlights the contradiction between the weaknesses of state capacity identified in Asgisa – ranging from crime prevention to industrial policy – in supporting economic development and the emphasis on state programmes and policies to address the same constraints.
- International evidence suggests that state *strength* is more important than state *scope* in determining long-term growth. What matters for competitiveness is not minimal government but competition-enhancing efficient government. Business must do more in shaping these decisions and speak more often with a unified voice.
- Coordination, capacity-building, planning and consultation in policies and projects would be facilitated by
  - greater use of official 'green' and 'white' papers on government policy
  - expediting implementation of regulatory impact assessments
  - expanding public–private sector partnerships
  - making Nedlac more effective
  - enhancing and strengthening the role of local government.
- What is needed from the public sector is to build confidence in

its strategic thinking, in dealing with poor performance, managing change effectively, learning from mistakes and working with government departments. This tells us that raising the rate of growth in South Africa and achieving a fairer society have much to do with strengthening state capacity where it matters, or otherwise devising new and innovative mechanisms to ensure effective delivery. It would be more realistic and relevant if in future we spoke to a greater extent about the need for a *delivery state*.

- Changing domestic and global economic circumstances present a clear and urgent choice if South Africa is to avoid a 'low growth trap' in the years ahead. Either strengthen public sector delivery, keeping government affordable and the tax burden reasonable, or face a continued failure to ensure delivery, leading to rising costs, reductions in services and greater financing challenges. In other words, either real economic growth with all its benefits, or the yoke of low growth and its creeping socio-economic costs and welfare dependency. We want to turn many more South Africans into victors over adversity and deprivation rather than victims trapped on welfare.